For Theo (8), Milo (6), Rex (4), and Lila (2)
who already know the power of fashion…

…and to the future Fashion Icons and all the dreamers who live for fashion.
Never forget Fashion Lives in us all.

FASHION ICONS 2

FASHION LIVES
WITH FERN MALLIS

Rizzoli
NEW YORK

New York · Paris · London · Milan

FOREWORD

I first met Fern Mallis in 2016. My friend and agent, Ivan Bart, walked me over to her table at the Council of Fashion Designers of America (CFDA) Fashion Awards to introduce me. As soon as we started talking, I knew she was an important person to be around, not only in fashion but also in life. I was immediately drawn to her kindness and honesty, and also to her wisdom. Fern is someone who is always excited about what is new and interesting in the fashion industry, and she was one of the first people to advocate for me in a space where I was not conventionally viewed as someone who could be successful in this business.

We share the belief that beauty is not one-size-fits-all, but is instead a vibrant world that welcomes and celebrates people of all different backgrounds, perspectives, and body types. For decades, Fern has committed herself to growing that community and capturing its most iconic voices. She has championed positive progress in ways that have defined modern fashion and elevated the industry's diversity, inclusion, and innovation. In this second volume of *Fashion Icons*, she celebrates the many creative voices advancing these ideas.

It's her incredible talent for making people feel comfortable that makes these stories so wonderful to read. Fern allows her subjects to open up and reveal aspects of themselves they might not have before. As an interviewer myself, I love seeing her skills in action—more an insightful conversation between two friends than anything else. Readers are gifted untold stories, life lessons, career highs and lows, and are witness to the power of reinvention. This book is not about a single collection or moment in time, but the personal journeys behind these fashion legacies, and the grit and determination that got them where they are today.

Fern is often referred to as the Godmother of Fashion. It's an apt title, given her selflessness and dedication to creating a better fashion world—all those who have had the honor of knowing her, watching her, listening to her interviews, or reading her work are the better for it. I am eternally grateful for the opportunities I've experienced thanks to Fern's incredible influence and creation of New York Fashion Week. Considering everything that Fern has accomplished so far, I can't wait to see what's in store for her next! **—Ashley Graham**

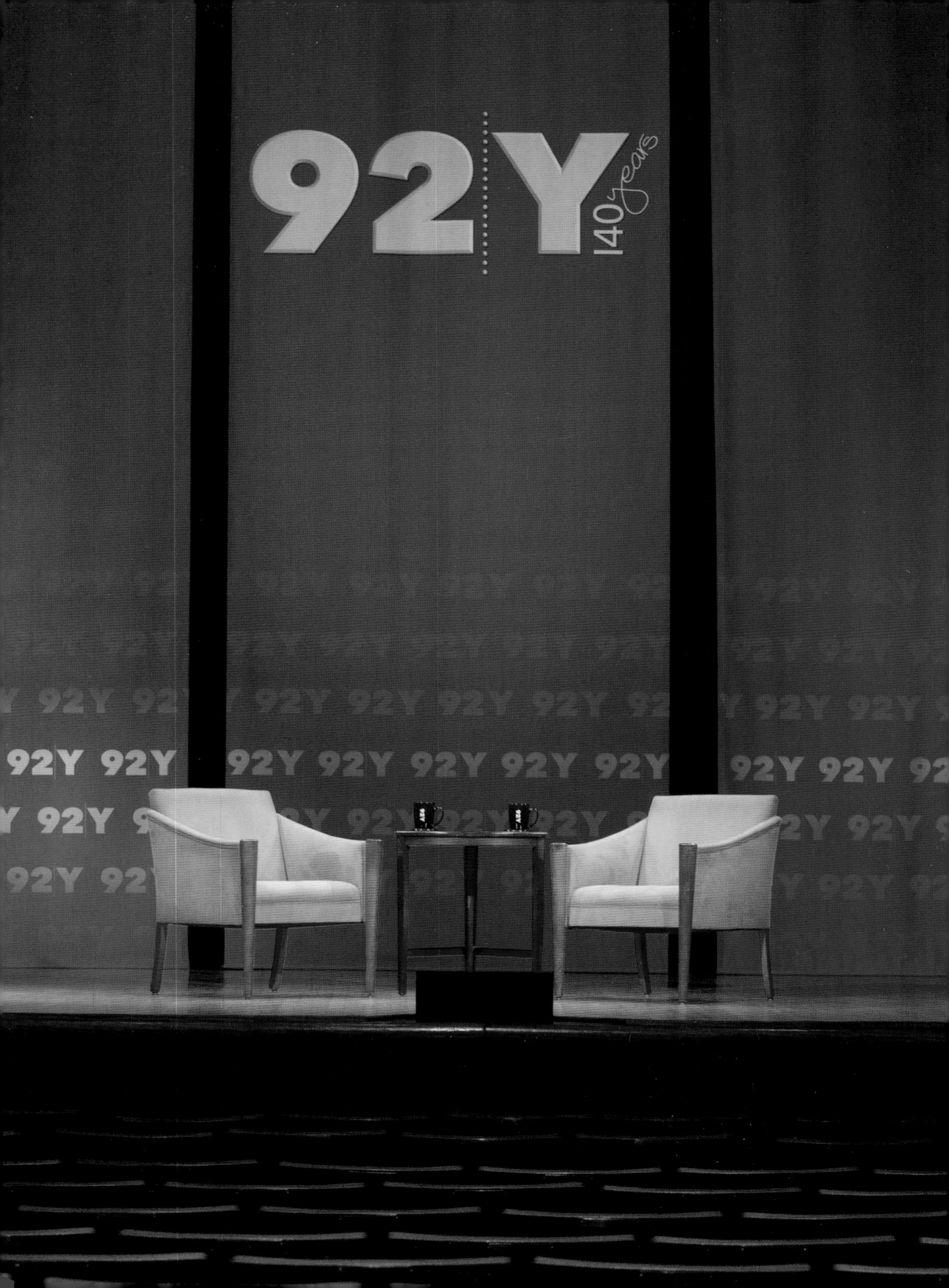
92Y
140 years

TABLE OF CONTENTS

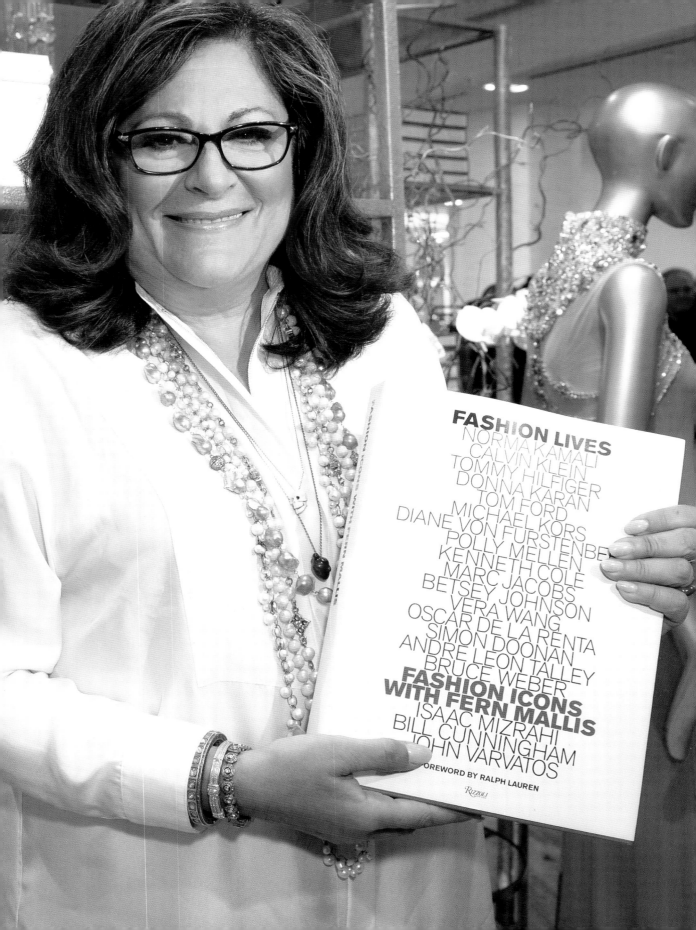

INTRODUCTION

This story starts in 2010, when I came to a crossroads in my life and career. I organized New York Fashion Week in the Bryant Park tents and ran those shows for twenty years, first as executive director of the CFDA and then as senior vice president of IMG Fashion. When Fashion Week was evicted from Bryant Park, I decided it was also my time to move on. As the tents came down in Bryant Park for the last time, I realized that nothing in fashion lives forever.

But what was next? After twenty years of doing something I loved, and that truly made a difference, how do I "reinvent" myself?

Out of this time of uncertainty, and thanks to my great friend Timothy Greenfield-Sanders, who introduced me to Betsy Berg, who introduced me to Susan Engel, came "Fashion Icons with Fern Mallis" my sold-out conversation series at the 92nd Street Y, New York City's hub for culture, politics, the arts, entertainment, and now, fashion. I never dreamed how successful this series would become. Over the past ten years, I have interviewed over fifty Fashion Icons, launched a YouTube series called *Fashion Icons: The Archive*, and achieved what has become one of the accomplishments I'm proudest of in my career: the *Fashion Icons* book series.

Fashion Icons 1: Fashion Lives with Fern Mallis was published in 2015. This first volume contained nineteen seminal conversations with America's leading designers, editors, photographers, and tastemakers—all the key players that put American fashion on the global map. I can still remember the book's star-studded launch party at Saks Fifth Avenue in New York City. Never in my life could I have imagined seeing my book, my name, my face adorning all of the store's famed Fifth Avenue windows. I had to pinch myself when my friend and Fashion Icon Bill Cunningham rolled up on his bicycle and took photos of me looking at the windows for the first time. (He was supposed to be upstairs with the other guests of honor, but he couldn't resist working the event.) My first book has now gone on to have four print runs, along with a special edition in Japanese. I am proud that my book is in the Library of Congress.

Then came another time of uncertainty: 2020. It was a year that changed all our lives as the world was engulfed in an unprecedented global pandemic. COVID-19 literally shut down the whole world, and fashion was one of the industries greatly impacted. We lapsed into wearing sweats, leggings, hoodies, and athleisure wear. I watched as my friends and colleagues pivoted their brands to adjust to the new "virtual" reality of everyone working from home, attending meetings, weddings, galas, and memorials over Zoom, and having happy hours over FaceTime. We all took a hiatus from our workwear, our colorful cocktail attire, and our one-of-a-kind ball gowns. "Fashion Icons" was on hiatus, too, as the 92nd Street Y followed COVID-19 protocols and shut down live, in-person events.

Uncertain times have a way of presenting new opportunities. Thanks to Rizzoli's Charles Miers and Anthony Petrillose, the visionary art director Sam Shahid, my research lead PC Chandra, and the support of Gigi Ganatra Duff at Nordstrom, I realized that this was the right time to create a sequel to my *Fashion Icons* book.

As I rewatched these interviews, I kept hearing similar themes emerge. These conversations were the mostly untold stories of the grit it took to achieve these Fashion Icons' career highs, the perseverance and passion they needed to overcome career lows, and the innovative thinking that led them to their second, and sometimes even third, acts. It was an aha moment. These stories define most of the Fashion Icons' careers. Each Fashion Icon has weathered their storms and ultimately triumphed. Their stories are now more relevant to share than ever.

So fasten your seat belts and get ready to have your passport stamped as this volume of Fashion Icons goes global. You will learn the real stories behind some of the world's most iconic designers: from London, to Paris, to Milan, and back again to the States. I also share my story, on the occasion of my birthday, when the tables at the 92nd Street Y were turned, and my pal, the smart and sassy Bevy Smith, interviewed me!

So while it may be true that nothing in fashion lasts forever, I believe the memories and the lessons learned from these Fashion Icons will endure. **—Fern Mallis**

Special thank you to the Billy Farrell Agency and the Patrick McMullan Company.

It was very pleasant. When we grew up, the doors were open. You could play in the street all night. We didn't have cell phones. We were good kids.

Your dad was a garmento, but your mom was a Turkish Donna Reed?

Well, more like a Turkish Martha Stewart.

Growing up, my parents were both world-class handball champions, and my mother was a big track person. They were very athletic. Then that kind of stopped.

My dad was a big basketball player. Through him, I got to love basketball, and he coached a team. He was playing ball when the NBA hadn't quite happened yet. There were teams in the Garment District; the different houses had basketball teams. He played at Union Temple in Brooklyn. He blamed me for stopping his career because he said when I was in my carriage, he'd take me to the schoolyard and I would cry too much and he had to stop playing ball. But it became part of our lives, following basketball.

A big part of your life was the fact that your dad was a garmento. You grew up going down to the Garment District. Back then, it was quite different than it is now. It was actually a really bustling, thriving place with lots of languages being spoken and lots of gruff men who were telling dirty jokes and smoking lots of cigars.

It was a time when "garmento" was not a bad word. I think of "garmento" as a very loving term. The Garment District was filled with rolling racks of fabrics and garments being wheeled down the streets. It seemed like everybody knew each other on the street. Everybody was friendly.

It was a haven for me in those days. My dad sold scarves and his buyers were mostly the fashion directors in the New York stores. He never wanted to be a traveling salesman where he would have made a lot more money. He always said he wanted to be home when we had school occasions and birthdays. He didn't want to be on the road missing everything.

A very doting father.

Yes, and my mother was like fire. She was a ball of fire.

Is that where you get it from?

I think I have a little bit of both of them. I mean, my sister Joanne [Metcalf], who's unfortunately passed, had more of my mother's fire. My sister Stephanie [Mallis] is more of my father's reserved, Renaissance kind of person. My dad was a brilliant scholar, I mean, he read so much. You couldn't challenge him on religion, on travel, on governments, on history. You couldn't play trivia with him. He won all the time.

It was an interesting home. They painted a lot. My mother loved going to the theater. Broadway was their thing. They went to the theater all the time.

That's back when you could get a ticket for five dollars versus five hundred, right?

Whatever it cost, they went. They went all the time. If she saw something she liked, she would immediately buy tickets for me and my sister.

I remember she bought tickets for all the kids in the neighborhood to see *Bye Bye Birdie*. That was the first play that almost any of them had ever seen. When *Fiddler on the Roof* came out… she got us to see it with her again. I still have all her *Playbills* in my garage in the country. I don't quite know what to do with them. If anybody has a suggestion, please ring me.

When they would go out to the theater, we'd wake up, and on the dining table would be a palette of watercolor paper, pastels or charcoal or watercolor crayons, different paints, always something for us to create and be visual with.

That really fed your creative side, your artistic side?

Totally. We took art classes at the Brooklyn Museum. Now you go to there for the CFDA Awards.

Things have definitely changed. What was one of the biggest perks of being in a family that worked in the Garment District?

I had a lot of scarves, a lot. I still have a lot of scarves. One of my uncles was in women's sportswear, so we got a lot of that, too. One of the lines they had was an old cowboy western line, H Bar C, if anybody remembers that name. We used to have really great cowboy shirts and stuff. The other uncle was in textiles. We had a lot of fabric if we needed to make anything.

But the scarves… I could have had my own YouTube channel teaching everybody how to tie scarves eight hundred ways if the technology was available then. I was the scarf queen, without question. That was a perk.

You mentioned when we were backstage that you were also named best dressed in your school.

Yes, at James Madison High School. I won best dressed when I graduated. And other luminaries who went to my high school were Chuck Schumer and Ruth Bader Ginsburg. It's a very cool school. Chuck and I were actually there at about the same time. I think he looks a lot older than me, though. RBG was before my time.

Definitely. He doesn't have that good Turkish blood that you have, baby.

I met him when he was running for Senate, because my mother loved him when he was a congressman in Brooklyn. He would call me "Madison" because of the high school.

What were some of the lessons that you learned from being at your father's knee while he was working in the Garment District?

Well, going to work with my father was a real joy. I went every chance I could. Whenever

Why was she able to go to Pratt for interior design, but you couldn't go to FIT for fashion?

She lived on campus. She didn't live at home. He said, "Just because you're going to be at Pratt, you shouldn't be deprived of a campus experience," which I thought was very, very smart of him. When it was time for me to go to school, I knew that they were spending a lot of money on Pratt. I said, "OK, I'll just go to Brooklyn College."

He said, "No, you or your mother have to move out of the house, and it would be easier for you to go away."

The SUNY schools were a really great program. The biggest city with a university was Buffalo. At that time, Buffalo was like the Berkeley of the East. It had the most extraordinary professors and theater programs. It was a revolutionary time. It was Vietnam War time. It was an extraordinary experience.

I became very good friends with Ron Silver, who was in the theater department, Peter Riegert, a producer friend, Rob Lieberman, and Steve Sunshine, who became a big producer at *Extra*. They were all up there at that time. We all became pals.

What do you think would have happened had you attended fashion school? You're able to be in fashion, but you're also a savvy businesswoman. You know about the art, but you also understand the commerce quite well. Do you think that that's the beneficial part of you having gone to Buffalo versus FIT?

I've never really stopped to wonder what it could have been if… There are a lot of people who said, "You should have become a designer. You could have been Donna Karan." But I don't regret the education at SUNY Buffalo. The experience was great. While I was there, I joined *Mademoiselle* magazine's College Board.

Yes, a very big contest. It was kind of like the career gal's debutante ball. If you were able to win that, you had a huge coming-out in the business.

For you guys who may be too young to remember *Mademoiselle*, it was a really amazing young women's magazine. It was quite a literary magazine during its heyday. They had a great contest, where the prize was that you got a chance to guest-edit *Mademoiselle*.

Now, some of the people that won that contest, besides our Fern, were Sylvia Plath, Ali MacGraw, Peggy Noonan, and Betsey Johnson. It was a very rare kind of contest. Were you at all intimidated to even enter? I always think about the *Mademoiselle* college competition being like the place where the Seven Sisters kind of girls went.

To be on the College Board, you just needed to fill out an application and send it in. You would get mailed questionnaires about beauty products and different things and were asked to share your comments, so they have some survey that they could show advertisers. We became like their free focus group for the publication: "This many college students like this, and this many like that." We were their demographic.

If you wanted to escalate on the College Board, you could write poetry, write an article, enter photographs, fashion or graphic designs. Since I was in the fine arts, graphics, and advertising program, I designed a direct mail piece that *Mademoiselle* would send out to lure subscribers. It was something that folded out in all different ways. It was kind of fun and fabulous.

I got a call one day from somebody at *Mademoiselle*. They said, "There's an editor who is going to be in your area. Can she come visit you?" I didn't know that these meetings were interviews with potential guest editors. I spent a day with a nice editor and the next thing I got was a telegram; this certainly dates me…

Wow, that's even before my time.

… A telegram telling me that I was selected as one of the twenty guest editors for 1969. Opening that up in my mailbox, was an aha moment. I couldn't believe it.

That meant I had to be in New York for the month of June, so I never went to my graduation because this was more important. We were put up in the Barbizon Hotel for Women, which is now Equinox gym on Sixty-Third and Lexington.

I always say that this contest, if it happened today, would be a reality-TV show. It would be twenty girls from all over the country, living in some glamorous high-rise apartment, fighting for the job, or the boyfriend, and you know, killing each other. You'd be watching all the drama, but it really wasn't that. We were a great group of girls.

Paint us a picture of the way you looked. So is this, like, a pillbox hat, gloves, knee-length skirt? What's the look?

No, that was the editor in chief of the magazine. That was Betsy Blackwell. We had regular clothes. We had hot pants and shorts. We wore fun things. It was a very mixed fashion statement.

… At the Barbizon, they let you come in there looking like a hippie floozy? I mean, all the things I've ever read about the Barbizon; it was where girls, when they came to New York to go and get jobs, it was a safe place for them to go. It was like a dormitory for career girls.

But we were twenty *Mademoiselle*, young, upstart editor types. There might have been some leeway. We all dressed well. Clothing was always something that I loved, and I dressed well, so it wasn't an issue.

I was the guest art editor working for the art director, Roger Schoening. We put together what was then known as the college issue, the back-to-school issue.

Now, "back-to-school" means get another hoodie or sweatshirt or something. But at that time, you bought new clothes to go back to college. It was a wonderful experience. We met lots of interesting people. We went to Israel for a week and climbed Mount Masada in long green wool three-piece knit things before they had a chairlift up there. Every year, travel is part of it. We had lunch with Mayor Teddy Kollek in Jerusalem.

There was a photographer, George Barkentin, who had a big party for everybody in his studios. I know Arthur Elgort is here tonight. Arthur was one of the big *Mademoiselle* photographers whom I met at that time in my life. It was a fun experience.

You took that fun experience, you took that opportunity and you created a better opportunity for yourself. You actually landed a job. You were the only one who landed a full-time paying position out of all the girls.

Yes, I was the only one called back. I went to Europe that summer after the guest editor month. That was what you did after college. You went to Europe with a Eurail Pass. We'd wait for mail at American Express offices, hoping to hear from our parents and maybe get some money in an envelope.

That was the trip where you went into every church, cathedral, museum, and you didn't need to do that again. On subsequent trips to Europe, I just went shopping.

Where'd you go on that trip?

London, Paris, the South of France, Holland, Italy, Greece… I mean, you just went everywhere.

Did you have any dalliances while you were there?

Yeah [SMILES SLYLY].

Do tell, Fern.

It was kind of hard to not get seduced in Greece. I've always been a sucker for European men. They are just more interesting and exotic.

It was the very first time I actually ever wore Indian kurta shirts. I was like, "Oh, my God, that's the most fabulous thing I've ever seen." I think I got them from a man. I was like, "Can you give me your shirt?"

After that summer abroad I came home and I thought I would be pounding the streets to go to an ad agency to get a job. I could have become the next Mary Wells Lawrence. That's really where I thought my strengths were, but my mother said *Mademoiselle* was always calling. "You know, they have a job." I took the job in the college competitions department.

I'm going to backtrack a second because I just remember a funny story about when I was a guest editor. One of the things we did was to meet different industry professionals. Our group went to see a designer who turned out to be Stan Herman.

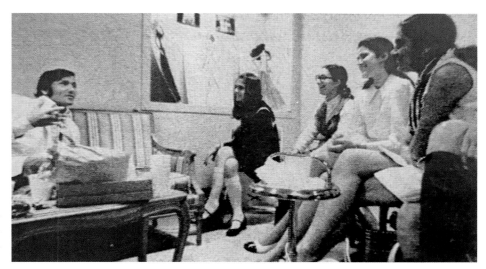

Fern Mallis meeting Stan Herman for the first time as part of *Mademoiselle*'s guest editor program in 1969.

Wow. The icon of the CFDA.

He was designing Mr. Mort. Years later, when I went up for the CFDA job, I told him, "I met you twenty years ago when I was a *Mademoiselle* guest editor; we came up to see you."

He said, "Oh, yeah, I remember."

I said, "No, you don't" [LAUGHTER].

But to me, that's a story that plays through my life. You never know where people turn up again in your life.

That's why your mantra of "be nice" really comes in handy.

It absolutely does. The people that you think you're never going to see again, that you hate in a job: you go somewhere else and before you know it, they're the CEO there or they're in the next office.

Anyway, I started working at *Mademoiselle* and going to college campuses meeting the next round of guest editors for a year or two. At a time when they were burning bras on campuses and a *Mademoiselle* editor going there didn't quite make sense.

Then I moved into merchandising, which meant going to the department stores. I went to every department store in America. This is before Macy's bought them all. They were all regional stores, you know: Higbee's, Meier & Frank, Burdines, Liberty House in Honolulu. We were doing events, makeovers in stores, promotional things for different advertisers.

You were at *Mademoiselle* for six years. Believe it or not, guys, people used to stay at jobs for years, sometimes decades. Now, six years is an eternity. No one stays at a job for more, really, than two years. If you stay more than two years people think that you're a low-achieving person. People get jobs and they have three months experience. But don't get me started on millennials.

After *Mademoiselle* you took a job as the fashion director at Gimbels East, which is not to be confused with the Gimbels on 34th Street. Gimbels on 34th Street was

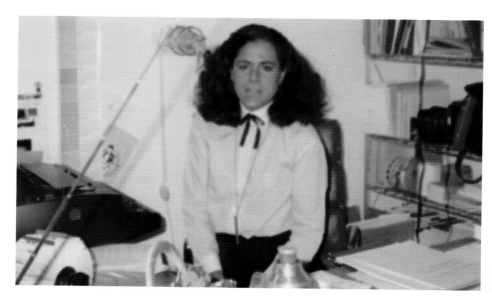

Fern Mallis at her public relations office that she shared with Bromley Jacobsen Architects.

made famous by Hollywood and *Miracle on 34th Street*, but you were at Gimbels East, which was on 86th Street and Lexington Avenue. It was a more high-end version of Gimbels, yes?

Yes. It was a very beautiful store. It was designed to basically cater to an audience, which was in the highest-income zip code on the Upper East Side. We had our own fashion director, our own buyers, and our own budgets. I remember having my first all-red office with rattan furniture in it.

I was responsible for windows, and displays, and going into the market. It was when going to Calvin Klein's shows and Diane Von Furstenberg's shows was very hot. We created departments for all of them.

You know the designers Larry Laslo and George Stavrinos? I was giving them their first jobs to do illustrations for our ads and hiring people to design fun windows, just surrounding myself with a lot of my creative friends and bringing them all into the picture. It was a wonderful job until Gimbels was bought by Saks Fifth Avenue and it was all consolidated.

That's when you struck out on your own?

I had a short stint on Seventh Avenue for a company named Cinnamon Wear, which had a big presence at Henri Bendel. I hated being on that side of the fence. I hated being in the showroom having to sell to people. I also got fired from that job.

That was also a memorable moment and learning experience for me. I was fired Christmas week. The showroom was at 1412 Broadway. I remember walking into the lobby, with all these trays of cookies and platters for holidays. I was so depressed. I thought, "If I'm ever in a position to have to let somebody go, I will never do it at a holiday."

Then years later I come back to 1412 Broadway, which is where the CFDA offices were. I came back triumphant into the building.

You returned, rising like a phoenix from the ashes. You start your own PR firm called Fern Mallis Public Relations. What was that like for you, being a female entrepreneur at that time? It's still very tough to be a woman in business and have your own firm. We're still battling sexism right now. Women are still paid far less than men. What was it like for you?

Well, it's very nice when you say I had my own firm. It sounds like I had a real business. I had me, and I had a desk in my friends' office—Scott Bromley and Robin Jacobsen, who are architects and interior designers. Robin is no longer with us. Scott is my BFF.

They had an office on 59th Street between First and Second. At the time, they were designing Studio 54. It was a very heady time in that office, having Steve Rubell and Ian Schrager coming in and out.

I started doing PR because I thought I had "411" on my forehead. All my friends would ask for my help: "Can you tell me where to get balloons for a party?" "Do you know a good place to host an event?" "Where do I get this printed?" "Can you introduce me to this editor?" I eventually realized I could get paid for my answers. I worked at a desk in the corner of their office.

Then Scott and Robin's insurance agent said, "Would you hire my daughter, please? She's at Vassar." They hired her for a summer job. Then after her senior year, when she graduated, she came back to Bromley Jacobsen and we hit it off really well.

I hired her—Jane Hertzmark, who is now Jane Hudis. Jane is now a global group president of Estée Lauder Worldwide. Probably the most important woman in the cosmetics business. She was my assistant for six years. She worked on my typewriter return. We had pea soup every day on that typewriter return, with crumbs in the keyboard.

I started doing fashion PR first. Selma Weiser of Charivari was a client at the beginning, when Marc Jacobs was a stock boy there. I was helping her to do little openings after work to get people in the store. They only had one little store on the Upper West Side, on Broadway. Eventually the clients evolved and were primarily architects and interior design firms, textile and furniture companies.

You took that creativity and that passion and you made that into a business as well.

That became a very successful business. At the time I was doing that, we were like the KCD of the interior furnishings industry in its heyday. We had all the best clients. Everybody wanted us to work with them.

We were throwing confetti in invitations and glitter all over things; mailmen hated us. You would get these press kits and they would explode on your desk. But you remembered it. You went to our events. You went to our parties and they all stood out.

We were doing openings in Chicago at the Merchandise Mart, in Los Angeles at the Pacific Design Center. Then we got this big client called the IDCNY, the International Design Center in New York in Long Island City, and began working with I.M. Pei & Partners, Gwathmey Siegel Architects, and Joe D'Urso. Massimo and Lella Vignelli, who became friends and mentors to me.

Massimo did the subway map for New York City.

… Among many other things. Michael Bierut, who worked for the Vignellis, became a friend who's done every graphic need of mine through my career. Including when I got to CFDA; he designed the ubiquitous logo with the red "F."

You pull these people through your career that do good work, and they stay with you. They become the loyal people you can count on, in a pinch, all the time.

Well, speaking of great people and that era, we're now in the 1980s. It's when we get the scourge. What would initially be called a gay cancer that turned out to be AIDS. Life changed forever. For me, working on AIDS charities was the first time I ever really understood about true philanthropy. I know for you as well that's when you got really very involved, especially being on the board of DIFFA.

DIFFA was an earth-shattering and remarkable experience, because we all got together in the interior furnishings industry, at a time when nobody in the country—the president, even the *New York Times*—would even mention AIDS.

Part of what Bill Cunningham did, and he cried when we talked about it, he would go to every

Clockwise from top: Fern Mallis and Scott Bromley on Fire Island; Fern, Scott, and Robin Jacobsen in 1979; Fern in the lobby of the IDCNY; Fern at DIFFA's Edible Architecture fundraiser. Next page: The "TV House" on Fire Island in 1978, with Jerry Melmed, Ralph Gambaro, Scott, Bob Currie, Peter Strauss, Robin, and Steve Chambers. Everyone in this photo except Fern, Scott, and Peter was lost to the AIDS crisis.

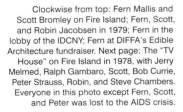

AIDS benefit and party and he put it in his party pictures in the *New York Times*, just to keep something out there about that.

The interior designers were dying quickly. At that point, because of my friendships, I spent a lot of time on Fire Island with Scott, Robin, Steve, and all my friends. We all had a wonderful time. Then all of a sudden people started dying, and we were going to a funeral, not once a week, but three times a week until it got to the point that people said, "We can't keep doing these big memorials. This is just crazy."

It was horrifying. I can't even count the number of people that we lost. But we needed to do something to raise money and awareness. This was before amfAR even started. DIFFA really was at the forefront. We raised money to buy a commerical refrigerator for Ganga Stone who was cooking for people and it became God's Love We Deliver. Susanne Bartsch did a Love Ball.

We did unbelievable events. I did something called Edible Architecture. I got every architect and interior designer to give me a drawing. We turned every single one of those into a three-dimensional piece of art, made of cake. Chandeliers were all made of gumdrops. It was one of the most exciting things I ever worked on. We raised half a million dollars at Sotheby's and sold everything.

At the IDC we did the ultimate warehouse sale, which really became a forerunner of Seventh on Sale. It was all the furniture companies taking booths, and we designed great aprons, and everybody sold their stuff. I still have furniture in my house from that sale. I got all my things from these big sales.

We needed to do it. I was at the Design Center and I had a boss there who wouldn't shake any gay man's hand. He was afraid that he was going to get infected.

One great event we did at the Design Center when I worked there was the first Comme des Garçons fashion show in New York, in Long Island City in the garage. We did great things when I was at the Design Center. I loved that job.

I think the DIFFA events opened the door for so many other charities. The breast cancer organizations learned so much from the AIDS groups.

Your philanthropy led you into a really incredible job, that of the executive director of the CFDA.

I was fired from the IDCNY because the real estate crash at the end of the 1980s caused everybody to stop building, and nobody was buying a million square feet of furniture anymore, so of course the first thing they do is let the creative people go. Instead of the businesspeople. That always makes me crazy.

I took a temporary job doing PR again at Loving & Weintraub with Mary Loving and Harriet Weintraub. I came with my three-roll Rolodex, which doesn't exist anymore. I shared an office with Leslie Stevens, who then eventually started LaForce + Stevens.

I was reading *Women's Wear Daily* about how the CFDA had just done Seventh on Sale and they were looking for a new executive director. I went to that first Seventh on Sale with a dessert ticket because I couldn't afford to go to the main event.

It was chaired by Donna Karan, Calvin Klein, and Ralph Lauren, with Anna Wintour. Robert Isabell designed the Armory and every designer had their own little space. They were selling everything below wholesale prices. Tickets were sold for two-hour shopping times. Checkout lines were around the block all weekend.

The CFDA raised $5 million and didn't know what to do with it. Carolyne Roehm was president, and she resigned. The executive director was a friend of Perry Ellis's, who came from the textile business, and he was gone. There was a really small office behind the elevators at 1412 Broadway and they were searching for a new director.

That's when I said to Harriet and Mary, "Maybe I should throw my hat in the ring?" I called my friend Jeffrey Banks and asked, "Who should I call?" Somebody said, "Call Donna Karan." Then I was told to send a résumé to Stan Herman and Monika Tilley; they were the search committee. That's when I reconnected with Stan.

But they didn't automatically give you the job. They put you through it. They said you had been out of fashion for ten years, right?

They had five finalists that they had already picked. They'd seen hundreds of résumés and met fifty or so people. I came in, they liked me. That's when I had this meeting with Stan, Calvin, Carolyne, and Bill Blass. Bill looked like my father so I was comfortable with him. Calvin knew me from Fire Island. Carolyne was very pleasant. They said to me, "Why should we hire you? You haven't been in fashion in ten years."

I said I never stopped wearing clothes. I never stopped shopping. I never stopped looking at magazines. I said it's either in your DNA or it's not. I grew up in this world; I know it.

I had proved that I organized the interior furnishings industry—all the architects and designers coming together for big events. I could take a stab at doing it for the fashion industry. That meeting obviously went well. They told me that they wanted me to do it. I had to come to the next meeting, which was the entire board of directors meeting to ratify and vote in the candidate. That was also on my birthday.

Wow. Good things happen on your birthday.

It was in Carolyne's showroom, with a big conference table, the size of this stage. It was every name you could imagine at the table, from Ralph, Donna, Bill and Oscar de la Renta, Patricia Underwood, Mary Ann Restivo, Herbert Kasper, and even Eleanor Lambert, who started the organization. For the next ten years, or however long she lived after that, she called me "that woman."

She wasn't a fan?

Not really. I think she was very jealous that I got Fashion Week organized.

She had done the fashion calendar so many years.

She did fashion shows at the Plaza Hotel for the trade press, small press shows. Which were great. I thought she'd be thrilled that we finally got this to work, but not really. But we made sure we gave her the press list every season for Fashion Week.

This page, from left to right: Richard Gere and Fern Mallis at 7th on Sale San Francisco in 1992; Fern, Stan Herman, and their team at the original CFDA offices in the early 1990s. Next spread: 7th on Sale as illustrated by Robert Risko in the *New Yorker* in 1995. Fern is featured in a seafoam James Purcell gown.

But in any case, it was a very heady meeting. I wasn't a shoo-in. People challenged me about my beliefs and what I could do and wouldn't do for the organization. Oscar gave me a very hard time about raising money for DIFFA, and said, "How can you spend time raising money for DIFFA? We need you to do this for the CFDA."

I said, "Don't ask me to stop raising money for my friends who are dying. That will not take one iota away from what I will do for the CFDA." I stood my ground with him.

Mary McFadden said to me, "You're also involved in this Furnish the Future thing; what is that?"

I said, "Funny you should ask that, because I only got involved in that because there was a meeting in your showroom and I wanted to see your showroom, and that's the God's honest truth." You know what it's like getting rid of furniture in New York? It's a nightmare. You used to be able to call Furnish the Future. The trucks would come and take it to Brooklyn, where homeless families who were set up in housing could go and get sofas, tables, chairs, accessories and make a home.

By the end of that meeting they said, go out, they're going to deliberate. I came back into the meeting and the CFDA board of directors had a cake and sang "Happy Birthday." I got my job.

You're at the CFDA, and you decide to create 7th on Sixth.

It was market week in New York. Fashion Week was market week, and if there were fifty shows, they were in fifty locations. Nobody talked to each other. Uptown, downtown, all over town. If you had a show at the Pierre Hotel in the morning and somebody had a bar mitzvah that night, you had to take everything down. If you wanted a show the next day, you put everything back in again and paid full price again.

But that week Michael Kors had a show in an empty loft space down in Chelsea. Designers love empty, raw, concrete spaces. If you have been to shows, you know when they turn the bass music on, it's so loud that if something is not nailed down it shakes.

Well, the ceiling shook, really shook, and the plaster started coming down on the runway on the shoulders of Cindy [Crawford], Linda [Evangelista], Naomi [Campbell], Claudia [Schiffer], all the one-named supermodels. They get paid the big bucks and they just kept walking.

But the plaster chunks landed in the laps of Suzy Menkes from the *International Herald Tribune* and Carrie Donovan from the *New York Times*, and I heard years later that it broke Carrie's favorite Chanel lipstick that they didn't make anymore. She wrote the next day, "We Live for Fashion, We Don't Want to Die for It."

That became the shot heard from Sarajevo. I said, "I think my job description just changed." I just started the job. Stan became the president after I was hired. He said he could work with me and we did, for ten years together, and he stayed for sixteen years.

Organize, modernize, centralize became the mantra for the shows. The first place we got organized was the Macklowe Hotel, now known as the Millennium, which we did for two years, to see what could work. It wasn't big enough and it wasn't right, but it gave us the foundation and incentive to get the industry organized.

Also in the summer of 1992, we had the Democratic Convention in New York. That was the convention that nominated Bill Clinton to be president. I sat on a citywide committee about how to entertain all of the delegates and media coming to New York.

We put on a fashion show in Central Park under a big tent on Sheep Meadow. Every designer was there, with models, and included Oscar, Bill, Ralph, Nicole Miller, Isaac Mizrahi, Todd Oldham, Michael Kors, Betsey Johnson, Joseph Abboud, Alexander Julian, Arnold Scaasi… you name it, everybody. At the end of the show, we were all standing on the lawn and they said, "Is this what you're talking about? A tent like this?"

I said, "You got it. That's what we're talking about."

That September I went to observe the shows in Milan and Paris. I met with everybody I could and came back with all my research. We had massive meetings with everybody. The young designers were like, "I don't know, I need a really cool place that just has my identity," and "Will Calvin show there?"

Calvin, thank God, was sitting in the front row. He stood up and said, "Absolutely, I'm going to be part of this. We all have to do this together." The first couple of years Calvin, Donna, and Ralph all showed in the Bryant Park tents.

Bryant Park at that time was not the Bryant Park that we see today.

No. It was just on the edge of completing its renovation. It was Needle Park. There were rats. It was a mess. Then it became one of the most beautiful urban renewals in the city.

Stan's offices are at the corner of Bryant Park. He was instrumental in working with Dan Biederman, the founder of the Bryant Park Corporation, and getting us into the park. It was like the backyard of the garment center. Everybody could walk there. It was finally centralized.

I mean, it was amazing. It was such an extraordinary experience, putting that together.

It really was a heady experience to walk up those steps to Bryant Park. You were in the temple. You got sponsors, which is something that we had never seen before.

Well, that was my first stab at making this happen. We tried to put a budget together and hired a freelance producer who literally sat in a closet in our new office.

We had moved into a bigger office thanks to help from my friend Scott Bromley. I think Melanie Seymour might be here, who was my first assistant at the time. We hired this guy who had done exhibits for me at the IDCNY, and we put a budget together, then I started dialing for dollars.

The first person I got to give us money was the chairman of Evian, thanks to Cindy Lewis, who was publisher at *Harper's Bazaar*. She introduced me to Mark Rodriguez. The company was in the process of rebranding their water. He saw fashion as a great opportunity, and said, "How much money do you need?"

I said, "$100,000." I'm making up numbers, and he said, "Great."

The next person I called was Anna Wintour [editor in chief of *Vogue*] to explain to her what we were really doing and to show her plans. She said, "Well, how much do you need?"

I said, "Half a million."

She said, "Let me get back to you," and she called S.I. Newhouse [chairman of Condé Nast], and she called me back later that day, because she's fast. She said, "We'll give you $100,000."

I said, "Great, thank you. We'll take it."

Then I called Claeys Bahrenburg, who was the group president at Hearst. I said, "*Vogue* is giving us $100,000." He said, "*Bazaar* will give you $100,000."

Then I called, what's his name? The guy from the *Enquirer*. David Pecker. David Pecker was the chairman of Hachette Filipacchi. I said, "*Bazaar* and *Vogue* are giving us $100,000." He goes, "OK, *Elle* will give you $100,000."

Then Hearst called back and said, "Can we have *Town & Country* on board, too?" I said, "You sure can!"

I called friends at Clairol and we got them. Jane, who was my first assistant, was now heading up Prescriptives at Estée Lauder. I said, 'Jane, it's a great new brand, you know, this is perfect." She gave me $100,000 and so we got Estée Lauder involved.

Was it ever that easy again?

No. But for a while it was like, ka-ching! Ka-ching! Ka-ching!

Then I called General Motors. I was like Michael Moore: "Can I talk to the president?" They put me through. That's where you learn that sometimes you just ask. I spoke with his secretary and told her what we were doing, and she said, "What a great idea! Can you send more information?"

Then David Pecker said, "We have all the car and driver magazines here. I'll get you General Motors," and he did. We got General Motors and that's how Fashion Week started. Then we got the *New York Times* involved, and Moët & Chandon, and several others.

Tenacious dialing for dollars. Then in 2001, IMG acquired 7th on Sixth. It's 9/11. It's Fashion Week. What was that moment like for you?

It was the worst possible experience. It still makes me cry. I was home that morning because I wasn't going to the Liz Lange 9 a.m. show so I could watch CNN, which was doing a special all week backstage. I wanted to see it on the TV.

Clockwise from top: The NYFW Bryant Park tents in September 2001, designed by Stephen Sprouse; Paris Hilton, Steven Kolb, Stan Herman, and Fern Mallis front row at John Varvatos's NYFW show in 2007; Fern standing outside the NYFW tents in 1995.

Then there was breaking news. Like everybody, I saw that a plane crashed into the World Trade Center's twin towers. I said, "Uh, oh, I'd better get downtown." I didn't know what was going on. At the corner of 68th and Park you could see smoke filling the sky.

I got to the tents, and the severity of what was happening became real. Guests were coming out of Liz's show. People were starting to find out what was happening. I remember going backstage to Douglas Hannant and Oscar de la Renta, who were having the next shows. They were all busy setting up. We were getting as much intel as we could from Ty Yorio from Citadel Security, who was masterful during those days.

I went into these venues and I said, "Stop everything you're doing. Everybody, please, quickly take your belongings. Go home. Go be with your loved ones. There's been a terrorist attack in New York. We're not having any shows here today."

People were looking at me like, "Is she crazy?"

It was unbelievable.

At Oscar's show, all these women were backstage at tables having lunch. Oscar wasn't there yet. There are people to this day who stop me and say, "You know, you were the first person who told us all about this."

We were the largest public event in New York, right behind the New York Public Library, right by Times Square, by Grand Central, there were bomb scares everywhere. We were running out of that place and just watched Armageddon walking up Sixth Avenue. We thought that we would turn the tents into some retrieval center or something. There were millions of dollars of equipment that had to be protected. It was just such a nightmare from one minute to the next.

Thousands of press were in New York for the shows. Journalists took off their heels, and went down to ground zero, and were reporting a very different story firsthand. It was quite remarkable. From all over the world, they were in New York at that time because of Fashion Week.

People were stranded in New York.

Giorgio Armani was stranded in New York. The city was shut down.

We sent all our Evian water down to ground zero. We sent our people to put tents up down there and help create structures to protect things. I remember calling KCD, who was doing our press, as it was happening and saying, "Let's get this press release out about what's going on here."

Kerry Youmans [from KCD] was on the phone. Their offices were in the Milk Studios. He started screaming while I was talking to him, "Oh, my God! Oh, my God! The building just came down. The buildings came down in front of my eyes." It was just unbelievable.

IMG, which was presenting the shows for the first time since the acquisition, was like, "Wait a minute. We need to check what the legal liabilities are for our sponsors if we stop the shows." I'm like, "I don't care what they are. We're not having fashion shows here. Everybody's got to get out of here."

It was a crazy time. We shut down the tents, which had a fabulous Stephen Sprouse–designed graffiti front, and we all know what happened from there.

The next season we put up tents with an organic American flag design that Stephen Sprouse had done for Target, and we had Mayor Bloomberg cut a ribbon with all the designers in front of the tent to let the world know we were back.

… And we came back stronger than ever. That was a tough day.

Which brings me into another tough day. IMG began changing the face of New York Fashion Week, and taking it from a place where you started it to help and support creative fashion designers, to it being all about making more money.

Ultimately, at the end of the day, I respect that it is a business. I respect sponsorships. I know how important they are to make things happen. But in the last few years of my tenure there, I felt like the only word you heard in the corridor was "EBITDA."

It was time for a change. All the great swag bags we used to put together for the media were now going to the sponsors and their guests. I mean, everything was about sponsors. "How can we make sponsors happy?" Sponsors, sponsors, sponsors. We had created this project for designers, to put the designers front and center. It became a conflict of interest for me.

By that point I'd also spent several years going all over the world for IMG. I went to India and consulted on Fashion Week in Mumbai for ten years. We acquired Fashion Week in Moscow. Fashion Weeks in Sydney and Melbourne, Australia. We created Fashion Week in Berlin, and I consulted on projects in Mexico City, Toronto, Singapore, Dubai, Tokyo, as well as creating Fashion Weeks in Los Angeles and Miami. There were some great times. Now, Ivan Bart is doing it. I love Ivan and I wish him all the best with wherever it continues to grow.

I'm glad folks are clapping, because this is my favorite part of your journey. I'm a big fan of women who take what's at their hands and really create something for themselves. Thank you.

Fern Mallis accepts a proclamation from New York Mayor Michael Bloomberg in 2002, kicking off the return of NYFW after the September 11 attacks.

At this point you're over fifty. You've achieved great success in doing so many different things. But you weren't a journalist. What gave you the notion that you could do something like "Fashion Icons with Fern Mallis"? That you could pull it off? I love that, because you put your name in the title, my love, and it's about damn time…

I didn't know that I could do this. It was never something on my wish list. I knew it was time to leave when the tents were exiting Bryant Park and going to Lincoln Center.

I was glad I left. Timing is everything. I took time off to smell the roses, as they say, at my house in Southampton. It was nice to spend more than a long weekend there, and figure it all out.

As it says in the introduction in my book, *Fashion Icons 1: Fashion Lives with Fern Mallis*, I entered what was called the "coffee phase" of my life.

What I mean by that is that, all of a sudden, I was getting calls from people, "Hi, can I meet you for a cup of coffee? I have this new idea. I'd love to talk to you about it." "Somebody said you'd be good for this. Can we have a cup of coffee?" I mean, everyone's calling for coffee, but nobody wanted to buy me lunch or dinner.

I had coffee coming out of my ears until I had tea with Timothy Greenfield-Sanders, the photographer, who's a great pal, who always took our press photos. Timothy introduced me to a friend, Betsy Berg, who is an agent and who does speaker series and stuff. She and I had lunch. It was a step up.

She said, "You know, I think that you should meet a neighbor in my building. They do these speaker series at the 92nd Street Y."

I said, "I know the 92nd Street Y. I used to go to the architecture series all the time there with Paul Goldberger. That place is extraordinary."

I met with her neighbor, Susan Engle, for coffee at Nespresso on Madison Avenue. She said, "Fashion is such a vital part of the culture of New York. Would you ever consider doing

Fern Mallis and Bill Cunningham at *Fashion Icons with Fern Mallis* at the 92nd Street Y in 2014.

38

something with us?"

I said, "I guess I could try it."

She said, "Do you think you can get some good people?"

I said, "I'll give it a try."

The first designer I asked was Norma Kamali because Norma was a friend of forty years. I got my feet wet with Norma on this stage. The next one was Calvin. Calvin really opened the door for me. I remember asking Calvin on the stage, "Why are you doing this? You have nothing to promote; you've been out of your business for ten years. You have no fragrance to hock and nothing to sell."

He said, "I'm doing it because the 92nd Street Y is such a great place, and I'm doing it because you asked me."

… And I thought, "Good answer."

Yes, absolutely.

When Donna was on her way to the 92nd Street Y, Calvin said to her, "Just have a good time. Just enjoy it. You'll love it." Honestly, I'm as proud of the series as I am of the tents at Bryant Park.

Certainly. Like I said, I love this one because it has your name on it. That's important for a woman to have something with her name on it, something that has your real stamp.

Now, to have a book in the Library of Congress, published by Rizzoli and beautifully designed by Sam Shahid, is a really cool thing.

The book launch was one of the best book launches ever. It was at Saks Fifth Avenue and the book was featured in all sixteen windows on Fifth Avenue and both side streets for nine days. There was a party with every designer. The sketch of me on the back of the book was done by my niece Alexandra Metcalf. And we're hoping to turn this into a book series.

Wow. I know the answer, but I have to ask you: who was your favorite guest?

I have two favorites. One, without question, is Bill Cunningham.

Bill was such an extraordinary, special person. He doesn't open up and doesn't talk much. Many of you probably know the story of how I got Bill to agree to do this. I'd been begging Bill since the series started. We'd been friends a long time. I'd beg him, "Bill, please, please, please, you have to do this." Well, you'll have to read about the rest of this quest in the *Fashion Icons* Book I, which we held up printing so we could include his interview.

My second favorite one was Leonard Lauder. Leonard was extraordinary. He's a remarkable man, and he talked about supporting women in business. He has built this sandbox with all these women playing in it together, competing, yet they all like each other. They're all making money for the company, and for themselves.

He shared so many stories about how he built the company: the lessons he learned from being at the University of Pennsylvania, about collecting postcards, about starting a film club, and then starting another film club because that film club was booked up.

Then he realized how he could have one brand, Estée Lauder, which was his mother's, that they built in their Queens kitchen, and then create another brand, Clinique, and it won't hurt that first brand.

Look at what this man's accomplished. He's as nice as they come, just such a sweetheart. I loved that interview with Leonard.

Who is your dream guest that you have not secured just yet?

Ralph is the one that makes me nuts because he graciously did the foreword to my first book in a minute, and was happy to do it. I love Ralph and worked with him on Fashion Targets Breast Cancer very closely for years. We're really fond of each other.

There was a moment when I would have liked to have done Karl Lagerfeld, even though I think it would have been a difficult interview. I'm looking forward to Bethann Hardison, whom I've known forever, and know is going to be great.

If you could go back in time and pick a fashion icon that's now deceased, who would you select to be on the stage with you? I'm talking about from any era.

Maybe Halston. Tom Ford just bought his Paul Rudolph–designed town house in New York.

Fern, you continually reinvent yourself. I have a saying, "It gets greater, later." I love what you've been able to do with this series and I love that you have the book. But I want to see the TV show. Actually, I want to see the streaming show.

Help me do it; I'll do it with you.

Do we have any TV executives in the room? We should go and talk to Apple. But you would be open to something like that.

Are you kidding?

Yeah, OK. In a heartbeat. I know you've done a lot of TV.

I was very good judge on *Project Runway*.

You were a great judge, a great judge. But you know, TV is kind of running out of time.

Yes. TV, podcasts, Instagram. It's a whole new world.

You've adapted to it quite well. I'm very impressed. Most people in your age range, honestly, don't even want to try.

In my age range?

Well, no. Think about it. I don't know that many people that are over the age of…

Be careful, Bevy.

I'm trying to be careful. Even I'm long in the tooth to be a social media maven. But you took to it. What do you enjoy about social media? Because you really are a part of it.

I'm curious. Apparently I have a lot of people wishing me happy birthday on Facebook. I love seeing my nieces, my family, everybody's trips, and my little nephews. I feel like I have so many friends who, while I've never even met their kids, I've watched them grow up on a screen this big [MAKES A SMALL SQUARE]. When I meet them, I'm going to go, "You don't know me?!"

We are going to get audience questions right now. First, the illustrious Mr. Mickey. My fairy godfather. He sparkles plenty.

Fern Mallis, Isaac Mizrahi, and Kelly Rowland starring in Bravo's *The Fashion Show* in 2009.

MICKEY BOARDMAN: Happy birthday, Fern. Fern is the person who first took me to India and I've been there seventeen times. She is responsible for my addiction, so thank you for that.

And now you are a bendy, twisty yogi!

MB: Exactly. Fern, what was the first fashion show you ever went to? If you could tell us your impressions of it? Do you remember?

FM: The first fashion show I ever went to was when I had a summer job. It was at Ohrbach's on Thirty-Fourth Street. Ohrbach's used to bring in all of the couture collections from Europe and copy them. It was quite extraordinary. It was a real big deal to get clothing at Ohrbach's. I remember my sister Stephanie and I had an Yves Saint Laurent suit. The long tuxedo jacket, with a sheer blouse, and pants. It was from Ohrbach's. I think that was the first fashion show I saw.

STAN HERMAN: Happy Birthday, Fern. I would like you to tell everybody a little bit about "Swan Lake." I think that's an important part of your life and I'd like to hear about it.

FM: "Swan Lake" is also known as Big Fresh Pond in Southampton. When I got the job to be the director of the CFDA, Stan said to me, "You know, I have a little cottage on my property, a little green camp. There have been renters in here for the last ten years and they're not coming back. Do you know anybody who wants to rent it?"

I'd spent years renting in the Hamptons. I said, "Well, maybe me." I agreed to take it.

I came out Memorial Day weekend, and proceeded to clean it up, paint it, and add my touches. Lots of flowers, fabrics, and baskets hanging everywhere. It literally is a little green cottage on the edge of a lake that is beautiful, magical, like *On Golden Pond*. That's how Stan and I really became such good friends, because we spent so much time together on weekends and in the summer. I was in this cottage for six years. Ivan Bart and his husband Grant Greenberg are temporarily living in it now.

Then Stan told me about another house on the lake. I remember being at that house and saying, "Well, should I do this? What am I going to have at the end of ten years at CFDA, a closet full of clothes to show? Let me put roots down and buy a house." I never thought I

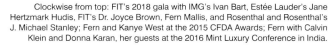

Clockwise from top: FIT's 2018 gala with IMG's Ivan Bart, Estée Lauder's Jane Hertzmark Hudis, FIT's Dr. Joyce Brown, Fern Mallis, and Rosenthal and Rosenthal's J. Michael Stanley; Fern and Kanye West at the 2015 CFDA Awards; Fern with Calvin Klein and Donna Karan, her guests at the 2016 Mint Luxury Conference in India.

could afford to do it. It was the best decision I ever made.

That place is very special. I sit with my little cat Dimples. If you follow me on Instagram, you see pictures of Dimples and the lake and the sunsets. I truly have Stan to thank for that.

FEMALE SPEAKER: Hey, Fern, Happy Birthday. I wanted to get your thoughts on sustainable fashion.

FM: Sustainable fashion is the new black. I think it's the most important thing happening in the fashion universe, and in the whole world right now. I think we all have an obligation to try to protect this planet and to live on it as long as possible. The fashion industry is a serious contributor to pollution, and I think that finally the industry is taking serious steps to correct this. It's not an easy solution or answer, but there are many steps for companies and designers to take, with everything from fabric, to sourcing, to the way things are packaged and shipped.

ROY CAMPBELL: Hey, Fern. It's Roy Campbell. Happy Birthday. When we were in fashion back in the 1990s, what I noticed about you immediately was, unlike a lot of people in fashion, you accepted everybody. You were gracious to everybody. You mentored everybody. How did you get that aspect of your personality and was there any pushback from the fashion industry about that?

FM: There's always pushback. Again, it's my mantra to "be nice." You never know who anybody is, really, and what they're really doing, and the shoes that they're walking in.

It's so much easier to be nice to people and let them in. I mean, when there's a crowd outside a venue, I would go to the line and pull people in from security, especially the people who we know needed to get into venues and were being denied because somebody didn't recognize them. It's just part of my nature to try to make things run smoothly and comfortably, and accommodate people.

When I was running the tents, we were in the service business. Essentially it was like building a hotel, and venues were rooms that were rented, and we needed to get people to go to the rooms that they were invited to be in. Anything to help make that experience better.

I always thought of organizing those things from a Disney perspective. Disney is brilliant at it. When you are in a line at Disney, they design everything so that your experience every step of the way is memorable and pleasant. It should be that way, and a lot of people don't do that. I would always walk through the tents and go, "Move that stanchion. Why aren't there more garbage pails?" Things that nobody else ever noticed, I noticed in there. That's the quiet part of what I was always doing. We always needed more garbage pails. "The signage is not high enough. You can't read how to go to that venue, and the bathrooms are flooded!"

I'd be in the tent and people would always say to me, "How come you look so calm?" It was my stewardess face. You know when the stewardess goes down the aisle with the coffee, and all of a sudden the plane does something crazy? The first thing you do is look at her. If she goes running to the back, you know you're in trouble. If she keeps walking with the coffee, go back to reading your book.

In those tents, there were a thousand eyes always on me for some reason. Watching me at

Clockwise from top: Fern Mallis's nieces Victoria Lampley, Alexandra Metcalf, and Brooke Lampley in the 1990's; Fern and sisters Joanne Metcalf and Stephanie Mallis in the 1980's; Fern with her family: Chris, Brooke, Theo, and Milo Papagianis; Michael, Victoria, Rex, and Lila Berens; and Stephanie in the Hamptons in 2021.

the information desk or at the front entry. If I was being hysterical about something people go, "Uh, oh, what's wrong?"

I always have my stewardess face on. A famous quote my father shared was "No two people should ever have to worry about the same thing." It's a really good one, because you have people around you who you're hiring to worry about that. So let it go.

Let it go. Thank you. We have time for one more, I believe.

FEMALE SPEAKER: Thank you. Happy Birthday, Fern. Hi, my name is Vanita del White. I'm privileged to meet you. Several times you've even retweeted me; thank you.

I wanted to ask your thoughts on the future of fashion, particularly the job market opportunity for entrepreneurship. I have the privilege of being a 2015 New York City Fashion Fellow, which I know you heavily supported.

FM: I think that's for another subject, another night. If I knew it, and had a crystal ball, I'd be really rich. To entrepreneurs, it's what I said earlier. You've got to find your voice and your passion, be focused, be creative, do it differently, and just stay with it. "No" doesn't mean "no" all the time.

When I spoke at FIT's graduation, I looked at the students and the audience and I said, "You know, the future is in the palm of your hands."

That used to just be a nice expression. Now, it takes on a whole new meaning. The world is in your hands. From the iPhone in your palm, you can unlock your doors, turn on the lights, book an airline ticket, and buy or sell anything.

The world is much better because you live in it, Fern Mallis. Thank you so much.

Thank you, all.

SINCE FASHION ICONS

Fern's proudest role is being the aunt to her very accomplished nieces Brooke Lampley, Victoria Lampley Berens, Alexandra Metcalf, and their children Theo, Milo, Rex, and Lila, and sister to Stephanie Mallis. Fern continues to serve on the boards of the FIT Foundation and the Carter Burden Network. During the COVID-19 pandemic, she took her *Fashion Icons* conversation series digital, launching *Fashion Icons: The Archive* on YouTube with the help of the 92nd Street Y, and completed this second volume of *Fashion Icons*. Fern splits her time between New York's Upper East Side and her lakeside home in Southampton (around the bend from Stan's house). Follow her on Instagram: @fernmallis

Ruben B 2021

VALENTINO GARAVANI

I've had the privilege of sharing this stage with many Fashion Icons, and they all had one thing in common: they were American designers. Tonight we get our passports stamped. I am thrilled to introduce the legendary, iconic, talented, charming designer, movie star, and author, Valentino Garavani.

While Italy may claim him by birth, he is truly a citizen of the world. In Rome, his Palazzo Mignanelli is located on the route Caesar took to the Imperial City. In New York City, his apartment overlooks Central Park and the Frick. Wideville, his château just outside Paris, is where Louis XIV's mistress lived. In London, his house is a nineteenth-century mansion on Lord Holland's original estate in Holland Park. Then there's Chalet Gifferhorn in Gstaad. The luxurious yacht T.M. Blue, named after his parents, Teresa and Mauro, gives him a home anywhere he wants.

When someone once said to him, "You have too many houses and rooms," he answered, "But too many for whom?"

He's dressed queens and princesses, First Ladies and sheikhas, and decades of Hollywood royalty, from his close pal Sophia Loren to Sarah Jessica Parker and Anne Hathaway. He has dressed more Oscar-winning actresses than anyone.

He has just published a spectacularly beautiful book, Valentino: At the Emperor's Table, *which depicts the richness of his life, his homes, his collections, and the table-tops he sets to entertain his many friends, or just himself. He often says, "I taught myself to appreciate beauty. I just like looking at beautiful things."*

… And my favorite quote, "I love a woman who eats food, has a body. That is a woman, and not a stick." His design mantra is actually quite simple. He just wants to make women feel beautiful.

Ladies and Gentlemen, welcome the one and only, the Emperor Valentino.

VALENTINO GARAVANI: You know almost everything about me.

FERN MALLIS: To really understand that journey and how you got to that place to do this book, and to become the living legend that you are, we start at the very, very beginning.

You were born Valentino Clemente Ludovico Garavani on May 11, 1932.

No, don't say this.

… Too late. In a provincial town north of Milan. How old are you?

I don't understand what you're saying [LAUGHTER].

I have a better question. How old do you feel?

Some days, very old. Some days, extremely young.

Tonight?

Valentino's 1964 fashion show at the Sala Bianca in Palazzo Pitti, in Florence.

Tonight, young.

Your astrological sign is Taurus. Are you a believer?

I believe in the zodiac. I like Taurus, not because it's my sign, but because it's a very good sign with lots of…

Stubbornness.

Taurus knows what they want and the big decisions to make. I am very proud to be a Taurus.

Great. My readings on Taurus said you are extremely interested in finance and it is likely you will amass a small fortune at some point in your life. You are very stubborn, but this stubborn streak gives you independence. You are dependable, persistent, loyal, patient, and generous. You are an excellent friend and you hold your few dear friends very close, and keep them guarded and protected. Your friends are treated like family.

Taurus loves to be the host, and the people who Taurus let into their lives are lavishly catered to. When Taurus decides to throw a party, they decorate and present everything lavishly. They will always pamper themselves and their close group of friends. They like to live lavishly and surround themselves with nice possessions and foods. It sounds like it was written perfectly for you.

That's too many things. The Taurus, you said a lot of qualities, but one that is not true. I'm not patient at all.

You are not patient?

I'm not patient. Usually, if I want the things done, I want it done immediately. If I have a desire, it has to be fulfilled immediately

Fair enough.

You mentioned too many good things.

Too many good things? I try to not mention the bad ones.

You are so nice. Thank you.

Back to your family. Your mother named you after the silent movie star Rudolph Valentino. Aren't you glad she didn't name you Rudolph?

I am just Valentino Clemente Ludovico. _

What did your parents do?

My father, he had a big, I mean big for a provincial city, shop where he sold electric cables. My mother, nothing. She took care of the house. She was not a great cook.

I thought all Italian mothers were great cooks?

Yes, but my mother, she preferred to stay in the shop with my father, and not to be at home cooking.

You made up for that. You have a sister. What was her name?

Wanda.

She wasn't named after anybody famous?

No. She studied. She got married quite young. She had two children, but unfortunately, she died quite early.

That's too bad. Tell us about her pink tulle dress.

When she married? I did a white lace dress with some pink underneath when she married. I was already in Paris as a designer.

Were you very spoiled as a child?

Quite a bit. Yes.

I read that you demanded to have your clothes custom made, and your mother agreed.

Custom clothes? Yes. Because at that time, you didn't have any boutiques, any places to buy ready-to-wear things. I remember very well that I used to have my shoes custom made.

... And I read you had jackets.

I don't know. You know, it's very difficult to explain, but since I was young, I always looked for beautiful things. "Beautiful things" is the phrase that I have repeated thousands of times during my shows, my collections, everything. Because for me, beauty is very, very important. Beauty is this table. Beauty is this glass. Beauty is all the people in the audience.
I love beauty. This has always been my religion.

I hope you don't think this table is "beauty."

No, but I wanted to say something nice.

Just checking. When you were very young, you went to the movies with your sister. Vivien Leigh, Hedy Lamarr, Lana Turner, Katharine Hepburn: those movie stars influenced you?

In the documentary that they did about me [*Valentino: The Last Emperor*], they had one scene where I spoke about my sister, and said she used to take me to see films. I was enchanted by them. I don't know, it was in the 1950s when I watched the film *Ziegfeld Girl* with Judy Garland, Lana Turner, and Hedy Lamarr. I was so enchanted with all the evening gowns, the sequins, those shiny things. It was then that I really realized that my way in life was to design.

I stopped my studies at seventeen and a half and I asked my parents if I could go to Paris. At that time for a child to ask to go to Paris was like somebody asking their parents if they could go to the moon. But they agreed, and I went, and I stayed for eight years.

Did you know anybody in Paris when you first went?

No, I didn't know anybody. I became friends with lots of people in the fashion business. We became, the three of us, together all the time: Yves Saint Laurent, Karl Lagerfeld, and myself.

You studied first at the École de la Chambre Syndicale de la Couture Parisienne?

I did nine months of study to perfect my design, to learn lots of things about couture, about cutting, about everything. I think it's very important for a designer not just to have an idea, but to know how to realize it.

You began applying for your first job and apprenticeships. You tried for a job at Jacques Fath and Balenciaga, and they gave you a big assignment, but you didn't want to design for others?

No, I didn't. I was at Jean Dessès and Guy Laroche, and afterward I decided that I could not go on designing for others. My father, I have to tell you, was extraordinary and gave me some money so I could open my own fashion house.

That's pretty fabulous. Tell us about your first apartment in Paris. You were in the maid's quarters, which I read you decorated from the flea market, *a marché aux puces*. Do you remember that first apartment?

I had lots of pieces of furniture and objects that I bought at *a marché aux puces*. My salary at that time in Paris was almost nothing. My parents used to send me money every month so I wasn't completely broke.

While you were there, I read that you went to Saint-Tropez for the summer, and it cost you your job?

Yes, I used to leave for the month of August and spend fifteen days with my parents, and fifteen days on the French Riviera. Most of the time, it was Saint-Tropez, Cannes. I was dreaming, because I've always been a very big dreamer, about beautiful things. I'm sorry if I keep repeating it…

It keeps coming back to that…

I would see all those yachts; they were not very big at that time. They were tiny. I was dreaming. Dreaming about yachts. Dreaming about everything beautiful. God gave me all the satisfaction one day when I got a yacht for myself.

You are now at Via dei Condotti with your own company, and you are producing your first show. Can you describe that feeling of having your very first fashion show?

My first show that I did in Rome, I remember that I did evening gowns thinking about

Clockwise from top: Valentino Garavani and Giancarlo Giammetti at their home in the 1960s; Valentino in his Paris apartment; Valentino with his school mates in Italy.

Jackie Kennedy.

Even then?

Yes. But I hadn't met her yet. But the big boom, Valentino's big boom, was in 1968, when we did the White collection.

For my White collection, everybody, all the magazines, everybody came to see me and I did the dress for Jackie when she got married.

But before you did that, you met a very attractive student studying architecture at the Café Paris on the Via Veneto?

Ah, yes, a gentleman called Giancarlo Giammetti, who is here tonight.

Absolutely. Do I dare ask you what attracted you to him? I mean, I think we all probably know.

He was the very light. I arrived in Rome to open this fashion house. He asked me if he could visit the fashion house. He came to see the fashion house, and finally said, "My gosh, what a boring life I have, becoming an architect and going home to study. I would love to come here and do something for the fashion house."

He came and he took care of everything; everything that was not the creation, and so we started together.

So without him knowing anything about business at that time, you just trusted him?

I never knew about business all my life.

But he just came in and figured it out with you?

Yes. He took care of the business. He took care of the publicity. Little by little, we arrived at something quite solid.

Then you moved your business to a tiny apartment on Via Gregoriana?

Elizabeth Taylor dances with Valentino Garavani at the Valentino: Thirty Years of Magic gala in 1993.

At Via Gregoriana, we started on the first floor. As time went on and on, we had the palazzo.

Before you got to the palazzo, you were at Via Gregoriana.

She wants to know everything.

You can't just jump around.

I never, never in my life say so many things like tonight.

Good.

I'm going to tell you which underwear I am wearing.

Please. Tell us.

No. It's too much.

Your first client in the new business that brought you lots of publicity was Elizabeth Taylor.

Elizabeth Taylor was in Rome for one year to shoot *Cleopatra*. She asked someone, I don't remember who, "I heard that you have a new designer that just opened his fashion house called Valentino. I would love to see his clothes."

We went one afternoon to meet her at this big villa. The villa was where Elizabeth was living at that time. I lived in a house close to that house. Anyway, we went, and I was left open-mouthed in front of this beauty. She was unbelievable. She was still Mrs. Eddie Fisher.

She told me, "I need an evening gown because in one month in Rome, it will be the opening evening of the film *Spartacus* with Kirk Douglas. I have been invited to this night. I would love to have a beautiful gown, an evening gown from you. But I have to tell you, I already have one gown from Christian Dior. If your dress is beautiful, and if it suits me, and I like it, I'm going to wear your dress." I tried to do my best and she wore my dress.

I went to that evening premiere, and the person taking care of my publicity asked, "Ms. Taylor, would you agree to have Mr. Valentino take a photo with you?" She said, "If he gives me one dress, yes." She was very demanding. Finally, I said, "Yes, of course."

Two days after, without any appointment, she came to my salon the day of my show. There were two rooms, quite big, full of people, to see the show. She arrived at that moment and it was a big disaster because all the people who had come were so enchanted to see Elizabeth Taylor, and they had to wait for hours to see my collection. Finally, I said, "I promised you one gown; choose what you like," and she chose the most expensive one.

She wasn't stupid.

The most expensive one. I gave it to her, of course, since she wore the white gown that I did for the premiere of *Spartacus*. I saw her once more, when she was having lunch at the seaside with Richard Burton. This was the beginning of their big love story. She disappeared for several years. I did not have any news, but of course I knew where she was. But we did not have any contact.

One day suddenly, I received a telegram. My secretary asked me, "Ms. Taylor would like to invite you tomorrow to the Grand Hotel for lunch." I was very surprised. I went and we had lunch, and she said, "You know, I thought about you because I need a beautiful evening

gown. The Rothschilds are doing a beautiful ball, the Proust Ball in Paris, and I would love to have a dress."

I made this dress, and it was the reunion between Elizabeth and me. She was very successful that evening. By the way, when Christie's did the sale of all her jewelry and the clothes, my dress from the Proust Ball was there and it was sold for quite a bit of money.

So giving her those dresses at the beginning was a very good investment?

Very good.

Shortly after that, you showed in Rome, which was the big fashion city.

I showed several collections in Rome in a big, big way. On the square, outside with forty girls, two hundred pieces. Now a collection that is very big may have only forty pieces. But this was a very, very good time. After that, I decided to go to France to show.

You also came to New York and met all the social ladies, which started a whole new business for you.

In the 1970s and 1980s, I dressed the most beautiful ladies in New York. Really very, very beautiful. In my documentary, they showed in *Women's Wear Daily* all the faces of the people that I dressed.

You dressed Begum Aga Khan, Jacqueline de Ribes, Jackie Kennedy, Lee Radziwill, Audrey Hepburn, Gloria Guinness, Marella Agnelli, Princess Margaret, on and on. It was a good group.

You then met the new *Vogue* editor—this was in the 1960s—Diana Vreeland. I read that she ordered a dress and sent you a note that said, "Even at birth, genius always stands out. I see genius in you. Good luck." Do you remember that?

She was one of my closest friends. I remember arriving in New York from Rome. My first telephone call was to Diana. She invited Giancarlo and myself to have a drink, to speak about everything. She was really somebody. She admired what I did, but she also liked me as a person. We had a very, very, very good relationship.

That's an important relationship to have. Then I read a quote which I thought was wonderful. It must have been around that time that the mayor of Rome said, "There is the pope, and there is Valentino. In this city, I don't know who else is as famous."

You know, it's very difficult for me, after all these decades, to say something about my career. To say something about my name, and what I did. But I have to tell you, I think I am one of the happiest, and luckiest, and most fortunate people in the world. I have absolutely everything, and sometimes I ask myself, "Did you do something to deserve all these things?" and of course I say to myself, "Yes."

Do you remember getting the request from Jacqueline Kennedy to see your clothes? She asked you to send clothes to the Waldorf Astoria when she was in New York. She ordered six of your haute couture black-and-white pieces that she wore during her year of mourning after President John F. Kennedy was assassinated.

Absolutely. She chose black-and-white clothes. After four years, she continued to order dresses. She went on an official state visit with Robert Kennedy in Asia. For that trip, I still don't know the total quantity of coats and dresses I made for her, but she wore them on top

Opposite: Diana Vreeland and Valentino Garavani in 1982. This page: Jacqueline Kennedy Onassis wearing a dress from Valentino's acclaimed White collection on her wedding day to Aristotle Onassis in 1968 (also pictured: Caroline Kennedy).

of the elephants and camels. There is the very famous dress with one shoulder in the pale green. This dress has been worn by lots of movie stars for the Academy Awards…

It's a beautiful dress. In 1968, one of your most famous dresses was worn by Jackie when she married Aristotle Onassis. Tell us about that dress?

That dress. She had already ordered several dresses from that collection. When all the magazines came out saying that she would marry Aristotle Onassis, automatically *Women's Wear Daily* called to ask, "Did you make the dress?"

I said, "No, I have no idea. Nobody called me to make a dress." Then she went to some-body, I don't remember who, to order a hair band to put in the hair. It was ivory colored. They mentioned that the dress was in my collection, and they were right.

It was just the dress she had already bought in her closet?

Absolutely.

Amazing that she didn't come to you for a new dress.

You know the most amazing thing? The dress was in the collection in short and in long for evening. The month after the wedding, we sold thirty pieces of the same dress.

That dress got a lot of publicity.

Yes.

It was an evening at the opera house in Spain that influenced your signature red color, which I had to wear tonight. Tell us how red became so identified with you?

If I had a million dollars every time that I talked about this, I would be Bill Gates. Bill Gates, I would be!

I went to Barcelona to see some designer. They invited me for the opening of the opera

Valentino Garavani and partner Bruce Hoeksema at the launch of the Valentino Virtual Museum in 2011.

house. That evening, I was a young guy, enchanted to see all the ladies that evening, and I was really attracted to the red color. I said, "One day, when I become a designer with my own fashion house, I would do red as a lucky color."

Well, I feel very lucky tonight.

You see!

Over the next ten years there was great growth in your company, including store openings in New York, Paris, and Tokyo; menswear, licensees, and fragrances. In 1973, you and Giancarlo also met another young handsome fabulous Brazilian man who became part of your team, Carlos Souza?

Yes, he is here tonight. He takes care of publicity and the image of Valentino, and he does it very, very well.

I read that you said you liked the 1960s and 1970s; you hated the 1980s. You thought women looked vulgar. Can you explain that?

I don't know. I went back through all my collections. What I did in the 1980s, I hated those dresses. Ladies were out of proportion with shoulders that didn't belong to their figure. The hair, it was all terrible, very short. The shoes, they were not good. They looked like puppets. I never liked it. I love the 1940s, I love the 1950s. I loved the 1960s very much.

In the early 1980s you also met your partner Bruce Hoeksema, a former model. Now Bruce does luxury handbags. Can you tell us anything about Bruce?

Yes, Bruce. He worked a lot in the fashion house on the business side, but he also had some creative ideas and one day he wanted to stop. He opened a beautiful boutique in New York for jewelry and bags and he's still doing this. He's here tonight.

That was a beautiful store on Madison Avenue.

Yes. Unfortunately, he had to get rid of that boutique because the space was rented by Apple. Apple, they paid the most amazing premium for the rent. So he moved. He is going to open very soon at the… Oh, my God, I forgot!

The Four Seasons.

Four Seasons, yes. Downstairs, a beautiful boutique.

Then in 1982 Mrs. Vreeland invited you to show your collection at the Metropolitan Museum of Art.

Yes, and I did a dress for her.

Was it red?

No, no, no, it was black and white.

Then you began to dress many of the stars for the Academy Awards. You also were designing cars for Lincoln.

They interviewed me on the red carpet three years ago at the Academy Awards because I think I was the only designer at that time that dressed several people when they won the Academy Award.

That's more important. You also were designing uniforms for Italy's Olympic teams?

Yes, we did. One thing that you didn't mention, because again I'm ahead of you, I also did costumes for the ballet. That was the most beautiful thing in the world.

You liked doing that?

Yes. I did the Vienna State Ballet and the New York City Ballet two years ago. You were there?

No, but I read all about it. I'm going back a little bit to 1986, when you won Italy's highest honor, the Cavaliere di Gran Croce [Order of Merit of the Italian Republic].

What I thought was more interesting that year was when you took on McDonald's when they opened near your villa and where you were working. You didn't like the smell of the fried food coming from McDonald's?

Maybe. You know, I have to tell you, it was not very elegant what I said. I don't like that restaurant so much because I am very particular about food. It's better to pass this question.

Can you describe the *Thirty Years of Magic* show that was held at New York's Park Avenue Armory? It featured Bette Midler, Aretha Franklin, and Placido Domingo. Over two weeks, 70,000 people saw it.

This was one of my evenings that I remember with lots of pride and lots of joy, because having Aretha Franklin, Placido Domingo, and Bette Midler sing "Happy Birthday" to you is a very rare thing.

It was record-breaking crowds that saw the exhibition.

Unbelievable. Sophia Loren was there. I am very lucky because I had lots of evenings with people that I would dream about. It's very pretentious what I am going to say, but when they know that I am there, they come.

That works. You can't blame them. I would come if I knew you were there.

Thank you.

You bought Château Wideville, which is on over a hundred acres. Had you been shopping for a house and you saw that one?

This page: Valentino Garavani surrounded by members of the New York City Ballet wearing costumes that he designed in 2012. Opposite: Julia Roberts in Valentino after winning the 2001 Oscar for Best Actress in *Erin Brockovich*.

Hundred and thirty acres.

No, because I had a house in London and I was crazy for the London country. I went to visit so many houses, but they did not work. Finally, a friend of mine said, "You know you have to be careful because in England if you don't have hunting, nobody comes for the weekend because they just go to shoot." I am against this and I changed my mind.

One day on Madison Avenue, I saw a beautiful home in the window. I said, "This one is the house that is in my dreams." I went to see it in Europe, in France, and after many conversations, many discussions, this house became mine.

I love that you found it on Madison Avenue in the window of a real estate office.

You see.

I also loved reading that you got a call from France that said that there was an explosion of roses, hundreds of thousands of them in the garden, and they must be seen now. You said, "You cannot ignore the roses. When they demand to be seen, you must go."

You know why? I had this house for quite a bit of time, but having a collection and shows—it's eight shows per year to prepare—and I was away from the house. Every month, you have different flowers blooming and they change. Finally, the last two years, I got to see everything I have in that countryside.

It sounds extraordinary. Apparently, there's a million rose bushes, in all colors. In addition to the roses, however, there are three hundred cherry trees, fields of lilacs, freesias, lilies, sunflowers, irises, wisteria, daffodils, gardenias, bright purple lavender patches the size of football fields, and tulips from the Queen of Holland.

It's a good cutting garden. Do you garden?

No. But I know exactly what's in the garden. I do not cook, but I know exactly what's used in the food.

You did finally buy a house in London in Holland Park and you renovated that. How much time do you spend in London?

Let's say four months a year, and five months in Paris, and the rest New York.

The least amount of time in Rome now?

Very little now.

You are also the first of Italy's famous designers to be listed on the stock exchange. Let's talk about when you had a cameo role in _The Devil Wears Prada_ with one of your favorite actresses, Meryl Streep.

Yes. You are so lucky, all of you, that you are American, and have such an unbelievable actress, because she is unique in this world. Nobody has somebody like Meryl Streep. I love her because she's a great actress, she's a great human being, she is very simple. Sometimes she comes for lunch at my house. She loves to go to see the cook and to ask for the recipe.

She's amazing, amazing, amazing, and I'm a great, great fan of hers.

Did you enjoy having a cameo in that movie?

At that time I was in New York with the collection, so for me it was quite simple to film the scene. To be there and to say, "Hello. How are you? Do you like the collection?" was very simple.

I'm sorry, but you make me feel naked tonight.

We're dressing you up. But did Anna Wintour get upset with you for being in the movie?

No, I don't think so.

Let's talk about the party that you created on the forty-fifth anniversary of your business. Clearly that party set a new bar for every anniversary event. The *Valentino in Rome: 45 Years of Style* was three days of extravaganzas.

It was an extravaganza, but it was also a show for my friends and the people that love my things. It was my chance to give back to them. What I put together for the three days was really amazing.

I was very lucky to have the authorities in Rome give the permission to do the first evening at the Temple of Venus, just across from the Coliseum. I did the first dinner there, and people could not believe what they saw because it was so unique. The night after we were in Villa Borghese, the central park of Rome, with a huge tent that was all Chinese. I wanted to do something totally different, something that was not Roman. It was all Chinese that evening, and it was really exceptional.

I was very, very glad, and very happy that I gave this opportunity to all these people. This was in July, so they had all their summer to speak about it.

… And they did.

They did.

… And the winter after, and the year after, it went on. But you also announced at the end of that year that you would be retiring.

I announced that in January 2008.

In 2009, we have to talk about *Valentino: The Last Emperor*, the documentary, which

Pages 61–62:
Valentino Garavani
arrives at the
Valentino: Thirty
Years of Magic gala
with Sophia Loren
and Giancarlo
Giammetti in 1993.
This page:
The Valentino
Virtual Museum.

Clockwise from top: Promotional image for *Valentino: The Last Emperor*; An aerial performance at Tempio di Venere in Rome commemorating forty-five years of Valentino in 2007; Valentino Garavani at his final collection premiere as creative director in 2008.

actually started filming several years prior to that.

Yes.

How did you and Giancarlo decide to let Matt Tyrnauer come in and film?

I don't know. They asked us to make a film. I was so busy, and Giancarlo, too. He was very, very busy. We did not focus very much on the questions. We let the cameraman go around filming. I was filmed when I went to the loo, you understand?

They were worse than me?

[LAUGHTER] Finally, when the film was finished, I saw the rough cut here in New York, and I was not so crazy for it. But the film was there.

It was presented on the second evening, at one of the biggest film festivals, in Venice. I was very small in my chair and I did not know what to think about it. I said, "My gosh, what ladies and gentlemen want to see me run around a dress, fitting, changing something?" But anyway, the film went on, and on and on, and at the end I had ten minutes of standing ovation.

So you got higher in your seat?

I was higher in my seat, but I was not finished because immediately the film went to Toronto. Everybody told me that in Toronto, they were not like Venice, that they were very difficult. But I had a standing ovation five minutes more than in Venice.

Five minutes more?

Yes. Finally I decided the film was successful and that people like it. I had young people, middle-aged people, old people tell me that they love this documentary.

It's an extraordinary movie. I think it set a new bar for documentaries about designers and people in the industry. It was such an extraordinary insight into your life and relationship. It was a love story on all counts.

Now I realize that of course. Very late, but I realized it.

Did you have a final say on what was in the film?

No, no, no, no. The film shows something quite personal. I was screaming. I was yelling. Usually, I'm not like this. But the moment is the moment, and they filmed everything.

I had to accept it. I saw my face in certain discussions, in certain realizations of my collection, and yelling at Giancarlo, yelling at everybody because I was not happy to have people around filming.

We are grateful that movie was made and we appreciate it.

Thank you. Thank you very much.

Now let's talk about the book *At the Emperor's Table*. When did you decide to do this book?

A long time ago, because I always loved a beautiful table. When I want to buy something, it is always something for the house. I start with china, I start with everything that is part of the table.

When you see china that you like, do you buy a service for ten, for forty, for sixty?

For one hundred people. But it depends. This is what you see in Christie's, in Sotheby's, in the antiques dealer. Sometimes you like a service that is so beautiful, but you have just ten plates. I buy it because I can use it just for myself.

When you see them, do you decide this is going to go to London, this is going to go to France?

Absolutely.

I want to see that storage closet. You have to have a warehouse to store all these things?

It's better that I don't.

I mean, just the glassware, the flatware, all of the accessories for the table…

I am very glad because in this room tonight, I have part of my staff that came to see me, and they are perfect. They take care of every detail of my houses, of the glasses, of the china, of the flowers, of the table, everything.

Where is the team? We should have them stand up and acknowledge them. That's a nice job, to take care of all those beautiful things for you. When you did this book, were you involved in overseeing every shoot?

Yes, we did it together. We put together the tables, together. I discussed the food with them. The book came together very fast. I want to tell you something that maybe you don't know yet. I always prepared my shows with lots of strength, lots of belief in myself. I believe in my dresses so much. Every day, every moment backstage, when I was putting together my creations on the models—and there were a lot of creations—I was always very happy. I was not nervous at all because I love what I did. I would say to myself, "But maybe there are people that won't like it. OK, I don't care. I love it. I created it, and they have to accept what I put on the runway."

But when I do something like the book, like the film, I am always just as demanding of myself. Those things are not part of my creation of clothing, but they are as good as my dresses. For instance, with my last book, *Valentino: Themes and Variations*, I was too concerned about it being too much of a show-off…

Too lavish?

Yes. But to my surprise, people loved it.

I think they do not want to see a bare table from you. They want to see one that is beautiful. Do you have a favorite recipe in the book?

No, I like a lot of things. Speaking about food, I am a very simple man, and I eat very healthy foods. You told everybody my age. Look at me. I eat very properly.

I love that the recipes in the book have very little sugar and butter, and that's how you run all your kitchens.

Yes, absolutely. They are all things that I have daily.

There must be some meal in that book that's your favorite.

You know, as an Italian, I love pasta. I love rice very, very much. I love fish. I don't eat meat. I don't eat many other things. I eat lots of chocolate and lots of sweets.

That works. Are one of the homes, or table settings, or one of the seasons, the most

Clockwise from top: Valentino Garavani at his home in France, Château Wideville, on the cover of his book *Valentino: At the Emperor's Table*; Valentino hosting a casual lunch in the château's gardens with long-time friends Carlos Souza, Charlene Shorto, and Giancarlo Giammetti; a table setting at Valentino Garavani's Holland Park home.

Valentino Garavani at the premiere of the 2016 Valentino collection designed by his protégé Pierpaolo Piccioli, surrounded by friends Dasha Zhukova, Giancarlo Giammetti, Eugenie Niarchos, Jessica Hart, and Bianca Brandolini d'Adda.

beautiful to you?

Yes. There is a picture that I took in my house in France. In the big garden, I have a corner that is called the White Garden because it's just white flowers. I have a sort of gazebo with just little tiny roses, and I did a table under this trellis, and I think it's the most beautiful in the book.

That sounds beautiful. I can picture that. The book is wonderful. Tell us about the mice and swans because there's a lot of stories in the book about the swans on your tables.

This is because one day, a long time ago, I saw some beautiful swans, and there were some mice with them. I loved it so much. Sometimes I do a table with only the swans on top.

I actually have a house in the country that I call Swan Lake, because there are two swans on the lake. I have many, many swans in my house, which is why I asked you about your swans.

Good. I love you now.

We've bonded over swans. I want to talk about the pugs. Tell us about your dogs?

My favorite. I mean, I love animals. This to me is the best thing in the world after human beings, but immediately after.

That's close.

It's a pity they don't speak, because they have eyes like us. They look at you. They are afraid when they are abandoned. When I go in the car sometimes and I see little animals on the streets, I don't know what to think.

The animals I have, I take care of. Unfortunately, I lost three of them just now because they were quite old, but I still have three.

Will you get more?

No, I am too old.

You are not too old. Do all of them travel with you, the three of them?

Yes, they travel with me.

So the three are in New York now?

Yes.

I just have to ask you this question about your working relationship with Giancarlo Giammetti. How important is it to have a partner who can run your business for you? For young designers, that's a big issue for them.

It is part of the luck that you have in life. I was very lucky that everything went together like jewelry that you fit together, and you move together, in a way. Do you understand?

I had the chance to have Giancarlo Giammetti. I had the chance to have other people around me. I had the chance to be an optimist. I had the chance to do lots of things. They helped me a lot in my career.

You are very fond now of the designers who are working at the House of Valentino. Are there other designers who have worked for you through the years that you've mentored or that have gone on to open their own businesses?

Yes, my boy [Pierpaolo Piccioli] and my girl [Maria Grazia Chiuri] were my assistants for handbags. They worked with me for close to thirteen years. They have seen me do every fitting, every detail, and they learned a lot. Today, they are going on with the Valentino name. My two designers who now lead Valentino do a very good job because they respect what Valentino means. I was so concentrated in my design and in my creations. I have lots of assistants, but I never asked them to do something instead of doing it myself. I was too concentrated, too jealous, on my drawings, on my creations, on my decisions.

Do you miss designing the clothing?

No. The way people work now is difficult because life has changed. They work in a different way now. They're still successful. But what I did, and what many other colleagues of mine did, it doesn't exist anymore.

Are there any young designers working out there now in the industry that you watch, or you follow, that you're fond of?

There are people. I don't want to mention their names because they are all good. I don't want to make anybody jealous.

I don't think there has been one designer on the stage who ever mentioned another designer when I asked that question. It's very interesting. What about the young actresses that you admire?

Actresses? Meryl Streep.

Any other people that you love?

I have lots of friends. Anne Hathaway, Jennifer Lopez, Kiera Knightley, they are all friends of mine. I have a list of many people that I love. They are beautiful. They have lots of talent.

I see them in my private life and they have lots of good qualities.

I know that you are very fond of some of the newer models out there now. I was told that you adore Gisele Bündchen.

Gisele, for me, she's the top of the top.

Fantastic. Do you have any regrets in your life?

Very good question. It's very difficult to answer. Very difficult.

Is there anything you wished you had done when you were younger?

When I was younger, I was, now that I think about it, I don't know if I was a normal person. Maybe not. I was dreaming constantly. Dreaming. Dreaming about everything.

You have some new questions?

I have some new questions from the audience. Who is the Jackie Kennedy of today?

I like Michelle Obama very much, very, very much. She has the most beautiful arms in the world.

This is true. What do you dislike or find not beautiful?

Ugly things.

During this trip to New York, have you seen something that was extraordinary? Something beautiful?

I went to a sale of paintings at Christie's. I saw a beautiful painting.

I read that you bought the Richard Diebenkorn for $9.7 million.

I did not buy anything for $9 million. No.

But your friend did?

My friend? Which one?

Giancarlo?

I don't think so. I don't know. He did it without my approval [LAUGHTER].

What is most exciting about the process of designing: the beginning, the creation, or seeing the design on a model at the completion?

You have many, many, many moments. I never like to see the first fitting, because I am very strong when I explain to the seamstresses my designs, my drawing. I really detail every single proportion. The first fitting is always awful. I ask them to do it yourself, and you come here with the second fitting.

Through time, you see the dress is born. You see it better and better, until in the end, you either change things—that has happened to me very rarely—or otherwise you love it. I think there are lots of moments. It is very fascinating, very fascinating. I really don't regret one second what I was, because I had the most beautiful, enjoyable time in the world.

What do you think about women today and their style?

I have to tell you that I am very glad to see beautiful women, beautiful. Because you see on television, you go to the theater and you see it on the stage, they are very, very beautiful. I am not so enchanted when I see on the street lots of people all dressed in black. I don't like that so much.

Clockwise from top: Valentino Garavani hosting *The Devil Wears Prada* star Anne Hathaway on *T.M. Blue*; Valentino and Sarah Jessica Parker in 2011; Valentino on holiday with Bianca Brandolini d'Adda.

This is our last question. Who should play you in a movie of your life?

I don't know; I have to find an old gentleman.

The movie would be somebody younger that would then age. You don't want to start with an older gentleman.

I don't know. It's very difficult.

You can think about that one.

I can think about it, and I will let you know.

Well, on that note... I promised Mr. Valentino we would not take too much time this evening. But thank you, this has been wonderful.

Grazie.

SINCE FASHION ICONS

Valentino continues to be a citizen of the world. He divides his time between his many homes and his yacht, *T.M. Blue*. His Instagram is a virtual time capsule, highlighting his greatest collections, runway shows, awards show moments, and the behind-the-scenes stories from his decades-long tenure as the creative director of his eponymous brand. Still by his side is his best friend and former business partner, Giancarlo Giammetti, and his life partner Bruce Hoeksema. Follow Valentino on Instagram: @realmrvalentino

LEONARD LAUDER

I have been after Leonard Lauder for more than two years, trying to get him to join me here, to share the extraordinary stories of his fascinating life and career. He has just recently returned from a month long honeymoon. So there is always hope, and there is always time for love. Congratulations.

It is his love of family, business, art, and culture that we want to learn more about. He has been called the "moral center" and "chief teaching officer" at the Estée Lauder Companies, where he is now chairman emeritus. The company manufactures and markets prestige and luxury skin care, makeup, fragrances, and hair care products, and has annual sales over $10 billion. His brand portfolio includes the flagship Estée Lauder, Clinique, MAC, Bobbi Brown, La Mer, Origins, Jo Malone, Smashbox, Aveda, Bumble and bumble, and their most recent acquisitions, Le Labo, GlamGlow, Frédéric Malle, and Rodin. It is the home of designer fragrances from Tom Ford, Donna Karan, Michael Kors, Tommy Hilfiger, and Tory Burch. Leonard is a "brand builder," and he acquires brands that are about people with entrepreneurial talent.

Leonard has said, "you only regret what you don't buy," and "collecting is a passion, possibly an illness, or an obsession, or all of the above." He recently pledged eighty-one paintings, works on paper, and sculptures valued at over $1 billion to the Metropolitan Museum of Art. It is one of the greatest gifts anyone has ever given, not just to the Met, but to New York City, and to all of us. We are truly the beneficiaries of Leonard's possible illness: his generosity, humanity, and philanthropy.

Ladies and gentlemen, let's give a very warm welcome to the one and only Leonard Lauder.

LEONARD LAUDER: What a welcome. Can I leave now?

FERN MALLIS: No. We are so thrilled to have you here. You know I was pestering you to get on this stage for a very long time.

Easy…

Leonard, we always start at the very beginning. We are going to go back a few years. You were born on March 19, 1933. That makes you how old?

Eighty-one, almost eighty-two. I'm en route.

Your birthday is soon. You're a Pisces. You probably don't believe in astrology, do you?

We created a line of compacts at Estée Lauder with twelve different kinds of signs of the zodiac. It was a blowout and sold out. I said, "Here's the chance to make Pisces big."

Is anyone here a Leo? It was the number one seller of all. You've just heard my astrology story.

Well, some of the Pisces strengths are: being compassionate, adaptable, accepting, devoted, and imaginative. One of the weaknesses is being oversensitive. Pisces have formidable intuitive ability, are independent, and inspired by life's events. Their creativity

comes shining through and they dream of an imaginary world of happy people and happy endings.

They need other people to keep them grounded and on the right track. Pisces is the most sensitive sign of the zodiac. Pisces goes out of their way to help a friend, and I've heard that about you many, many times over. You are sensitive and loyal, and take a friend's problem and make it your own and often suffer with them. Does any of that ring true?

I think so. My brand-new wife, Judy Glickman Lauder, is here. My bride, Judy, where are you? We were married on January 1, New Year's Day. So, we are brand-new. Now, Judy, after hearing all that? You can still run.

She's not running anywhere. She's a lucky lady.

I'm the lucky guy.

You grew up on the Upper West Side. Where exactly?

I was born in the Women's Hospital on 110th Street, just off Broadway. I can't remember exactly, but the first apartment we lived in was on 78th Street and Amsterdam Avenue.

My earliest memories are of the crib I had. If I could remember the crib, then I was kind of young. Anyway, we moved a little bit after that, every two or three years. But in those days, everyone moved around. After living in an apartment, we went into a series of hotels, which had cleaning services so my mother would not have to make the beds.

I heard when you were living on the Upper West Side, you also used to go to the Tip Toe Inn on 86th and Broadway. Was it all about the egg creams?

No, no, no, the matzo ball soup. My father used to take me to the Tip Toe Inn every Sunday for lunch. I would order the most expensive thing on the menu, which was shrimp cocktail. He laughed and he said, "You eat like a buyer."

I thought a buyer was someone who ate a lot, and expensively.

That came true though, didn't it? You have one brother, Ronald, who is younger than

This page: A Lauder family portrait taken in 1968. Opposite, from left to right: Leonard Lauder at Camp Arrowhead in the 1940s; Estée Lauder with her sons in 1944; Leonard in New York City in the 1940s.

you by how many years?

Eleven years.

Were you very close as young boys growing up?

I was sort of Ronald's older brother and surrogate father. My mother was working very, very hard and so was my father. I went with Ronald to his parent teachers association days. I went to Bronx High School of Science, and Ronald also went there, eleven years later.

I went with him on that day. I saw my old English teacher. She looked at me and said, "How nice to see you again. Where are you practicing?"

I'd never become a doctor, as all my classmates did.

What was home life like back then, having a working mother who was making face creams and beauty products? Did you understand what she was doing at that early age?

Really, I understood everything. I went to PS 87, which is on 77th Street and Broadway, and we lived on West End Avenue and 75th Street. I would come home every day for lunch, and she would cook me a hot lunch every day for the entire time I lived at home. No matter what happened, she was there to cook me lunch. To this day—you've heard about people who love nursery school food—I love lamb chops with a baked potato with lots of butter, mashed up with salt.

Thank you, Mother [BLOWS A KISS IN THE AIR].

That was her specialty?

That was it. Yeah.

Every day you had lamb chops?

No, no, no. It changed.

There weren't a lot of working moms at that time. Was this ever an issue for you, that she was always so busy?

When she came to school, she would get all dressed up. She would wear a fur coat. I said, "Why can't you dress like all the other mothers?"

I didn't understand, but the fact is, she looked great, and she was a great mother, and never

stopped being a great mother. Later on, when I went to work with her, it was very tough being a son, working with a mother who was the boss. Except she said she was the boss and I thought I was the boss.

… And that's another story.

I want to go back to PS 87 because I read that when you entered first grade, you had to bring in five cents to open a savings account at the bank. You continued to make only deposits, and no withdrawals, through all those years.

That's true. We had to bring five cents in and they opened up a savings account at the Central Savings Bank. The building is still there, on 73rd and 74th Street and Broadway. You would know it, it was a great building.

I kept that savings account going through my entire time in school and then I went to the US Navy. It had built up. I can't say it was considerable; however, we needed to make a payroll at Estée Lauder, in the late 1950s. My parents were away in Europe, and there was no money in the bank for Estée Lauder.

I went into that savings account, and I cleaned it out and made the payroll. I have no regrets.

Did the company pay you back?

What's the next question [LAUGHTER]?

In 1939, your mom and dad divorced, when you were about six years old.

Divorced or separated, I had no idea. All I knew is that they parted. The answer that they gave me was that my father needed to be closer to the business. I accepted it for what it was worth. However, I saw him every weekend and he was a great father, and she was a great mother.

I can't say anything other than the fact that I love them both. I love that period of my life.

… And then they remarried several years later.

Yes.

How exactly did you become infatuated with postcards?

I love postcards. I love the way they were done. I used to get an allowance of five cents a week. One time, I took my nickel and went to Woolworth's and bought five postcards of the Empire State Building. I just love the way it looked. I don't have those cards anymore. I don't know what happened to them. But the fact is that I loved it so much that I bought it five times. I started my collection.

My mother would go down to Florida during the winter to sell her cosmetics. I would go with her, and she would take me out of school, and she would put me in a school down there. I went to all of the art deco hotels. I was a little kid. I put my hand over the counter of the check-in desk. I took a handful of postcards. I still have them and I love them.

Were they stored in shoeboxes under the bed?

I stored everything under the bed. Let's not go there, either.

Now, we're curious about what's under the bed. Tell us about meeting a stamp dealer who collected German postcards?

I used to go to stamp dealers to buy old postcards. I would pay… they were very expensive, one cent each. Sometimes something was really expensive, five cents each. There was a stamp dealer on 42nd Street of all places, between Sixth Avenue and Broadway, and I would go there every once in a while. He would have a shoebox full of old postcards. One day, a postcard collector walked in. He started to explain to me exactly which was which, and what was what.

I love the education, I love learning, and I was hooked. From that time on I collected picture postcards. Now, relax, picture postcards are cheaper to buy than Picassos, so…

I read somewhere that your late wife, Evelyn, at the time called your postcards your mistress.

That's right.

When you were young, your parents let you travel freely around New York City. Two to three times a week you went to the Museum of Modern Art [MoMA]. What did you love about the films they showed?

I was fascinated with old films, with the cinema. Since I went to school on 77th Street and Amsterdam Avenue, I could take the trolley downtown, and then the bus later on. I would go to MoMA two or three times a week to see the movies. I would arrive early. I'd walk around, and I'd see all my favorite pictures.

To this day, I can still remember seeing Pavel Tchelitchew's *Hide-and-Seek*; some of you may remember that picture. Or Peter Blume's *The Eternal City*, about Mussolini. I'll tell you something. I loved doing that; that's what got me started loving art. Wandering up and down through the galleries of MoMA.

You would savor a painting over and over again, and said that you would make it yours. Very early on you were interested in the history of France from 1900 to the beginning of World War I. What was it about that period that intrigued you?

You have to remember that Paris was the leading city in Europe, if not in the world. They had their Universal Exposition in 1889, which is when they built the Eiffel Tower. Then the Exposition in 1900. Did you know that fifty million people went to Paris in 1900 to see that show?

I got fascinated about that period in Paris. Art nouveau was just coming out. It was called Bing, after Siegfried Bing's gallery. Fashion was changing. Everything was changing. To this day I'm fascinated with the period.

Let's go to Bronx High School of Science, which is one of the best schools in New York. I read that in high school you spent every afternoon working for your parents' business in their first factory, which was in an apartment building on the corner of Central Park West and 64th street.

Boy, you did your research really well. Yes.

It was a rented space that had been a restaurant.

First, it had been a restaurant. They rented the kitchen. That was where the first factory was, and then as the business expanded, they rented where the office was. I worked there every

Page 82: Joseph and Estée Lauder in Palm Beach in the 1950s. This page: Leonard Lauder with his postcard collection.

afternoon if I wasn't playing soccer, because I was on the soccer team, too. I got paid well, twenty-five cents an hour.

You put that in the savings account?

I did.

You delivered packages on your bike. You typed every invoice during high school. How many people were working there at the time?

Mother never went to the factory. My father never went where she was. That's why the marriage lasted so long. Two people worked in the factory.

She was buying boxes and jars?

My father did all that. I'll tell you something. He was a very wise man. At the very beginning we had no money and no credit. He had to pay in advance for the components that they bought. He, at one time, put that money toward boxes from someone in Long Island City. They didn't ship the boxes and didn't answer his phone calls. He took me out one Saturday morning, and I was going to go with him to the box company to get the boxes or the money. I was with him to see what it was like to struggle and to build the business, bit-by-bit-by-bit, and that lesson has never left me.

Your mother was influenced by her uncle, John Schotz, who was a chemist. She worked with him at the very beginning. Describe what that was like. How do you create beauty cream?

The truth is, I don't know, because all I know is that he was Uncle John. She would buy his products, she would sell them, and give facials to people. Schotz was her mother's maiden name. Her mother was Hungarian.

By the way, in our first office after I had gotten out of the navy, I was in our little office and the secretary came in and said, "Mr. Lauder, there's a Mr. Pierre DuPont waiting for you in the reception room."

I came out, and there was a well-dressed man wearing a pair of spats. I said, "Mr. DuPont?"
He says, "That's me." It was my mother's uncle.

I said, "Well, how did you get the name Pierre DuPont?"

He said, "Well, when I came into the United States, the man who was taking my name couldn't spell my last name and heard the name DuPont. I thought that was a nice name. So you can tell your friends that you're with the DuPonts tonight."

Your father handled the lawyers, and the trademarks, and building the business in the beginning?

My father did all the production, and all that. It was a good partnership.

… And your mother was checking out people's medicine chests, and bathrooms, and cabinets to see what colors they had to make your boxes the right colors.

I'm the one who looked into the medicine chests. She had better manners. It was a good partnership. She did the fashion, the styling, and she dealt with the editors. My father dealt with the manufacturing, the production, and the finances. It really worked very well.

She started by going to beauty salons. She had a captive audience there. She was great at touching people's faces.

She would have a little concession there. She would go and do facials.

I'll tell you something. Do we have a moment for a little story? She had a concession in a place right near where my office is now, a place called Florence Maurice, the home of the ashy blondes. Don't ask me why I remember that, but I do. Anyway, a woman came up to the little counter that she had. My mother said, "Oh, that's a lovely blouse that you're wearing. Can you tell me where you bought it?"

She said, "My dear, there's no sense my telling you where I bought it, because you couldn't afford it."

When you hear a story like that… it resonated with her over the years. That's one of the things that drove her. That is a story that stayed with me for my whole life, and stayed with her for her whole life.

Absolutely. She also had an expression, "Telephone, telegraph, and tell a woman."

Right. That's a sales thing. Now, listen, she was very funny. A woman would say, "Do you have a night cream?" She didn't have a night cream yet, and she said, "How does the cream know whether it's day or night outside?"

"Don't have anything smaller?" a woman asked. "Are you going on a trip?" she responded. She was really very funny.

She figured all that out. In 1946, when you were thirteen, she finally cracked her big account at Saks Fifth Avenue, her first big prestige department store. Describe that and what that meant? How soon after that did the "gift with purchase," her invention, happen?

Forgive me, 1946 is when they officially went into business. But 1948 was when

they started to sell to Saks Fifth Avenue.

Why do I remember it? Because I helped them stuff envelopes to send out to all their customers, a little gold engraved card, "Estée Lauder Cosmetics are now available in Saks Fifth Avenue." They closed all the beauty salon accounts, and moved into Saks Fifth Avenue alone. The rest was history.

They decided when they went into business that they should advertise. They went to see some advertising agency. They had no money, maybe $50,000, at that time. The advertising agency said, "That gets you nothing; please go away."

So they came up with an idea. It was my mother's idea. "Let's give samples. Not little ones; let's give a big sample of face powder. Let's invite people into the store to get a box of face powder free."

It would be a sixty-day supply of it, and if they liked it after the sixty days, they came back and bought it again. They gave that away. Then they gave away some cream. Then after a while, they said, "You know, let's make it a little bit larger. Let's do something else. Let's say you have to buy something to get the gift." That's where the so-called gift with purchase came from. It was a brilliant idea, brilliant. It's what really drove the company for years.

There were two things. One was the "gift with purchase." The other was in 1953, when she invented Youth-Dew bath oil, which was a bath oil that doubled as a skin perfume. It had an incredible fragrance, the sexiest thing that you've ever smelled in your life. I promise you.

Listen, I married Judy, who uses it. If there are any single women here, let me give you some advice, OK?

Believe me. Trust me.

OK, so, the fragrance was so good. Something like twenty years later, the hottest perfume in the world at that time was a new fragrance by Yves Saint Laurent called Opium. Has anyone ever smelled Opium? That's Youth-Dew! That's it. I promise you. So anyway, Youth-Dew drove the company. One more minute?

Go ahead.

We did so well with it, so well, and at that time we were not incorporated. Our accountant said, "You have to do something because you're paying all your money to the government." Remember back then, tax rates were very, very high. I think like 80 percent at one time.

We formed a corporation called the Fragrance Products Corporation, which I underwrote. That's another story. The Fragrance Products Corporation sold all of our fragrances, first Youth-Dew and later Estée Lauder fragrances. Then the Fragrance Products Corporation bought a little cosmetics company called Estée Lauder. The Estée Lauder of today was a company that started years ago as the Fragrance Products Corporation, from one sexy fragrance.

Wow.

If you use it, and it doesn't work, write me a letter. OK?

Is Youth-Dew still a huge seller?

It's huge. Yes.

I'm actually wearing Modern Muse tonight since I couldn't wear clothing from the designer like I always do. I went and had my complete makeup and fragrance done by Estée Lauder at Bloomingdale's.

Fern, I love you. Thank you for doing that.

I had to do it for you.

By the way, in case some of you didn't realize it, I'm a salesman.

You went to Wharton at the University of Pennsylvania. What did you study there?

Business. But wait, I'm not finished with you yet. You think that she's running this?

Not a chance.

Anyway, every Sunday morning, my parents would read the Sunday *Times* in their bed. I came in one Sunday morning, when I was starting to apply to colleges, and my father said, "Here. Here's the classified section."

Are any of you old enough to remember the classified section in a newspaper? He said, "Look under 'Help Wanted—Chemist,'" and there were maybe thirty or forty lines. "Now look under 'Help Wanted—Businessman.'" There were no lines.

He said, "You are going to become a chemist, and you're going to make the creams."

I went to business school. I never became a chemist. I can hire a chemist, which I did, and we did OK.

I do want to talk about something that you did when you were in college. You created the Cinema Club, and you designed the posters for it. This is something that I think is quite remarkable. You made a very small profit on that venture when you were in college.

A flier for Leonard Lauder's first business, University of Pennsylvania's Cinema Club, 1954.

Do you remember what you did with that money?

I bought books for the University of Pennsylvania library. However, I've got a handle on this, Fern. I'll run this, OK [LAUGHTER]?

Go ahead.

All right. At the Cinema Club, I sold a membership for $1 and for that you got to see ten films. It was so successful that we had something like 2,200 members, but we only had a capacity of 1,000 people. I was terrified that someday everyone would show up. I decided that I would run a competing film society. I called it the Film Art Society, and I sold three films for $1.50, and I did very well there, too.

From that came the idea, later on, of creating Clinique to compete with Estée Lauder. If I could do it with the Film Art Society and the Cinema Club at Penn, I could do this again later on with Estée Lauder.

I owe my experience to that. I can tell stories forever. We'll serve breakfast later on, so settle down [LAUGHTER].

That's great, how that happened. But at that early age in college, when you make a little profit, and you can fit the money in your pocket, you went and bought all the history of cinema books, and donated them to the university. That's early on, showing something about the kind of man you are.

You are not going to invite me here again, so I'm having a lot of fun.

Anyway, the Film Art Society showed experimental films. We showed one film called *Fireworks*. This was a picture with a man wearing a sailor's uniform. He opened up his flap and he pulled something out. He took a cigarette lighter, and lit it. It turned out it was a firecracker.

At that, half a dozen people jumped up in the theater and ran out. The next day, I received an invitation from the dean of student affairs to visit with him. We had a very nice chat, and he said, "Did you preview that film?"

I said, "No."

He said, "Leonard, let's make a deal." The deal was that I would preview all the films, which I never did really, but OK, but anyway. That was Dean Robert Pitt, a nice name.

Eleven years later, my brother Ronald is applying to the University of Pennsylvania. I'm taking him down to Penn for his interview. We walk in there. Dean of admissions Robert Pitt puts his arm around Ronald and said, "Ronald, if you are half as successful as your brother was here at Penn, you'll be great. You're accepted."

I think the entire Lauder family has gone to the University of Pennsylvania?

Except for my niece, Jane Lauder. Jane, are you here? She went to Stanford. Jane, you did OK, too.

When you got out you went to the navy, and you were very handsome in uniform. You learned a lot about management skills from the navy?

The reason I went into the navy was that in those days, the draft was around, and all my friends were being drafted. They became clerk types for two years. I said, "I'm not going to go into the army for two years to learn how to type. I want to do something where I can learn something that my parents can't teach me."

That was leadership.

I applied for the Navy's Officer Candidate School, and went into the navy and did very well. I was on an aircraft carrier, then a destroyer. It was a great duty. I loved being in the navy. I know we're not going to have the draft anymore, but I'll tell you something, being in the military in those days made you a great American. I thank the United States for taking such good care of me, and for educating me.

When you came out and joined the company officially, you started to create a sales force, research and development labs, and you brought in professional management at every level. You always talked about hiring people who are smarter than you.

Right. Listen, you can't get anywhere without people who are smarter than you.

Can I give you another story? When I was a kid, I was pretty smart. I thought I was smart, anyway. When I went to Penn, I was number three in a class of 750. I thought, boy, I was smart.

Then I want to the Navy Officer Candidate School, OCS. I was put in a section with twenty-four men, of which four or five were PhDs, some had military engineering degrees, etcetera. Of the twenty-four men, I was number twelve out of twenty-four. Here I came from being three out of 750, to twelve out of twenty-four. That taught me the greatest lesson in my life. The lesson is, no matter how smart you think you are, no matter how good you think you are, there's always someone around who's better than you.

I vowed that when I got out the navy, I would only hire people who are better than me. That doesn't mean that they may have been smarter than me, but they were better than me. To this day, if you hear someone say, "I'm not hiring that person; they're overqualified," forget it. Always hire great people.

That's great business advice. You've also said that you are only as successful as the people who work for you want you to be. I think that's a great one.

I write people little notes, congratulating them, if they've done something well. At Estée Lauder, people call them the "blue notes."

Today we had a great presentation at our board of directors meeting from the people at MAC. The minute I got back to my office, I sat down and I wrote everyone a little handwritten note telling them how great they were. If you tell people that have done well for you how much you appreciate what they've done, when the time comes if you want to call someone out, they'll take it. They want you to succeed, because you're congratulating them for what they've done.

Great advice. In 1959 you married Evelyn Hausner, who was born in Vienna, Austria. How and where did you meet Evelyn?

On a blind date. Well, that's another story.

I told you that I did well at Penn? I decided that I was going to go to Harvard Business School. I applied to go there. I went up there on a Saturday for an interview. It was a bad day, or what-

Top: Evelyn Hausner and Leonard Lauder on their wedding day, 1959;
Bottom: Evelyn and Leonard in their New York City home in 1987.

Clockwise from top: Leonard Lauder with sons William and Gary at the 21 Club in 1981; The Lauder family gathered for William's graduation from Trinity School in 1978; Leonard with his sons at a young age; Leonard and Evelyn enjoying time with their grandchildren.

ever it was, because the guy who interviewed me, I never saw his face. He was looking down and cleaning his nails.

He said, "Mr. Lauder, what makes you think you're so good? Why should we accept you and turn down so many others?"

I'd never been asked that question before. I said, "Well, you know, I think I'm going to be pretty successful. I understand how things are done, and I think I can be very helpful to the school" [MOTIONS BEING SHOWN TO LEAVE].

So, I'm not going to Harvard. I applied for the US Navy. My friend and I went for a one-week vacation before I went into the navy. He met a girl, and she's the one who fixed me up with Evelyn Hausner, whom I would never have met if had gone to Harvard. So, Harvard, thank you!

…And that admissions guy has to be really pissed off. Also, your mother must have approved of her right away?

She loved her. The fact is, of all the girls I ever dated, she's the only one that my mother ever approved of and liked.

Evelyn joined the company answering phones first, and then later, she created training schools for the store sales staffs. She was the first PR director of the company, is that right?

She was the first everything: first training director, first PR director, first marketing director, first everything! We would work together. Understand, the company was tiny. There was Evelyn, and myself, and there was my mother when she was there, and a secretary. That's it. Evelyn would answer the phone, "Estée Lauder." Someone would say, "May I speak to the audit department, please?"

She said, "One moment please." She pressed the hold button, changed her voice, and said, "Hello, audit department."

That's the way you do it.

By the way, she didn't use the name Lauder. She used her maiden name, Hausner, because we didn't want to have people think it was just Lauder, Lauder, Lauder, Lauder.

I had to interview some people who were trying to sell some advertising. About a year or two later, we were at Carnegie Hall. By this time she was eight months pregnant, and the guy says to her, "Hello, Ms. Hausner. How are you?"

She said, "You see, I made him marry me."

You know, for years everyone thought that I had gotten my secretary pregnant. So don't kid. Don't fool around.

I have a wonderful anecdote about Evelyn. Many years ago, when I was at the CFDA working on Fashion Targets Breast Cancer, which we know Evelyn was so extraordinary with, she was being honored at Duke University. I was doing fashion shows for the Duke Cancer Center to help them raise money. I would come down with designer clothes from the CFDA members and they were modeled on the runway by cancer patients and survivors.

When Evelyn was being honored, I remembered she called me and said, "We're flying down on the plane. Would you like to come down with us?"

Well, yes, of course, I'd love to fly down on the plane with Leonard and Evelyn. I went to Teterboro and got on the plane. It was the pilot and just the three of us. I remember you were sitting in the back of the plane, I think writing checks or something...

I was writing blue notes.

... Blue notes, that's what he was writing! Evelyn and I were sitting, chatting away. Then we were hungry, so Evelyn opened up a cabinet and took out trays of food and unwrapped them. Evelyn is my stewardess, serving me food. I'm thinking, "This is really an out-of-body experience."

Then she opened up her cosmetic case and started to do a manicure. She was applying Nail Tek. I said, "What are you using?"

She goes, "Don't tell anybody. It's really good"

You're not going to publish that story, are you?

Another cute story is from a friend of mine, Timothy Greenfield-Sanders, the photographer, who has a home near yours in Putnam County.

He's my neighbor.

Your house is on a pond. It's a very modest house, simple and unpretentious, designed by a friend, Thad Hayes. He said that he was at a dinner with you and Evelyn one night and said to you, "What does your mother think of this house?"

You said her answer was, "Can't you tear this house down and build a real house, like your brother?" You picked up a knife and gestured stabbing yourself.

"Why don't you buy yourself a real house, like your brother." Oh, my God. But listen, that's Estée.

I was going to ask you about how you made the decision to create a company like Clinique, but you explained that with the Film Art Society.

I tell you, Estée Lauder was getting so big. I was afraid, because we were growing so fast, like 20 to 25 percent a year at the time, maybe even more like 30 to 40 percent. I was afraid that the people we were selling to, like Saks Fifth Avenue and Neiman Marcus, would demand that the growth keep going.

I was afraid that if we had to keep that amount of growth going, that we would have to do things that weren't right for the company like promote more, etcetera. I wanted to bring another company along, that would compete. I said, "You know, if I was going to compete with Estée Lauder, what would I do?" I thought about all the things that I would do, and that's exactly what we did.

Clinique was a big hit. Then one of your biggest mandates was saying, "I want to go international," which was a big deal. Harrods was the place you wanted to be. It took about three years to crack that.

She wanted Harrods. Frankly, I didn't know about Harrods, but she knew about it. We had a distributor there who tried to sell to Harrods, and Harrods said, "No, we don't want this."

Leonard Lauder with Estée Lauder Companies' Breast Cancer Campaign Global Ambassador Elizabeth Hurley and long-time Estée Lauder model Carolyn Murphy in 2019.

She said, "Let me do it." She went to see the buyer at Harrods and an hour later, there was a deal. The distributor was so insulted that she would go around him and make the sale that he couldn't make that he resigned our account.

Well, today the company in the UK does about $800,000 worth of sales. If that distributor is still alive, eat your heart out [WAGGING HIS FINGER].

You also said, "Think small. Thinking small brings big profits. You can do anything if you're small enough," which kind of sounds contrary to the scale of the way you do business.

It depends on what you think is small. Like I mentioned, today we had a MAC presentation. They have the smallest distribution of any of our brands in the whole corporation. But what they will do is sell to very few stores, and try to do as much as possible in each one of those stores.

If you take, for example, a company like Procter & Gamble, their average sale per door at a Walmart or something, would be between $30,000 and $50,000 per door. The average sales MAC will have are about $1.8 million per door. If you have a hot brand, and you don't over-distribute it, if you hold it tight, that's thinking small to me.

I see. Following that, you took Estée Lauder to Russia and to China. Where else were the big markets that you opened up first?

Well, Russia and China came much, much later. The first market was Canada. Then came England, then came Italy, and then came Germany. By the way, the Italians are the ones who grab on to new things and embrace new things the quickest of anyone. We did very well there.

The UK is an interesting little story. When there is a Conservative government, business is slow. When there's a Labour government, our business picks up tremendously. You may think that's contrary, but it really is true. It always has happened there. I think it happens around the world, too.

Can you talk about 1995, when the company went public? Why did you go public, and was that a difficult decision for you?

Well, listen, there are many reasons, as time goes on. There are some pressures in the family. We all felt it was a good thing to do, and so we did it. I went on the road shows and sold the stock.

For those of you who are in the investment world, you know that there are road shows, and large audiences, and one-on-ones. I was at an investment house somewhere on Park Avenue with my flip charts. This was at a one-on-one. I was flipping my charts. There was this young woman in her early thirties looking at me. I smile and I said, "Yes. Are there any questions?"

She said, "Yes. If your products are so good, how come you have so many lines on your face?" That's the thrill of going public.

Do you remember how you answered that?

No [LAUGHTER].

We talked about MAC a little bit. Tell us about that decision to acquire a small Canadian cosmetic company, created and owned by two Franks who were makeup artists. The face of their Viva Glam line was a drag queen named RuPaul. That must have been a big risk for a company like yours?

Look. I'm a nice Jewish kid from West End Avenue. What do I know about drag queens? I said, "Look, the world is changing. If I keep on doing the same thing, it's boring."

MAC had developed this strange business. All the people who work for them had their hair dyed pink, or green, or blue. They had tattoos here and there. They had face jewelry here and there, on the tongue. Instead of saying they're creepy, I said, "Wow, that's great!"

We bought the company and started to slowly build it. But the key thing was to keep MAC, MAC. Very often people buy a company and try to change it into their own image. I wanted to change ourselves to make us like MAC. MAC today is now twenty years in, and is as much MAC today as it ever was.

After the success of MAC, were you then shopping for new creative brands, or were they lining up outside the building to talk to you?

No one was lining up, but do you remember the Estée Lauder/Clinique story? I launched Clinique to compete with Estée Lauder. I bought MAC and the first thing I said was, "Who's the number one competitor of MAC? It's Bobbi Brown." I bought Bobbi Brown six months later.

Boy, were the people at MAC like, "Oh, my God." As edgy as MAC was, Bobbi was different. It wasn't a replica. No one really understood what I was doing, to tell you the truth. I did, but no one else did.

Well, I'm glad you did. We all love Bobbi. All of your acquisitions become part of the Estée Lauder family. Are you a family business or family in business?

You did your homework. William, Jane, and her sister, Aerin, went to a consultant and spent the whole day talking about, "How do we explain ourselves?"

They said, "We're not a family business, we're family in business." We still are a family in business. Even though we may have the controlling interest, we've never, ever used the power of our vote to make a decision that the professional management didn't want to do.

We're there, and it works. I'm having a lot of fun. In fact, I've got to tell you, they don't pay me much. You're laughing, but you should see my paycheck. When my son William became the executive chairman and Fabrizio Freda the CEO, I got a call from Dick Parsons, who was head of our compensation committee, and he said, "You know, we have no job description for a chairman emeritus. So how are we going to pay you?"

I said, "Pay me a per diem." So they pay me a per diem, and I maxed out a certain amount of money, believe it or not. It's not much. But look, I do get some dividends. What I say is that I would pay Estée Lauder to do what I do. I love it so much.

Do you want to address a little bit about the contribution that some of the family members make to the company: Jane, Aerin, and William, and Gary got away...

Gary's on the West Coast doing venture capital. Everyone does their own thing.

At the very beginning, my mother and father said, "You know what you and Ronald should do? You should sit in one office with a partners desk." Now that doesn't work. Each of us does their own thing. I started, and then Ronald, who was, as you know, eleven years younger. He came first after he graduated from school. He went to Belgium for a graduate degree in business and worked for a factory there. Then he and a man named Raymond Bermay launched Estée Lauder in France.

Then he came back to New York. Along the way, we're having some challenges at Clinique. I came to him in about 1971 or 1972, and I said, "Look, I'm having a hard time, would you do me a favor? Could you go in?" By that time, the general manager of Clinique was Carol Phillips, who had been the senior editor at *Vogue*. Carol and Ronald worked together and built Clinique into the business it is today. I owe a lot to my brother Ronald, because he helped make Clinique what it is.

Now, I love women, and I'm not talking about my sex life. I love women in business. All of the people who were working in cosmetics in the field were men; they were salesmen. Ronald created the title "account executive" and we hired women who were well educated and wanted to do this. To this day, I think we have something like 96 or 98 percent of people in the field who are female.

There's a lady who worked for me and she was the account executive at Bloomingdale's. She said, "You know, all the men I work with, all they want to do is get promoted. I don't care about getting promoted. What I want to do is do the best job possible."

That resonated with me over the years. I love women. I want to hire as many women as I can. If they're good, they're really great. Anyone want a job here?

But it's true. You have some of the best and brightest women in your organization. You have always been a strong proponent of women in leadership roles. All those women

From top: Toasting Estée Lauder Companies going public at the New York Stock Exchange in 1995; The AERIN fragrance launch at Saks Fifth Avenue in 2013; Celebrating the Melville (New York) Research Park, still in operation today as the brand's manufacturing and testing facility.

who are actually competing with each other, they all play in the same sandbox, and play well together and they do the best job to make the company successful. That speaks to your leadership.

Some of them didn't do so well at the beginning. Do you remember Jeanette Wagner? Do you remember Carol Phillips?

Yes.

In business, they could kill each other. Kill each other. I think Jeanette invited me to have lunch in a summer home in Sag Harbor and I went there. There was Carol with her at lunch. Carol is her neighbor. They killed each other and competed with each other during the day, and on the weekend, they were friends.

I can't not go forward without acknowledging Jane Hertzmark Hudis, who was my first assistant when I started in public relations. She is now the executive group president at Estée Lauder.

Jane was your assistant?

Her first job was working for me for six years. I never ask her who was the better boss, because I know that you've had her for a lot longer than me.

Jane, who is the better boss [LAUGHTER]?

This is a great quote I read about Leonard: "Clearly, Leonard has one of the best minds in the business. Estée is like the Queen of England, and Leonard is Margaret Thatcher."

That's a great compliment, by the way. She was a great lady.

… And a leading competitor was quoted as saying, "Estée would be nothing if it weren't for Leonard. He is the brains behind the organization. Honest to God, Leonard did it all. I'll give you her Youth-Dew. I'll give you her 'gift with purchase.' I'll give you her standing in line to see buyers. But he developed it into a company that far and away today has the largest share of prestige beauty in department stores anywhere."

Look, I have to tell you, it takes two to tango. The company would not be in existence today if it wasn't for the years of hard work that my mother and my father put in. I owe it all to them. The only difference is that there reaches a point when you go this far, and then someone else has to take it to go this far up.

In business, people say most businesses run out of steam. But I was able to come in there. I learned from both of them. They got me to where I was. But I was different. I didn't try to be like them. I tried to be totally different from them. Somehow or other, it worked.

It worked and you always said, "Listen to your mother." That's good advice. Let's move now to cubism. You have been collecting art for forty years. Did you consult with anyone at the beginning, or was it was just what you loved?

I always had someone working with me. I had my own taste. I mentioned earlier my time at MoMA. I went there again and again, and I learned. I read a lot. I read, and read, and read, and then my eye was honed. I hired advisers. One adviser is Dr. Emily Braun, who is a distinguished professor of art history at Hunter College. She has worked with me for nearly thirty years. Sometimes I agree with her. Sometimes she agrees with me. Sometimes we disagree. But together we were able to do some great things.

I would say that probably 50 percent of the collection was put together strictly by me going here and there, and 50 percent was the two of us, more or less. I never really counted. Do you remember I mentioned to you earlier to hire people that are better than you? She was better than me.

Were you originally buying them to hang in your homes or buying them knowing it was a collection and putting things in storage?

I hung everything. I'm not going to pay all that money and put it in a warehouse. By the way, it's not that I want to say, "Look at my Picasso." I come home every night for dinner. We go into the living room or the library, and sit down and look at a painting for five or ten minutes. Maybe have an after-dinner drink, or maybe have a drink before dinner, then leave. I loved what I was doing. I really, really, really loved it.

After the first few years, I wanted to put together a museum collection because I believe that I was only a custodian of these great works of art. They were someday destined for a museum. Every painting I bought, I looked at from three ways. It was something I learned from my brother Ronald. When you buy a painting, there are three "oh's": oh, oh my, oh my God. I only bought "oh my Gods."

You know, museums are always putting things up, and then taking them down and putting them in the basement. I would say, "Will it make the cut? Will it be so good that is has to stay on display?"

For example, if you go into MoMA, you'll always see Van Gogh's *Starry Night*. When you go to the Louvre, you always see the *Mona Lisa*. I want to have things that, no matter who the museum director is, because I'm not going to be around in fifty years from now, they would say, "that painting has got to stay on display."

With that high bar, I think we bought some great things and had to overpay for most of them. It's the truth. I believe in that. I borrowed a lot of money, and I didn't sleep at night. In any event, it's not that it was an investment for me, because I never sold much, but I wanted to have a great collection to go to a great museum. I think it is in good hands now.

Did you always think it would be the Metropolitan Museum of Art?

No, I didn't think it was going to be to the Met. I went to various museums. Everyone made a great presentation to me. I said, "If it went to MoMA, they are a fantastic museum, and they have so much good stuff, it would only make them stronger and add strength to strength. If I went to the Met, they didn't have anything like that."

They literally stopped at 1900. I was looking to transform a museum, and I believe I did. I have always looked at everything that I've ever done in terms of, "How will that transform something?."

I believe we have transformed the cosmetics industry. We have transformed a retailing channel. That's one of the things I do, and I love it.

Leonard Lauder at home with Picasso's *Nude in an Armchair* in 2014.

Not only did you give them thirty-three Picassos, seventeen Braques, fourteen Légers, and fourteen Gris…

I did?

…you gave them a $22 million endowment to create a research center for modern art.

By the way, I didn't have to bribe them, but I'll tell you this, I didn't give them the $22 million. I gave them $10 million, and they put up $10 million. I wanted them to have skin in the game, because I wanted them to feel that they had as big an investment in that collection as I had. I think eight or ten trustees put up the money.

You were also chairman emeritus of the Whitney Museum. Is it true that you gave that museum $131 million to beef up its endowment?

That's what the newspapers say.

… And to keep the Marcel Breuer building from being demolished?

Well, they wanted to sell it and make it into a shopping center. I said, "You know what? Guys. Come on. No."

Tell us about all the artwork you have hanging in the company's headquarters. You have formidable art hanging at the Lauder offices.

My brother Ronald is a great art lover also. He's the one who pretty much watches after the company's collection, although I have a lot of stuff hanging there myself. It's good stuff.

Yes, it is good stuff. We are getting toward the closing questions here. What excites you most in business today?

Creativity. I love ideas, ideas, ideas. You mentioned Jane Hudis, who is in the audience. We were talking about an idea that she just created and sold one of our customers on. She was so excited about it. It's a great idea.

I had lunch with this guy in Palm Springs last week. I said, "What do you do?" He said, "Well, I play golf four days a week and I play canasta."

Not your speed?

Not me.

What keeps you up at night besides your new wife, Judy?

I'll tell you something. Probably the thing that worries me the most is that someone will not really fully understand what this, Estée Lauder, is all about. Because this is not just an idea of creating something and you sell it. There are so many things that go into creating a company, and creating a product, and an ad campaign, and the people who go around it.

What I had started off doing is telling the people who were working with me that I wanted to have Estée Lauder be the best company in the world. I did not say I wanted to be the largest. I did not say I wanted to be the most profitable. I said I wanted it to be the best company in the world. If that can be accomplished, then I feel that I have done something.

I have a lot of people who have learned that quality sells, and that you do not have to cut prices to sell something. Good thinking sells. Having a future vision sells. I'm creating a group of acolytes who say, "We can do great things."

… And so that's what gives me my thrills.

In Leonard Lauder's crystal ball, what do you see for the future of the beauty industry?

Well, I can only quote my mother, "When sex goes out of business, so will we."

Can you talk about what you think are some of the most important changes that you would anticipate over the next ten years?

You know something? Every time I look into a crystal ball, I see something different. Look, we are living in a world market. It used to be that if you have a plane in New York and flew to Los

Angeles, you saw 80 percent of the cosmetics industry out of the window of the plane. The world has changed.

China is now a major market. The fastest growing market today, believe it or not, is India. It's growing like crazy. What about Brazil? What about the Middle East? What about any of these places? What you're seeing now is a major change in the world. It's that change of the world opening up and thinking differently that I love.

Do you still eat a nonfat yogurt with a sliced peach and whole wheat bread for breakfast every day?

It's a Greek yogurt, nonfat. It has live cultures in it. I'll slice in half a banana and some strawberries, and in the summertime, peaches. I like whole grain bread, not whole wheat bread. But I like my coffee black, without cream or sugar. No sugar, please.

Is there anything you wish to do that you have not done yet?

Yes, there are places I'd like to go to and there are places I'd like to visit. You know something? If I sat down, I would have a list of books I still want to read, and movies I still want to see, and places I want to visit, and kids I want to see. My wife Judy has, if you can believe, sixteen grandchildren, and she's the most beautiful woman ever in the world. I want to see her grandchildren grow up.

I'll tell you something, I don't know what your religion is here, but a few days after our wedding, we attended the bar mitzvah of one of her grandsons in Sarasota, Florida. By the way, they're great. At the end of the ceremony, the rabbi, who was her son, called all the kids up who are under thirteen to the bimah. There was something like thirty-two of them out there. I said, "Holy Christ, can you imagine? Every high school graduation, every college graduation. I'm going to live long enough to see them all married and have their children."

I hope that's true. I think that beautiful story is the best way to end.

But we have a couple of questions from the audience. If you have a free day in New York City, what do you do?

What is a free day? It depends on the season. I have a bad back now, but my whole thing used to be getting up early in the morning of a spring, summer, and fall day, and taking a walk in the park for an hour or two. I love Central Park. It just gives me energy.

Then if I have time, which I always try to have, I'm going to go to a museum. I would go to the Whitney Museum, I'd go to the Guggenheim, or the Met, somewhere. I love museums.

Or I would go to a bookstore, but there are no more bookstores. But I love going to bookstores and just browsing. I would always come back with a shopping bag full of books, and no place to put them.

I love having lunch, and if you can eat outdoors, that's great. There are two or three little restaurants around our neighborhood that I love because I always see people I know there. I just love the neighborhood. I love neighborhoods.

Then in the evening, I'll have a great, quiet dinner with Judy. We love going out alone with each other. Or we'll go to the movies. Or we'll go to a Broadway show. But to me, New York gives me energy. I love New York.

It's a place that makes my spirits soar. That's what I'd do.

Other than Youth-Dew, what is your favorite product of all time?

I could answer that. The product that we have that people love is a product called Crème de la Mer. It's really, really good. That's a company that I chased for years because I loved the product and everyone said you could knock it off. I could never knock it off, so I had to buy the company.

Last question: if there was one bit of advice you could give your thirty-year-old self, what would it be?

Stay healthy. You're not going to believe this. I was a jogger. I ran every city in the world. The Champ de Mars, which is right by the Eiffel Tower, at dawn. Red Square in Moscow, in a snowstorm, in December. Seoul, Korea, and around the Emperor's Palace in Tokyo, etcetera, etcetera. I'm paying for that now.

I would say walk, don't run.

SINCE FASHION ICONS

In 2020, Leonard released his long-awaited autobiography, *The Company I Keep: My Life in Beauty*, about his life and the legacy of the Estée Lauder Companies. Mr. Lauder continues to live by his motto, "you only regret what you don't buy!" The Estée Lauder Companies have grown to more than twenty-five prestige brands, and they continue to acquire exciting new brands. He lives on New York's Upper East Side with his wife, Judy Glickman-Lauder, within walking distance of many of the museums he loves so much. Follow Leonard on Instagram: @thecompanyikeepbook

basking in the spotlight. I think you do. Public image is very important to Leos. They are always trying to make things right in the world. You have larger-than-life emotions and need to feel like you have accomplished something at the end of the day.

Thank you. That is me.

I like that. it seems to describe you well. Back to your beginnings in the Cleveland Park neighborhood of Washington, DC. You are from a fifth generation Washington DC family.

I am.

Your parents had very interesting jobs. Your dad, George William Gunn, was an FBI agent during J. Edgar Hoover's administration.

For twenty-six years.

Your mom, Nancy, helped create the library at the CIA?

Mother was only at the CIA for four years. After she had me and three years later my sister, she became a full-time mom. Later, she became a real estate broker and sold real estate for thirty years.

Did you understand what those jobs were about as a kid? Was your father able to come home after work and talk about his day at the office?

No. Dad did not. In fact, we rarely saw him. He had very long hours. My sister and I ate dinner with my mother. Dad would come home later and have dinner alone. I don't even think he would speak to my mother. That was not because of animosity; Dad just didn't talk about his work. I was very proud of him and would visit him in his office once a year with my sister. We would take a whole tour of the FBI, which was great.

Tim Gunn and his family before a trip to Paris: brother-in-law Jay Gundy, sister Kim Gunn Gundy, and niece Wallace Gundy.

For those of you who are younger, J. Edgar Hoover was not a presidential appointment. He was immune to whatever was happening in the White House or on Capitol Hill. I have a conspiracy theory about his death. He died in his sleep, and it was right on the cusp of the Watergate scandal. I believe he knew. I believe someone decided to do something about that.

… And he is the truth teller.

I mean, it's speculative. I don't know. But it seems very coincidental.

You mentioned your sister, Kim Gunn. She's younger. Are you close?

Very.

What does she do, and where does she live?

She also is a career academic. She and her husband were most recently in Vermont, at the Vermont Academy. They have been all over the place: University of Virginia, the Hill School in Pottstown, Pennsylvania. My brother-in-law just went into retirement. So they're now happily at their home at the beach. Bethany Beach.

We're all looking forward to the happy days of retirement, right?

I don't know that I am. I'm a bit afraid of it. You must be, too? Look at you. You'll never retire. They will have to drag us both out of here.

You were a very shy, inhibited child? You played with Legos and your sister's Barbie dolls? That couldn't have gone over so well with your parents?

It did not.

How did they react to that behavior?

It was more a matter of, well, I don't think my mother believed in sex, period. As a matter of fact, she's the one who told me about the birds and the bees, and I made the assumption that she and my father had had intercourse twice because they had two kids. My sister and I have the exact same birthdate. So I thought, well, once every three years…

I have to tell you something else. I'm getting off track. On the topic of my birth, I was born on July 29. My parents were married the October before, October 1952. If you count the months, it's dicey. My grandmother was at my mother's bedside when she was ready to give birth, begging her to cross her legs until August. Because then if you count it, it's ten months.

Wow.

Yeah, begging her. I also have a story about my grandmother's pregnancy.

Tell us.

Here's the story, as told by my grandmother. She didn't attend her weekly bridge club meeting. One of the bridge club members called her house and my grandfather said, "She just had a baby. She's in the hospital."

This person who played bridge with her weekly said, "She just had a baby? We didn't even know she was pregnant."

The logical question for my grandmother is, "You played bridge with these women every week and you never told them you were pregnant?"

Her response was the following, "That is none of their goddamn business."

That's my family DNA.

I mean, that's not so easy to hide.

Well, it was the 1920s. You had flowing dresses that cascaded from the shoulders.

Very interesting.

You're looking frightened. Fern may uninvite me from her living room.

No, not at all. I read that you changed schools a lot because you were having a hard time growing up?

I was having a terrible time.

You were bullied?

I got so used to that. It was called "being teased" back then. My big FBI agent, six-foot-two-inch, macho father…

… Never came to your defense?

… He never once took me aside and said, "Let me show you how to fight back." The consequence is that instincts kicked in. I'm a great biter and hair-puller. You'd better watch it. I'm good.

I hope that you add that to your…

My résumé.

Were they not upset when you came home, and you were beaten up a lot?

This is probably where my memory doesn't serve me well. I was in such emotional agony. Their response was to just have a stiff upper lip. Just deal with it.

… And make it work?

Yeah, make it work. Well, I didn't want to. That's for sure.

In your books you speak quite openly about a lack of sexual identity when you were growing up?

Very much so. For me, it was a matter of, I didn't know what I was, in terms of sexual identity, but I knew what I wasn't. I knew I was not attracted to women. I knew it.

We didn't rehearse this, so I don't know where Fern's potentially going. But at this particular time, I'll call it homosexuality, because that's what it was called at that time. If you were talking about someone being gay, you thought they were happy!

Exactly.

Homosexuality was treated as a psychiatric disorder, something that could be fixed. I thought I had enough trouble without heaping that on myself. I was in denial for a long time and just suppressed all those feelings.

Is that when you took all the pills that you could find in your house and attempted to commit suicide?

Well, that was not over my sexual identity. It was over just being miserable and seriously wanting to end things.

Can I also say about that experience, and it sounds awful, and I don't want to send a bad message to people, but the taking of the pills for me was euphoric. I was soaring in the sky.

I was so happy that it was over. It was waking up the next morning that was horrible.

What pills did you take?

I took a couple hundred aspirin. It doesn't work.

That hurts the next day. That's a really nasty stomachache?

Yeah, and more. Ringing in the ears, and fuzzy vision.

Your parents then just said, "Don't do that again"?

Well, no. It was the psychiatrists.

You went to Yale New Haven Hospital to deal with all of this?

It was for two years and three months.

Was this before high school, after high school?

It was during. I mean, it literally did save my life.

You are talking about Dr. Goldblatt?

I love that man. By the time I met Dr. Goldblatt, I had already been in the hospital for three or four months. He was right out of his residency. He was young. I thought, "I'll be on Dr. Number Five before you know it."

He would let me just sit. He wasn't leaving. He wasn't going anywhere. We just sat, and we sat like that five days a week, for weeks. Eventually, I figured out that he really cared. I started to open up, and we had an extraordinary relationship. I really do believe I owe my life to him.

Did you stay in touch with him?

Occasionally. When I came to terms with my sexual awakening and embraced it, I went to him to say, "Something's happened and I want to talk to you about it." I get emotional about it. He was so supportive. Extraordinarily supportive. He made me feel "this is OK."

Has he followed your career and all your great success?

I don't know how much of it he has. I know he is still in practice.

When you came to that sexual identity realization, did your folks come around?

I never told them. I told my sister. She's the only one in the family I ever came out to.

Are your parents alive?

No. My father died about eighteen years ago. My mother died three years ago.

I mean, my mother figured it out, especially once *Project Runway* happened. Well, no, it wasn't *Project Runway*. It was being the chair of the fashion department at Parsons. When I would go to visit her in Delaware, she stopped saying, "Oh, there's this lovely girl for you to meet."

But your dad passed away before all of that?

Yes. I have to say, when I had a special edition Barbie come out, a Tim Gunn Barbie…

Was it a Ken?

It was actually a Barbie wearing my ten essential items. I said to my sister, "If Dad weren't already dead, this would kill him," and it would have.

You were also a champion swimmer. Wouldn't that have helped your image? That's not a particularly gay sport.

From left to right: Tim Gunn with students at the Corcoran School of the Arts & Design; First Lady Rosalynn Carter holding an ornament designed by Tim for the White House Christmas tree in 1979.

Fern, I'm not so certain. There are a lot of really hot guys.

My father and I did not have the greatest relationship. A lot of it had to do with these tensions around the Barbies and wanting to play the piano. There were so many things.

In so many ways he really was a saint. He was determined to help me with this whole sports culture and he became the baseball coach. Even though he was the coach, he couldn't prevent me from being the last one chosen all the time. I would run home crying and it was embarrassing for everyone.

When I finally took to swimming, and was actually pretty good at it, he became a swimming coach. He wanted to be there for me in his own way. It was really touching.

We'll give him a few points. After high school, you enrolled in Washington's Corcoran School of the Arts & Design.

Well… I did eventually. There were a lot of colleges in between. I was this rolling stone. I was constantly looking for a place where I felt at peace, content, not threatened, and fulfilled.

That seemed to happen at the Corcoran.

Oh, my God. It was a whole new threshold for me. It was extraordinary.

You were surrounded by creative people and found that you actually had a creative gene in you.

One of the stints in college was a semester studying architecture, for which I had had a passion for most of my life. In fact, my mother would frequently recall our visit to Monticello, Thomas Jefferson's home in Charlottesville, when I was nine years old. I took my allowance money to buy a book of Thomas Jefferson's architectural plans. I actually still have it. She said, "This is a kid who is really driven by this."

But when I was studying architecture it was the olden days. You had to drop India ink into a stylus and pull it along a straightedge. If the ink bled, which invariably it did, you had to start all over again. It drove me bananas. I thought, "You know, even if I get through this program with a B.Arch or an M.Arch, I'm going to end up doing wiring and plumbing specs for gas stations." I wanted to be Frank Lloyd Wright.

Tim Gunn and friend Maxine Howe at Parsons School of Design London campus.

But things happen for a reason.

They absolutely do. You received a BFA from the Corcoran in 1976, and set up a sculpture studio.

With Molly Van Nice. The person I mentioned with the psychic.

Tell us about your job at the Corcoran admissions office.

My first job was assistant teaching to a wonderful teacher named Rona Slade. The following September, she invited me to come back and teach three-dimensional design, which I taught for years.

Then, about two years after that, the admissions director at the Corcoran left on maternity leave. It was as though no one ever expected her to leave. Unlike my grandmother, we could see that she was pregnant.

They said, "Would you take over her responsibilities?" I went to Rona first, just to ask, "May I do this?" I literally walked into an empty office with drawers that had nothing in them. I had to just invent things based on my own admissions experiences. I was grateful that I had applied and been to so many schools. I had a lot of experience.

See, that all somehow worked in your favor. In that position then, you were looking for new students. What did you see in a student's portfolio that would suggest that they would be a good candidate?

For me, it was always about: Who are you? What do you want to achieve? What are your goals and aspirations? And let's look at your background.

For me, it was always about how you utilized the resources that have been presented to you. I won't just look at a portfolio and make judgments. I have to know who this person is. It's very important to me. It was a conversation. A dialogue.

Parsons was next, in 1983. You were the assistant director of admissions at Parsons.

How different were the students coming to Parsons?

I had just turned thirty. I harbored a misconception, which was that the students applying to Parsons would be only the crème de la crème. But it was just like the Corcoran, only there were hundreds and hundreds of applications, as opposed to a hundred of them. Parsons is very selective. I was not used to rejecting anyone. Of course, it wasn't on my shoulders to reject them because everything was decided by a committee.

The committee would see everybody's applications?

Yes. Everyone's. All of us on the committee interviewed applicants and had to write up what was called a green sheet and rank them.

Here was the conundrum for me, and I learned fairly quickly in that first year. I was so used to nurturing and supporting applicants from my Corcoran experience that I was doing the same thing at Parsons. I was never dreaming that, "you mean this person who looks so great to me is actually going to be rejected?"

It was tough because the applicant comes back to you and wants to know what happened and what can they do to improve their application. It was a tremendous learning experience for me.

Was it a dream of yours to live and work in New York?

Yes, a real, serious dream. I arrived in late August. I went back to Washington for Thanksgiving. I was a hair shy of not coming back. I was so tormented by the frenetic cacophony and emotional craziness of the city. Every person who was panhandling, I was giving money to. If they had a dog, I was giving them more money. It was really getting to me.

One of my colleagues at Parsons said to me, "You have to get over this." She said the city is exactly how I described it: a cacophony of emotions and frenzy. I thought, "OK, I get it, and I'm not alone." I was like the long-distance runner hitting the wall. I hit the wall and things were much better after that.

Where was your first apartment?

Oh, my God, half a block from Macy's Herald Square. I was at 36 West 35th Street.

That's pretty noisy.

It was crazy. In my admissions role, I needed a rental car. The first day I had the car, I pulled up in front of the apartment to get all of my catalogs to go to my first high school visit. I came out front, and the car is gone

You would go to high schools to recruit students?

In my book *The Natty Professor*, I talk about that experience because Kit Chase, the admissions director, wanted to see how I was doing. I loved Kit. I really worshipped her. She was so charismatic and super at what she did. I wanted to please her.

We were going to three schools. When we went to the first school, she said, "I know I told you I would critique you at the end of the day, but this was the worst presentation I've ever seen in my entire life. We have to fix this now."

At the core of it was, I was talking about the process. I was talking about materials used. I was talking about the outcomes of the work. But I was not talking about design disciplines, and the careers, and where this can lead you. Frankly, it was coming from a place of ignorance. I didn't know. I had to learn a lot. It was stiff upper lip time.

How many years later did you become the associate dean?

In 1989. I was the liaison to our programs abroad, which at that particular time included our campus in Paris, which was founded in 1920, and our affiliate campus in the Dominican Republic, in Altos de Chavón, near La Romana in Casa de Campo.

You needed to go there a lot, right?

Well, a couple of times a year. This is the late 1980s; the electricity went off for twelve hours a day. We weren't certain we would have running water. It was a little rough and ready. But the campus was designed by a Fellini set designer. It was quite extraordinary. We were developing campuses or affiliate campuses in Seoul, South Korea, in Kanazawa, Japan, and in Kuala Lumpur, Malaysia. They were my charges.

In addition, I ran the full-time faculty searches and department chair searches for the dean. Overall, I was what other people called a Mr. Fix-It. I was constantly going into places that needed help curriculum-ly or pedagogically. I called myself a pooper-scooper. I used to say, "This place needs to stop pooping so much."

In 2000, the school's fashion department was in some sort of turmoil. Describe what was wrong, and what you were asked to do.

Well, initially, I was running a search for a new chair for the dean. In doing that, it was my responsibility to meet with the faculty, to meet with the students, to meet with the department's administration. I became aware very quickly that there was just flagging morale. It was awful.

Was this after Marie Essex?

This page: Tim Gunn on holiday in Venice, Italy, 1973. Page 120: Tim and Heidi Klum on *Project Runway* in 2017.

Marie was still there. Marie Essex was the chair who preceded me. She had been diagnosed with pancreatic cancer. She just couldn't continue to lead the department. I will also add that Marie was a Parsons graduate, as was her predecessor, Frank Rizzo, whom you know very well. I was this outsider, but I had spent a lot of time in the department in my associate dean capacity. So I was trusted and I was welcomed.

What's wrong with the department? Fern, the curriculum had not changed since 1952, when Ann Keagy was appointed chair. She was chair until Frank in the early 1980s. So she was there for thirty years. Owing to how famous the graduates are—Donna Karan, Marc Jacobs, Tom Ford, I mean, just to name a few—the department felt like, "Don't touch this special thing. This is a special secret sauce that shouldn't be tampered with."

Secret sauce? We had no computer technology! No fashion history! No dialogue! No critical analysis!

I went from running the search, to the dean deciding to abandon the search. Sending me in ostensibly for a year to offer up a diagnosis of what was wrong, and a prescription for how to "make it work," as I say. That first year I couldn't do anything.

You were going to do it for a year, but you wound up doing it for seven.

Seven and a half, and it is what I'm proudest of, professionally. The repositioning of that program was a bear.

Because you also jarred a lot of Seventh Avenue?

Including our pal Stan Herman.

You and Stan had a little tête-à-tête about that. You got rid of the designer critic program, which was a very well-known part of Parsons' curriculum.

The designer critic program has the designer come in and present a design concept to their group of students. The students make illustrations and technical flats for it. The designer critic comes back, and makes decisions about what will be done.

I'll use Donna Karan as an example. Donna was one of the good ones, so she won't mind. In fact, she was one of the people who kept nudging me, "Get rid of this thing!"

So Donna comes in and she's basically playing paper dolls. She's cutting out a jacket, and putting it with this top, or this pant, or this skirt saying, "Well, this is what you're going to do." She's making a collection because at the annual senior fashion show, the students basically show a Donna Karen collection.

The next phase is the muslin prototype. Donna comes back, and she sits with a pair of scissors, and she's changing the silhouette, and she's tearing out seams. But there's not really a conversation with the student. The student is basically a cipher sitting over here, watching.

Then Donna comes back for the final fabrics stage, and generally, the critics would bring their own fabric for the students. The students weren't even making textile decisions!

I watched as everyone waited, suspended in the air, because Donna's office would call to say she couldn't be back until the end of next week. No one can do anything. No one can move forward.

I've been a judge for that program.

Fern, you were a juror for this program forever. You would see the outcomes of that, and you would sit and watch all these clothes on parade, and say "yes" or "no" to these designs. There were seventy students in the senior year and each would make one garment a semester under the very controlling hand of the designer critic. We had a total of 140 garments at the end of the year. We'd have the jury show. We, in fact, paid attention to how the jurors voted so that the faculty could sweep in and fix everything. The faculty were fixing all the clothes. The department did not want anyone to be embarrassed by the quality of execution. I was in a total rage over this, as were the students.

I went to the juniors who were rising into their senior year at the end of the spring semester, and I said, "OK, guys. You have all come here for this designer critic experience. How would you respond if I were to tell you that I want it to go away?"

How did the students react?

They looked at each other and there wasn't a peep in the room. I said, "Doesn't anyone want to know what you would do otherwise? I mean, you are not going to sit around doing nothing for the entire academic year. You will design and execute a collection that represents your point of view as a designer."

Well, they went crazy. They were on their feet. They were applauding and cheering. And I said, "Wait a minute, I want to ask how many of you are terrified," and a couple of hands went up.

I said, "Every hand in this room should be up, because you are totally underprepared for this experience. If I were a responsible chair, I would phase in a new curriculum. The seniors wouldn't experience this for three more years. But I believe in you. I believe in your talents." This was going to be a tough, tall order, and they did it.

They pulled it off.

Stan came to the three days of jury shows. He did not believe in what was happening and he walked out of the jury show. We had a jury show over three days because we had so many clothes. We had 140 looks with the designer critic program. Suddenly we have seventy seniors making anywhere from five to seven looks each, and we had one collaborative collection, which is noteworthy.

He said, "I'm a juror at the University of Cincinnati. It's no different here now. Let's just talk about the textiles. These students used to have the most high-end, luxurious textiles to work with."

I would bring in three-ply cashmere myself. I said to Stan, "You're talking about something that has been revealed to me. These students know nothing about textiles and it needs to be part of the curriculum. It's essential." So, at any rate, we had a tense relationship.

It all starts with the fabric.

It all starts with the fabric. It's like sculpture. I mean, what are you making it with? The evening of the annual fashion show, Stan came up to me before the evening began, and he said, "I just want you to know it's been nice knowing you."

When the show was over, and Fern, you were there, there was a standing ovation. Everyone was on their feet. It was remarkable. Stan came over to me, gave me a huge bear hug and he said, "Never go back. Never go back." He said this was a staggering experience.

Stan and I did make up, thankfully, because I have such great respect and affection for him.

Stan is here. Do you agree with that story?

Sweetheart. Hi, how are you?

STAN HERMAN: You told the story very well.

TG: Thank you. And who were the student stars of that year? The Proenza Schouler boys, Jack McCollough and Lazaro Hernandez. Yes, Barneys bought their entire collection right off the runway. It was remarkable. It was a great moment.

Is that the curriculum that's still in place at Parsons?

To be honest with you, after I left Parsons in 2007, it was a matter of "don't mention the name of the dead pharaoh." I have no idea what is there now. Honestly, I'm persona non grata. I have not been asked back. They were great days.

We built a great empire.

While you were there you were doing some great work for the school and you got a call from producers of a new TV show. Was it Jane Lipsitz or Harvey Weinstein who called?

It was Jane Lipsitz and Dan Cutforth, who were executive producers at Magical Elves.

What did they tell you?

They told me that they were looking for a consultant for a reality show about fashion design. I said, "A reality show about fashion design? This industry has enough trouble without that." They said, "Well, just let us come in. A lot of people in the industry have said we should talk to you. We need five or ten minutes."

I Googled them, thank God for Google, and found out that they were the *Project Greenlight* producers. I knew that they had a serious sense of purpose and an integrity. We met, and I was impressed with them. They asked me one question that was especially penetrating. "How would you respond if we were to tell you that we want the designers on the show to create a wedding dress in two days?" I shrugged.

I said, "We'll have to create a wedding dress in two days."

They said, "You mean it can be done?

I said, "Yes, why?"

They said, "You're the first person we've met with who said it could be done."

I said, "But wait a minute, you're not going to get an Oscar de la Renta or Vera Wang gown. You're going to get a column without sleeves. But it can be done."

… And then I didn't hear from them.

Had they also gone to Pratt, or FIT, or the other fashion schools?

I'm sure they were talking to people all over the place. I did become their consultant. But the show was never intended to be shot at Parsons, ever.

How did that happen?

We were outfitting a loft space in the Atlas Apartments where the designers were living. The idea was to give them twenty-four hour-a-day access, which I was totally against. I thought, this is not good. Then it becomes a stamina test.

They'll be popping pills.

Yes, exactly! But we couldn't afford to outfit it at the loft space. We had almost no budget. We were taping in August. I knew that Parsons was empty, because the summer programs were over. Fall semester hadn't begun. I said, "You want to come over and look at it?" That's how it happened. It was all very serendipitous.

It was filmed that first summer. *Project Runway* premiered December 1, 2004.

… To three viewers. Really. We were almost canceled.

What was your expectation for the show at that time?

Fern, I didn't know what would air. I knew what I saw.

It's a whole other game in the editing room.

Exactly. There was a moment during the taping, when I was in the back of the Parsons' auditorium in the literal and metaphorical dark, so to speak, standing next to a woman I'd never met. I didn't know, she was someone new, visiting, I guess. She didn't know who I was. I'm sure she hadn't seen any rushes from the show.

We're watching the judges' question and answer session with the six designers, with the top three and bottom three looks. This woman turns to me, and she said, "Who is going to want to watch this?"

I said, "Oh, God, you're corroborating my worst fears."

Who was that woman? The president of Bravo, where we were first aired. I didn't know what was going to air. Oh, this is something no one's ever heard…

He's prepping us for this one.

She's an uber executive producer and had the first show on a disk. She showed it to Naomi Campbell. Naomi Campbell said, "This is a load of crap. Run as fast as you can and get away from this."

Heidi was really upset about it. She said, "What do you think? Have you seen the show?"

I said, "I haven't seen a thing."

I did not go to the premiere party on purpose. I never thought I would actually be in the cut of the show. I thought as long as the producers have the designers responding to me in the workroom no one needs to see me, nobody needs to hear my voice. I didn't go to the premiere, because if I am on the show, how will I look and what will the whole show be like? I thought it could be sexual escapades at the Atlas Apartments. I don't know. If I'm not on the show, I'll be totally humiliated.

I watched it the way I used to watch the *Wizard of Oz* as a kid. I was under the sheets, in my bed, and I'd peek out, and throw the sheets back over me. Peek out, and throw the sheets back over. That's how I watched it.

They did almost cancel us. No one was watching. Beginning in January, they aired three episodes and then decided just to keep repeating them over, and over, and over…

Which cable is very good at.

… And when the fourth show finally aired, the ratings had quadrupled, and then they kept increasing. When I went home for the Christmas holidays after those three episodes had aired, and all these repeats were happening, my mother said to me, "Every time I turn on that goddamn TV, that goddamn show is on."

I said, "Well, enjoy it while you can, Mother. This may be it."

How do you think it got its audience over those first few episodes?

I trust the intelligence of the TV viewer. People were really interested in the creative process, and the fact that the show does have integrity, and is committed to really propping up these designers and helping them.

What season did you feel validated the show?

I don't know that it's a season that validated it. It was when we were nominated for an Emmy for Season 1. That was the moment. It was Bastille Day, 2005. I remember it vividly. It was July 14.

… And fireworks were going off.

We were wrapping Season 2 on that day. I was running through the halls of Parsons, screaming, "We are nominated for an Emmy! We are nominated for an Emmy!"

How were you able to juggle your day job and the taping of these shows?

We taped during the summer. It's not to imply that we're not busy in the summer, but we didn't have classes. I gave Heidi my office. It was so easy for me to work where the set is

This page: Tim Gunn, Heidi Klum, Michael Kors, and Nina Garcia at *Project Runway*'s tenth anniversary show in New York's Times Square in 2012. Opposite: Heidi and Tim winning the Emmy for Outstanding Host For a Reality or Competition Program, 2013.

because I never had to leave.

You and Heidi won an Emmy for Outstanding Host for a Reality or Reality Competition Program in 2013?

Yes, I'm thrilled to say.

Where do you display your Emmy?

In my kitchen, so I see it all the time.

It doesn't just hold bananas or anything?

No. I'm entirely too respectful. It does sit next to my coffee maker.

A Nespresso?

It is a Nespresso.

You left Parsons and teaching after twenty-four years?

I had five years of teaching in Washington, so twenty-nine years of teaching total.

Then you became the creative director at Liz Claiborne. Was it about the money? Why did you leave?

You ready for this one, too? I've never told this story.

We are on a roll here.

You may never want to have anything to do with me. I was having a crisis. I will be candid with you. I was going through a reappointment process, which department chairs do. I had been presented with this need to be reappointed in the summer of 2006, and did my due diligence. I did everything that I felt was important to do. The dean to whom I reported kept giving me

Tim Gunn and Parsons School of Design board member Diane Von Furstenberg.

another broomstick of the Wicked Witch of the West to find. I kept finding them. Here it is. Here it is. Here it is.

Well, in mid-December, two things happened simultaneously. Another request for a broomstick, and a meeting with the then-brand-new CEO of Liz Claiborne, an incredible guy by the name of Bill McComb.

I had made an assumption about the meeting with Bill, having to do with the fact that I had a multimillion dollar ask out to Liz Claiborne to fund an accessory program for Parsons. I met with Bill. I thought, "How incredibly dynamic and engaging and smart is this guy?"

He is a good guy.

He then dropped it in my lap, this job. He said, "I want you to be my chief creative officer. I want you to be my first hire. This company currently has forty-eight brands. I need to whittle this down to our core competencies. I need someone the designers and merchandisers will trust. I believe that is you."

I said to him, "Look. I can't give you a 100 percent of my time. I have all these things happening." He was such a doll. He said, "I know that. But eventually these other things won't be happening, and then I'll have a 100 percent of you. I'm willing to wait as long as it takes."

Then I said, "OK, well, now I have to tell you the truth. Here's the real… here's my real concern. I'm terrified."

He said, "If you weren't terrified, I wouldn't want you. I'm terrified every single day."

It's just like those Parsons seniors when you changed the designer critic program on them.

Yes. I made the decision to leave. I had my letter of resignation in an envelope and I made an appointment with the dean. I go into his office and he says, "Ah, the envelope. You have the recommendations for me."

I said, "Well, let me put it this way. I have exactly what I think you want from me."

… And I loved his face when he opened up the envelope.

… And so you never looked back?

No, I haven't. Diane von Furstenberg called me after I submitted my letter. She is a Parsons board member and she's been a dear pal and a great mentor. She said, "You can't do this." I said, "Diane, I was made an offer I couldn't refuse." It was two things. I wasn't going to be reappointed. I'm quite certain of it.

I will share something with you, something I only told Diane. You bring this out in me. I feel like we're sitting here having cocktails, too. I had been at Parsons for twenty-four years. I was running what had become not only the largest academic program at Parsons, the largest academic program in the entire university. Parsons was one of seven divisions of the New School.

Parsons' fashion program was the cash cow for the university.

Absolutely. I was making $81,000. Do you want to know how much they paid my replacement? They spent a year searching for my replacement for $350,000! If they paid me $90,000, I probably would have stayed. Can you imagine?

What happened with Liz Claiborne?

What happened is the economy collapsed, and retail had a gigantic calamity. Thankfully, we were already on our way to whittling down these brands. When the real collapse happened, if we had still been forty-eight brands, I'm confident we would have gone bankrupt. We just wouldn't have survived. It was a matter of paddling and bailing as fast as we possibly could. It was crisis management, to be perfectly honest. It was a huge education for me. I'd never worked in the private sector.

It's sad to see what happened to the Liz Claiborne brand and company.

I also have a theory about legacy brands in America. They tend to not make it. They just don't. In Europe, they flourish. But here, they don't

This is something else I've never told anyone. When I was at Liz Claiborne, I actually tried to start a line. I was thrilled with it. I won't call it fashion. It was more about essentials.

When *Project Runway* moved to the Lifetime channel, did that change anything?

Initially, yes. There was a huge crisis because of the lawsuit between the Weinstein Company and NBC Universal.

That's the year I got to do *The Fashion Show* to fill in that Bravo gap.

Yes. We didn't know whether Season 6, which was our first show with Lifetime, would even air. I honestly thought that the show would be shelved. I felt sick for the designers because they had given up a lot to be on the show. It was tumultuous.

I have great respect for Bravo. But how Bravo has morphed, I don't think *Project Runway* would have remained a good fit because we're too feel good. Lifetime is not only deeply respectful of the show, they are very hands-off, and that was not the case with Bravo.

Heidi used to order the executives off the set. I love her.

How is your new judge, Zac Posen, doing?

Zac is getting it. I mean, stepping into Michael Kors's shoes is tough.

Why do you think there haven't been more designers who've really come out of the program and succeeded? Christian Siriano clearly is the one that's made it in the thirteen seasons.

I have a lot to say about it. I'll try to be succinct. One reason is the designer alumni can only be as successful as their ambitions and their resources permit them to be. The other is, it depends on how you measure success.

I look at Chloe Dao, the winner of Season 2. Chloe wanted to stay in Houston. She's committed to her family. She's grown her business fourfold. She's on QVC twice a year and it helps pay the bills. Chloe is very, very happy.

I think about Emmett McCarthy and the fact that he survived the whole economic downturn with his EMc2 shop on Elizabeth Street in Nolita. There are scores of others.

Christian is certainly a huge success. A good number of our seasons happened during the economic downturn and retail calamity, which was no time to start a business.

When I look back at the Coty Awards and even the CFDA Young Designer Award, when you look at that list and you go back about thirty years…

… A lot of them are nowhere to be found.

It's a tough business.

What do you think ultimately is *Project Runway*'s contribution to the fashion industry?

I believe it took that veil of mystery, and intrigue, and purported glamour, and fabulousness, and ripped the veil off. It said, "Look at it. It's gritty. It's daunting. It's incredibly difficult and demanding. Unless you have an unyielding love for this, do not do it."

I know that a lot of designers really loved it from the get-go because they could say to their families, "Turn on the show; you'll understand what I do." I believe it's been great for the industry. It's certainly been great for education.

How many people apply to fashion schools now as a result of it?

I don't know, but I do know the numbers are up considerably. When I was at Parsons, our department went from 242 applications to more than 800. If people watch *Project Runway*, and they want to go into the industry, my hat's off to them. Great.

That's the good news and the bad news. I think there are a lot of people who think anybody who can sew two pieces of fabric together can be a designer if they watch, and that's not the case.

It's not the case at all. During the auditions, I'm constantly talking about the difference between being a designer and being a dressmaker. No offense to dressmakers, but there is a difference.

What differentiates a good designer from a great designer?

Design for me happens in a context. Good design, it's societal, it's cultural, it's historic, and

Fern Mallis joining the *Project Runway* judges for the 2009 finale at New York Fashion Week's Bryant Park tents.

it's economic and political. Which is why good design is constantly changing, because all those elements are constantly changing.

What makes the difference between a good designer and a great designer? I think a lot of luck. I think a lot of just being in the right place, at the right time, and making the right decisions, and you just don't know. I believe if you chase it, it will elude you. I think it's a lot of luck.

You've been on every single TV show possible: *Sesame Street*, *Gossip Girl*, *Ugly Betty*, *Drop Dead Diva*, *How I Met Your Mother*. What was the most fun for you to do?

Wow. They've all been incredibly fun, I have to say. I wouldn't want to cross any of them off. I will say it was pretty surreal to be on *Sesame Street*. Very surreal.

My sister also told me she loves you on *The Biggest Loser*. Everybody tries to lose enough weight just to get to makeover week so you can make them over. You're so warm and genuine with them all. What is that like, watching these transformations?

It's emotional for them. It's emotional for me. I mean, to bear witness to these remarkable individuals who have been through such dramatic weight loss and haven't in their brains reconciled the fact that they are a new size and shape. They only realize it when they try on these clothes, because they've been wearing nothing but workout clothes. Things that are baggy and don't fit them.

They're looking at me, saying, "I can't put this on." When you see them come out of the dressing room… It's a huge joy.

On to your red carpet coverage of the Oscars. Who stood out for you?

I'm lucky to have done the official red carpet preshow for ABC for three years. It was incredible. But the most potent, stand-out experience for me was when I was doing it for the *Today* show. In that case, I had an eighteen-inch-wide swath behind a fake boxwood. You stay there,

This page: Tim Gunn visiting Jimmy Fallon at NBC's Tonight Show in 2017. Page 133: Tim interviewing Jennifer Lopez on the Oscar red carpet in 2012. Pages 134–135: The cast of Amazon's Making the Cut in 2020.

and you have a cameraman behind you, and a producer over your shoulder telling you who is coming.

Generally, I would know who was coming. But this one case, this exceptionally beautiful mature woman is approaching me. I'm looking at her while thinking, "Where is the producer?" She wasn't there. She stepped away. I'm thinking, "I don't really know who this is." She opens her mouth, and thank God, I didn't know in advance because I would have been in a puddle. It was Catherine Deneuve. Spectacular.

The voice gave it away.

Yes, her voice gave it away. Catherine Deneuve. My heart is going pitter-patter right now.

You are a frequent guest on the late-night circuit. Who do you love being with the most?

You know, I love them all, but talking about my heart going pitter-patter, it goes pitter-patter for Jimmy Fallon. I just love the fact that he's hosting *The Tonight Show* now, and you can tell that he loves it.

The *New York Times* just recently featured you in a column, and wrote about how you spend your Sundays. I love that you put on a suit on a Sunday to go to the Metropolitan Museum of Art.

It's out of respect for the work. They're incredible, great works of art. I can't stand there wearing shorts and flip-flops.

I used to dress up on airplanes. Now everyone just wears sweatpants.

There are times on planes when I'd be grateful if people were just wearing sweatpants. That's how bad it can get. I mean, sometimes I think it's just one big slumber party. They put on their pajamas, bring their own pillow. I guess… whatever it takes.

Let's get to your books. Do you write them?

Yes. But I have to say, I couldn't write them without Ada Calhoun. She is my disciplinarian. She is my truth teller. She is the most superb editor in the world. I babble and write, and she takes everything and shuffles it like a deck of cards. I don't have those organizational abilities. I love her.

In 2010 you wrote _Gunn's Golden Rules: Life's Little Lessons for Making It Work_. You called it fashion's 911. What's your number one rule?

"Accept responsibility for your actions." Another one I like is, "Take the high road." It's what you would say about being nice.

That's the book where you shared stories about _Vogue_'s Anna Wintour and André Leon Talley. Do we want to go there?

Do we?

I think the audience would like to hear that.

This was in the category of "Accept responsibility for your actions." I was asked by the _New York Post_, "What's the one thing you've seen in fashion that you will never forget?"

I said without hesitating, I said, "Oh, that's easy: watching Anna Wintour being carried down five flights of stairs from a fashion show." That was it. I didn't talk about her character. It was very matter of fact. It was on a Sunday.

On Monday, I was teaching in the morning. I came back to my office at Parsons, and there was a message that Ms. Wintour's office had called. I thought, "Oh, my God. This can't be good." I calculated when to call. I thought, "I'll call when I think she's probably out at lunch." I called at about two p.m., and she wasn't there. Thank the Lord baby Jesus. But _Vogue_'s director of communications, Patrick O'Connell, took the call and he told me that she demanded a retraction be printed. I said, "A retraction would imply that it's not true."

He said, "Well, it's not true."

I said, "Well, it is true."

Fortunately, I keep my appointment calendar. It was December something or other. It was Peter Som's show at the Metropolitan Pavilion. You know, it's that fifth floor with the freight elevator. I was there with colleagues from Parsons. Anna is a big fan of Peter Som. We weren't speculating how she would arrive, because she does not ride in elevators with mere mortals. We thought her posse will get her into the elevator, she'll ascend, and get out. But leaving? Everyone has to run to the next show, so how is she going to leave?

This is in the days when I had standing room. I'm proud to have standing room always. It really gives you a good view. It means you can move around. Colleagues and I had our eyes on her. How is this going to happen? Because we were expecting fisticuffs or hair pulling and biting. I didn't know.

She had two bodyguards, sitting on each side of her. They whisked her up. They went to this big open stairwell—the kind that you can look all the way down. They made a fireman's lock and she sat in it, and they rushed her down the stairs. I ran to the window because I thought, "Are they going to put her down on the sidewalk or take her that way to the car?" They took her that way to the car.

As I'm telling Patrick all these details, with each declaration he says, "Oh my, oh my, oh my." The next day, I thought, this is over now. I've validated at least that I was there and that she was there.

What happened next?

The next day he called me and he made a declaration, "I'll have you know that Ms. Wintour knows how to work a Manolo."

I said, "I'm not challenging whether or not Ms. Wintour knows how to work a Manolo. This was about speed, and these two guys got her down those stairs faster than her little Manolos would have taken her." Once again, his response is, "Oh dear, oh dear, oh dear."

The next day, he says, "Well, now we have to involve the lawyers." I said, "Good, because that means I can't speak to you anymore. You'll have to talk to the university's lawyers."

Someone, who has asked me never to mention his name again in this context and capacity, came into my office and said, "You look horrible." I told him how *Vogue* was tormenting me. He walked over to my desk, picked up the phone called, Patrick and said, "I was there. I saw the whole thing. So bug off."

I decided to take the high road. I wrote Ms. Wintour a lovely note, saying, "I never intended for this to cause you such distress." I didn't apologize. I sent her this huge bouquet of white flowers. White in our culture means peace. But in Asian cultures, it means death.

Let's talk about your latest book, *The Natty Professor: A Master Class on Mentoring, Motivating, and Making It Work!* What's the difference between mentoring and teaching?

That's a really wonderful question. I used to think there wasn't one until I became a mentor. I spent so many years as a teacher. As a teacher, I could tell my students what to do. I could lead them in a very demonstrable way. I could lead them to a conclusion. I could tell them to stop doing something. I could derail the whole process if I felt that was necessary.

As a mentor, you're more in the shadow. You are there to cheerlead, to be a truth teller, but only up to a point. When it comes to truth telling, I only believe in talking to people about things that they can change. Otherwise, they are wasted words. Why bother? If you have spinach in your teeth, I'll tell you. If you are coming to an event and you're fully dressed, and you don't have a change of clothing and it's the worst, most horrible garment I've ever seen, why would I talk to you about it? I would not.

I always want my students to only do their best. I would say the same is true about the mentees. But you are not making decisions for them. You are not designing for them. If they need that level of help, they're going to have to just probe, and search, and discover, because it's not going to come from me. They are wholly responsible for the decisions that they make. Also, I'm not grading them. I'm not judging them in the end.

The first five chapters of the book are broken up into the word "TEACH." The chapters

are: T: Truth Telling, E: Empathy, A: Asking, C: Cheerleading, and H: Hoping for the Best. With a final chapter of takeaways. What one takeaway do you want them to get from this book?

I have to say this book is not just for teachers. In fact, I hope teachers read it, but it's really for everyone, anyone.

Everyone in life mentors or teaches in some respect.

We are all teachers, we are all students. I hope that this shores up confidence in people about how they're navigating the world and their own sense of values. I believe that we share so much in common. I hope that it is a catalyst for spreading the word on education. There is a national conversation today about education. Everyone is concerned with it. I hope that the book doesn't sound preachy; it's not intended to. It's just my own experiences, good and bad.

Who is a mentor to you?

Fortunately, a lot of people. I've been very, very lucky. In terms of teaching, two extraordinary teachers I had at the Corcoran are people I've emulated in terms of my own classroom demeanor.

Tell us how the *Smurfs* movie influenced your clothing choices?

It did. I would not be dressed like this today if it weren't for Rita Ryack, who was the costumer of the *Smurfs*. It was nine days on the set, and it was pure joy.

Rita called me and said, "Just bring your wardrobe. I wouldn't dream of telling you how to dress." I brought a lot of suits and shirts and ties. She sorted through things and said, "Wear those today." So, I did.

I got home late that evening and the phone rang, and it was Rita. She said, "I've just looked at the rushes of today's shoot. That suit is not good enough. Tomorrow I'm going shopping. Meet me at a tailor on 54th Street at three o'clock."

So I did. I was in the dressing room and I started looking at price tags, and I said, "$4,500 for a suit? $300 for a tie? $450 for a shirt? I'm not wearing this stuff." She said, "You are, you're wearing it. Get it on, and get out here!" She was a strict disciplinarian, too, but a doll.

I came out and I said, "Surely, I'm not wearing all this stuff together?" The pattern mixing that I do now is because of Rita. I was not doing it then. I said, "I look like an ass."

She said, "You don't. We're going to get everything tailored and it's going to fit you beautifully." At any rate, it was a bit like the first time you have cilantro, and you think, what is this?

I hate cilantro.

Well, I used to. But now I love it. The same thing happened with this experience. I thought, this is horrible. I never wore a pocket square. Suddenly, it was like, "Oh, my God, I love this." I liked the way that I looked. I ended up going to Barneys, Saks Fifth Avenue, and Bergdorf Goodman to buy my clothes. I would leave the store after paying, and sit on the curb, literally feeling sick. Absolutely sick.

I've found a new company, thanks to Eric Wilson, and I'm saving a fortune.

Did you want to share that company?

It's the only thing I wear. I'm wearing it tonight, and they don't pay me for this. I don't believe in free stuff. It's a horrible name, but it's a company out of the Netherlands, so I think they didn't understand English well enough to know how horrible it is. It's called Suitsupply, one word. I mean, this suit was five hundred dollars, all of it. It is remarkable. The buttons work. Shoulders are set in by hand.

What's next on your bucket list?

A thing I have not done? You know, Fern, I'm going to be really blunt. I am so lucky, and so blessed. I feel it would be reckless hubris to wish for anything. If I do wish for something, I should be struck by lightning. Really.

I'm so lucky. If nothing ever happens again, I'm the happiest guy alive. Truly.

Which era would you love to see return to fashion?

There has been nothing like the 1960s. We ushered them in with mad men, and we ushered them out with hippies. In between, we have the miniskirt, we have the clear vinyl dress, we have the paper dress. What a revolution that was. I'd love to see another revolution like that—that really allows us to feel jolted. It would be fun.

Who is your celebrity crush?

Well, it is not romantic. I would give anything to have a cup of coffee with Meryl Streep.

Did you never meet her on the red carpet?

No, and I'll tell you why. It was the ABC official preshow for the Oscars. She was scheduled to come to us. I was on the stage with Jennifer Lopez, and Meryl Streep's producer told the Oscar preshow producer, "Ms. Meryl Streep will not follow Ms. Lopez."

I said, "If I had known that, I would've shoved Jennifer Lopez right off the stage. 'Get away, Jennifer. Get off the stage.'"

We'll have to get that message to Meryl.

She came to the Season 3 finale of *Project Runway* and she came through the backstage. I'm standing next to the entrance to the runway with the designers. She comes by and she grabs my hands and she says, "Tim Gunn, I'm so happy to meet you."

I said, "Well, thank you." I was in a puddle again.

So you got to meet her for a second.

I want more.

What would you advise to a woman in her early forties who wants to change her career completely, but is afraid to do that?

Throw the dice. Take risks. The more terrified you are, the more likely something fantastic is happening. Be terrified. It's a good thing.

Do you have any spiritual practices, like journaling or meditation?

How about drinking? That's my spiritual meditation. It's spirits.

It's very spiritual. If you were stranded on a desert island, what three items would you take?

A bar of soap, a toothbrush, and a bathing suit.

You are stranded alone and you need a bathing suit?

I don't even want the flora and fauna to have to look at me. Adam, I am not.

As a man who dresses with dignity, how do you feel about our current casual culture and its endangered sense of occasion?

You mean, the "slobification of America?" Yeah, it's grim.

What is the one biggest piece of advice you would give to a fifteen-year-old designer?

Be insatiably curious about everything, because it all becomes part of who you are as a designer. Every single thing you encounter and everything you study.

Curiosity is very important.

It's very, very important.

I think we've spent way more time than we were allotted tonight.

Well, thank you. I love you, Fern.

SINCE FASHION ICONS

After Tim and his "TV wife" Heidi Klum stepped away from *Project Runway* in 2017, the pair launched a new fashion competition series, *Making the Cut*, on the Amazon Prime video streaming platform in 2020. The winning looks from each episode are immediately available for purchase on Amazon.com. The judges on the program have included Naomi Campbell, Carine Roitfeld, Joseph Altuzarra, Nicole Richie, Chiara Ferragni, Jeremy Scott, and Winnie Harlow. In 2016, Tim took on a new hobby: fencing. This pursuit forced him to buy his first-ever pair of sweatpants (from J.Crew!). Tim lives on New York's Upper West Side. Follow Tim on Instagram: @timgunn

VICTORIA BECKHAM

How lucky are we to meet this very special, hardworking, and accomplished woman designer? She didn't start out by going to design school, but neither did a lot of designers. Her career started with a love of dancing and singing, long before ever auditioning to become a part of the biggest and most popular girl group ever: the Spice Girls.

She then met and married a footballer, and their life together has been an incredible journey and love story. They have four gorgeous children, who are either dropped off or picked up at school every day by one of their parents. Her most important and proudest role is as mother and wife. When she talks about her family, she actually does smile.

She reinvented her life as a designer with ready-to-wear, accessories, an optical brand, an e-commerce site, and a fabulous new store in London. All of this to critical acclaim from one of our industry's toughest critics, Suzy Menkes, who said, "I can't think of another celebrity who has been so willing and able to create a unique style. There is a vision and involvement here, and the foundation and flow of this collection could only come from her."

When Neiman Marcus's fashion director Ken Downing saw her collection, he called his buyers and said, "Do not walk, run to Victoria Beckham."

Tonight we will hear how hard work and perseverance took her from a girl band to becoming an entrepreneur, one of the 100 Most Powerful women in the United Kingdom, the fifty-second richest woman in Britain, a United Nations Goodwill Ambassador for AIDS prevention and education, and even the winner of the British Fashion Council's Women's Brand of the Year in 2011 and 2014.

Let's welcome the very talented, very busy, and very charming designer Victoria Beckham.

VICTORIA BECKHAM: That was so kind; thank you. My mum would be really proud.

FERN MALLIS: Thank you so much for being here tonight.

Thank you for having me, and thank you everybody for coming. There's a lot of you out there. I hope I'm going to say something interesting. I do feel the pressure after the introduction. I don't know whether to sing or to talk.

You can do both.

I'll do a bit of both.

Victoria is here in New York because she's been showing her pre-spring collection, and she's done that all day long. She's showing it to all the buyers and the press, to very good acclaim.

Yes, it's gone really well. I just like to talk. I like to talk about clothes, and it's been great. That's how I started out. When I first started presenting my collections, I would talk through the presentation. I took it back to that today. It's the first time that we've presented a pre-spring collection.

Fern Mallis:. Well, we're going to take you further back than that.

Oh, I hope I remember.

I hope you remember, too. We're going to start at the beginning. You were born Victoria Caroline Adams on April 17, 1974, in Harlow, Essex, England. That makes you how old?

I am forty-one.

You look fabulous. Are you freaked out about age, and what people attribute to age?

Not really. I mean, I think I've achieved a lot in forty-one years. I like how forty-one feels. I feel good. I don't like how it sounds too much. It doesn't sound great. But, you know, I am very proud of everything I've achieved. I've got four incredible children, a wonderful husband. I couldn't have done much more in forty-one years. I'm OK with it.

You're an Aries. I'm also an Aries. Do you follow astrology?

I don't. Your mother's birthday is the day after my birthday?

That's right. Aries are independent, generous, optimistic, enthusiastic, and courageous. They were also moody, short-tempered, impulsive, and impatient.

Does anybody think I'm moody? I mean, I'm just putting it out there. I'm never moody.

We got that on record. Aries often lead the way because it's the first sign of the Zodiac. They bring excitement into other people's lives. Aries are activists, although they do not always finish everything they've started. Some attribute that to their low tolerance for boredom and a lack of patience. Does any of that sound right?

I don't know, it's hard to say. A little?

Back to England. While you were born in Essex, you grew up in Goff's Oak, in Hertfordshire? How far from London was that?

It was about an hour and a half away from London. My parents still live there, actually, whereas we now live in Central London.

Your mother is Jacqueline Doreen Cannon. She was a hairdresser and insurance clerk, is that right?

She used to work in insurance before she had children, and as soon as she had us kids, she was a stay-at-home mum. David's [Beckham, Victoria's husband] mum was a hairdresser.

Your dad, Anthony Williams Adams, was an electronic engineer? I read that he was also a lead vocalist in a couple of bands before he met your mother?

He was. I think that's where I got my vocal talents from.

I bet that's exactly where those genes come from. How did they meet?

They just met when they were out one night, years ago. My parents are still together; they've been together for years and years and years.

How many years now, do you know?

Oh goodness, I can't remember. A long time.

Well, at least forty-one.

Well, yes, a long time. They're very happy. My mum and dad still sit in front of the TV and

Clockwise from top: Victoria Beckham with her parents, Jacqueline and Anthony Adams, in 1974; Victoria and sister Louise Adams sitting on the hood of their father's Rolls-Royce; Victoria with her siblings Louise and Christian Adams on holiday in Spain. Page 142: Victoria in costume for a performance at the Jason Theatre School in London.

hold hands, which is really, really sweet. They are great, they've always been great parents.

Is it true that you didn't like being called Vicky as a child? Do you want to tell them what "Posh" stands for?

When people used to travel abroad on boats, it stood for "port out and starboard home." That's what it actually stands for. But in England, if you go to a nice restaurant, they'll say, you know, it's a "posh" restaurant. If you like nice clothes, "posh" clothes. That's where I got the nickname. It was when I was in the Spice Girls that I actually got the nickname Posh.

Tell us a little bit about your grandparents? I read that they kept a penguin and a monkey named Jackie?

That is correct. Years ago, that was when my mum was really little, so I didn't actually meet the penguin or the monkey. I don't remember huge amounts about my grandparents because unfortunately they passed away when I was really young.

You have two siblings: a sister, Louise, and a brother, Christian. What is the age difference? Where do you fit in?

There is two years in between me and my sister, and four years between me and my brother. I'm the eldest, and we've always been close and we're still very, very close. My sister has four children that are all around the same age as our kids, and they are very close as well.

You were all interested in dance as children?

We were. My brother wasn't, but me and my sister were.

You wrote in your book, *Learning to Fly: The Autobiography*, that Louise was the pretty one and got more attention when you were growing up. Your mum crocheted outfits for both of you and dressed you alike.

My sister was very cute. She had lots of red curly hair. She was funny, and she was very outgoing. I was quite shy when I was a child. I was a bit gangly and a little bit awkward. She's great, my sister; she's so supportive of everything that I do. We're really super close. We have an incredible relationship.

You certainly made up for those days of feeling like you were not the pretty one, that's for sure. Your dad was quite successful in his business and he drove a Rolls-Royce.

He did, yes.

... Which did not make you and your siblings happy when going to school, being dropped off in that car.

I was so embarrassed. I just wanted to walk to school or get the bus to school because that's what everybody else did. My dad worked really, really hard, and it was always his ambition to own a Rolls-Royce. He was self-made. My dad always worked incredibly hard.

When he got this Rolls-Royce, he used to drive us to school in it every day, and I was just mortified. We used to beg him to drop us at the end of the road. He also had a van that he used to use for work. We used to beg him to take us in the van.

How times have changed, because I would much rather go in a Rolls-Royce now. For sure.

It probably gave you an early understanding of the life of luxury.

Absolutely. I remember how that car used to smell, and the sheepskin carpets that were on the floor. I remember all of that very, very clearly.

How old were you when you saw the movie *Fame*?

I can't remember how old I was, but I was such a fan. I had a velour tracksuit that was blue and it had gold "Fame" written on it. My sister had the same velour tracksuit, but in red. I had all the merchandise. I had the sticker books. I mean, I loved it. I absolutely loved it.

Your parents sent you to the Jason Theatre School in London when you were eight, and you went until you were about seventeen, because that movie so inspired you?

I was so inspired. I used to dance every night. I did tap. I did ballet. I did modern. I was dancing all the time. I used to really, really enjoy it.

Then you went to the Laine Theatre Arts College in Surrey to continue to study more dance?

Yes.

… And modeling?

No, I was never going to be a model. I studied dance and then I also qualified to be a dance teacher because my mum always said that I had to have something to fall back on if it all went wrong. That could be the next thing I do.

What does mum say about that now?

I mean, she's really proud of everything that I've achieved. If it does go wrong, I can be a tap dancing teacher. It's good to know.

I think they have tap dancing classes here at the 92nd Street Y. At that school, you went on your first Valentine's date with someone named Franco and you took your first bus ride to McDonald's?

Oh, my God! That was years ago, when I was at school. That was the first boy to ever ask me out, because I wasn't really very popular with the boys. That was just one date to the cinema. He wasn't interested in me.

Well, you made up for that also.

Well, you know, aim high.

Tell us about the lead role you had in something called *Bertie*?

Oh, no, that's very kind. I didn't have a lead role. I was a clockwork ballerina and it was a very small part. But it was fun. It was a musical. It was touring. I just wanted to be on the stage. Well, I thought I wanted to be on the stage.

Is it true that to celebrate that role you bought yourself a Prada bag and Patrick Cox shoes?

I bought myself the Patrick Cox shoes when I got the first paycheck from the Spice Girls. They were white slingback wannabes, and I queued up outside Patrick Cox on a Saturday afternoon with my sister. I bought us this pair of shoes that we would share because we've always shared everything, me and my sister. That was the first thing that I bought.

Are you friends with Patrick today?

I am. I really like him. They were white, patent.

So you considered yourself somewhat of a fashionista back then?

I've always loved fashion. When I was at school, I used to do a bit of customizing of the school uniform in the toilets at lunchtime. I've always loved fashion. When I used to watch my mum get ready, you know?

Did your mother dress beautifully?

Yes, she did. She was never into fashion but she used to make the best of what she had. She had big hair in the 1980s, and she had big shoulder pads, and lots of velvet, and lots of Raffinée perfume, and lots of makeup. I remember watching her get ready and I used to love it. I've always loved fashion. It's really what I always wanted to do.

But before you did that, you answered an ad in a trade paper called *The Stage*. It was looking for five girls who were "streetwise, outgoing, extroverted, ambitious, and able to sing and dance."

Other than ambitious, I was none of the above. I was very ambitious and I liked the idea of being in a pop group. It never came naturally to me. I always had to really work hard.

Tell us about that. You answered the ad and then what? You went through an audition?

I went to an audition. There were thousands of girls that turned up for the audition. There were queues around the studio; it was in a dance studio in London. Everybody stood up, one by one, and they were being taped, and everybody sang a song. Everybody except for me sang a pop song. But I sang… I think I sang "Mein Herr" from *Cabaret*, which is really, really not the right thing to do.

Well, maybe it was.

… But it got me in the group. I mean, it was very dramatic. It's so embarrassing, and you know that video is out there?

Somebody here is going to be searching later.

Oh, yeah. You won't have to search very hard.

Then it took how long to find the right five girls?

It happened very, very quickly. Very quickly. We were all put together.

Tell us how you got the name Spice Girls. How did that happen?

This is a funny story. We were going to be the Spicy Girls at one point, but then I think we realized there was a porn site called the Spicy Girls. We had to change it because obviously that wouldn't have been good. It was a lot of fun being in the group. I'm still very close to all of the girls.

How did each of you get the nicknames Scary, Baby, Sporty, Ginger, Posh?

Nobody put those images on us. We all just looked that way. I always dressed that way. Melanie Brown was always the scary one, wearing the leopard print. Emma Bunton was always the baby one with the pigtails and those bloody awful shoes that she used to wear, those big platform shoes. It was actually an English teenage magazine called *Top of the Pops*, they were the ones that gave us the nicknames. They put us all on a spice rack, and

Clockwise from top: The Spice Girls in Tokyo in the 1990s; The Spice Girls' reunion performance at the closing ceremony of the London 2012 Olympic games; Victoria Beckham on the set of 1997's Spice World.

would never have existed. They did put us together. Yes, we wrote the songs. Yes, we did all of that ourselves. But it was those two guys that put us together. It was probably a terrible thing to do, to just escape and not even say thank you.

Tell us about the importance to you of succeeding in America and how much that meant to you?

America was really important to us. We knew we had to start from scratch. I think a lot of bands failed when they came to America because they came thinking they're big superstars because they had had success in the rest of the world. We knew that wouldn't be the case. We came to America and we started from scratch. We just wanted to reach out to as many people as we could, because it was not just about the music, it was about so much more for us. It was about telling people it's OK if you're a little bit different. It's OK if you're not the tallest or the prettiest or the skinniest. It's OK to be who you are, whether you're a boy or a girl, or a man or a woman. We just wanted to reach out as widely as we could.

There was an optimism in America that you felt wasn't the same in the UK. Is that what was attractive to you here?

I've always loved America. It's always been important for me to spend time here, and to be successful here, because I love how optimistic you all are here. I love that, I really do.

It was Simon Fuller who also suggested that you date an athlete. He took you to the first Manchester United game where you met David Beckham, your future husband.

Simon was a huge Manchester United fan. He invited me to go to a football match with him. He introduced me and David after the game. It wasn't quite, you know, putting us together. He just introduced us after the game.

What was your take on that meeting?

You know what I really liked about David right from the start? When all the other players were in the lounge afterward having a drink with their friends, David was sitting with his mum and dad and his younger sister. I really liked that. I'm very close to my family. He's very close to

Victoria and David Beckham on a date in the 1990s

his, and I just thought that that was really nice; when everybody else was getting drunk at the bar, he was with his family, and his family is adorable. We just got to talk.

Was it a little bit of love at first sight?

Oh, absolutely. I believe in love at first sight. I really do. It was great. It was really great.

I read in your book that you had to keep it quiet. You were trying to find places where you could date and not be out in the public so much.

I mean, that was quite good advice that Simon Fuller actually gave to me. We didn't want anybody to know that we were dating because we knew that people would then be interested in the relationship. We had only gone on a couple of dates. We just tried to keep it quiet and really get to know each other, before we let anybody know.

Please tell me that this is true: after several dates, a big package arrived for you and instead of flowers, it was a big box with a black Prada bag?

He did get me a Prada bag. Yes, he did. That was very, very nice. Very nice.

This is a quote from you: your "spine turns to custard when he looks at me." It's a line from *Some Like It Hot*.

Oh, I haven't heard that, but it does. I'm very, very lucky. He's an incredible husband and a wonderful father. I mean, he is so good with the children. He really is.

Before you get to the kids, tell us how he proposed to you?

We were in a hotel up north, and he got down on one knee, and he proposed. He asked my dad before he did that, which was great and very appropriate.

Then, later that year, while you were on your American tour, you found out you were pregnant? You both clearly wanted a family. Brooklyn Beckham, your son, was born in March 1999. How did the name Brooklyn come about?

I actually found out that I was pregnant when I was in New York. I just liked the name. We were on tour at the time in America. We were performing in lots of amphitheaters around America. I remember it was really, really hot. I was wearing a PVC catsuit and a wig because my hair was just out of control because it was so hot.

I had such terrible morning sickness, myself and Melanie B, because she was pregnant at the same time. It was awful. It was absolutely awful. I was getting bigger and bigger and bigger, and I was still wearing a PVC catsuit, and platform trainers or something like that. It's quite tough being on tour and being pregnant.

Every night, I would come offstage and I'd say to our tour manager, "I can't go on. What happens if I just say I'm going home and I don't want to do this anymore?" Every night he would say, "You would get sued. Get the catsuit back on and off you go."

I would keep going and, without meaning to, would sound awful. I had had such terrible morning sickness. I was really ill.

At some point, he let you out of that catsuit?

After, I think, 103 shows. It was a lot of shows.

... And you named your son after what has become like the coolest place to live in New

York now?

Yeah, I did. It was always a name that I liked. I always thought if he decides he wants to shorten it, I like Brook as well. He hasn't. He's still Brooklyn.

Tell us who his godparents are, because that's pretty cool.

Elton John and David Furnish are his and Romeo's godparents. We've been very close with Elton and David for a long, long time.

Several months later you got married in Ireland. Can you tell us a little bit about that wedding?

It was really beautiful. The actual ceremony was tiny; we just had our family there. Then we had a party afterward where we had the football team and we had the other Spice Girls. But the actual ceremony was really tiny, and really romantic and beautiful.

You wore a Vera Wang dress?

I did. Well, the bottom part of the dress was Vera Wang. The top part was a corset that had been made by Mr. Pearl, who made incredible corsets.

Was it at the very first Christmas that you were married that you bought David a very special gift wrapped in a big bow in the garage?

Yes. Actually I was still pregnant. I hadn't had Brooklyn. We weren't married, and I bought him a Ferrari.

Good gift. It must be nice to have a Ferrari in the garage as a surprise present.

I spent everything that I had on that Ferrari. David always loved cars and I just wanted him to have something that he would never have bought for himself. It was very special. I loved him so much, and still do. I just wanted him to have what he wanted. We were much more extravagant in those days. I wouldn't do that now. I'm much more sensible at forty-one, that's for sure.

You then went on to have a solo recording career?

It wasn't great. You know, I did that because I thought that's what you do when you leave a pop group.

You also walked in some fashion shows for Roberto Cavalli. Then you were the British ambassador for Dolce & Gabbana.

Yeah, that wasn't great, either, walking on the catwalk. It was an experience. I remember phoning my mom and saying, "I'm really nervous. I'm going to be walking in this fashion show." She said to me—I can't remember how old I was. I was probably thirty—she said, "You've been walking for thirty years. If you haven't got it together now, then you never will. You should just get out there and do it."

But it was a fun thing to do. You know, I look back at certain things and yes, I cringe a little, but it was good at the time. It made me what I am now.

I read that when you met Donatella Versace and Naomi Campbell, Naomi asked, "Like, why do they call you Posh?" I could picture Naomi asking you that. You wrote that after Gianni was murdered, you met with Donatella and you stayed at the house on Lake

This page: Victoria and David Beckham celebrating the launch of the Beckham Signature Fragrance at Macy's Herald Square in 2008. Page 155: Victoria, Jennifer Lopez, and Marc Jacobs behind the scenes at his 2009 NYFW show. Page 156: Victoria at her Spring 2013 fashion show at NYFW.

Como. That must have been an interesting experience.

Yeah, and I spent a lot of time with Allegra and Daniel Versace as well. Donatella was always very sweet. When I was in the Spice Girls, she invited me to watch the fashion show. She flew me on a private plane, and then on a helicopter, and then she took me to the store, and then she gave me lots of clothes. That was incredible, really incredible. I've never taken any of that for granted. I've always really appreciated it.

It was quite overwhelming. It was a wonderful thing to have experienced, and so much fun. I had one of my best friends with me. I met Demi Moore and Naomi Campbell. There were so many incredible people there.

Did these associations get you to start thinking about the potential for your own apparel business?

It's what I always wanted to do, but I just wasn't really in a position to do it myself. It was a great experience working with other people. I also worked with Rock & Republic, where I was designing jeans and separates. I was working with Linda Farrow designing sunglasses. I was working with a Japanese brand doing handbags and jewelry. It was really great because I learned so much.

You did a fragrance then: Intimately Beckham. Is that fragrance still out?

We did it with Coty. The fragrance isn't out there anymore, but it was a huge success. Because of the success of the fragrance, it then enabled me to launch my own brand, to bring everything in-house because the fragrance did very well.

Doing all of those different categories, did you then start to have a staff working with you to help you do all that?

I had a very, very small team. Simon Fuller was my business partner and would let me use a few of his staff as well. We were a really, really small team.

In 2005, you moved to Spain when your husband went to play for Real Madrid. You gave birth to Cruz. That was your third son.

Yes.

You had Romeo in the middle, and then Cruz.

I have so many kids. It's a lot of children.

But how long did it take you to finally find that house in Spain?

It took a long time. We were living in rental houses. I was flying between London and Spain, because Brooklyn was at school. We were traveling a lot. It was good living in Spain because it really enabled me to knuckle down and lay the foundations of the brand that I have now.

I heard you learned Spanish with "Dondé esta Gucci?" ["Where is Gucci?"]

That was about all I could say.

That is pretty remarkable: managing three kids, moving around the world, and working on a burgeoning brand. You decided that you wanted to do your own dVb Style and dVb Denim, which launched at Saks Fifth Avenue. I remember that launch. There was a lunch you had at the Four Seasons for that.

Yeah.

Later in 2007, as your label and brand was coming into its own, you moved to Los Angeles. David signed a five-year deal with the Los Angeles Galaxy. You are in many ways a very private person, but you agreed to do a reality show, following you moving to LA. Why?

That was awful. I didn't enjoy it at all. Simon wanted me to do it and convinced me that it would be a fun thing to do. I suppose it was at the time. But that was actually before we moved to LA. We loved living in LA. I was really sad to leave, and we go back as much as we can.

Do you still have a house in LA?

We still have a house there. I still have my friends there. We're there all summer. We go throughout the year. As soon as the children have any time off of school, we jump on a plane and go straight to LA. It's the most incredible place. I was so happy there.

The kids love it there, too?

We all love it. We like to go hiking, and surfing, and you can't do either of those in London. Though we like living in London, and we have our family there, and my work is there, which is the main reason we're there. The kids go to school in London and we're very happy, but we love LA. At some point, I would love to go back.

Then in 2008, you were also the face of Marc Jacobs.

Yes, that was fun. That was really fun.

One of those campaigns was finally fun!

It was really fun. I love Marc. He's always been an inspiration and he's so great. When he asked me to do the campaign, I was so excited to work with Juergen.

Juergen Teller, the photographer.

At the time I don't think that I realized that he was poking fun a little. I don't think I realized that.

Was he really poking fun?

Yeah, he was! But that's cool. What was so cool about it was that it showed that I don't take myself too seriously. I like to have fun.

… And Marc doesn't, either.

Exactly. I'm still quite close to Marc. I think he's incredible. [Marc Jacobs's interview is in Book 1 of the *Fashion Icons* series.]

We had a terrific time here at the 92nd Street Y, Marc and I.

I'm sure. He's really interesting, isn't he?

He's a fascinating man, absolutely. That same year you produced your very first collection. It was a low-key presentation, with just ten key signature dresses, during New York Fashion Week. Similar to what you shared when you came out here, you were describing every detail to the editors and retailers who were actually blown away by your hands-on presentation and knowledge of the garments, the construction, everything about them. Style.com called it the buzz of New York Fashion Week. What was the signature of those dresses?

At the time, I was wearing lots of fitted dresses and so I wanted to stay true to myself. There were a few corset dresses and everything was very fitted. I did the presentations at the Waldorf Astoria Hotel here in New York. I would just have groups of people come in, whether it was the press or the buyers.

I didn't know if anybody was going to like what I was doing. I had two models. I didn't have stylists and things like that at the time. The girls would walk toward where we were all sitting and I just started talking because, as I said, I like to talk. I like to talk about clothes. It was never done because I wanted to prove anything to anybody other than myself.

People started to really like the fact that I would narrate through the collections.

Why New York Fashion Week and not London Fashion Week?

Because I was living in LA, so it made sense. Also, at the time, the buyers and the press that came to New York, not all of them were going to London. It just made sense for me to do it here.

… And that started the full-on Victoria Beckham collection?

Yes. Like you said, it started out with ten dresses, and with me talking through the collections. I did it at the Waldorf for a couple of seasons. Then I moved to a beautiful house somewhere else—I don't know where I am in New York.

There were more and more people that were attending the presentations. Then they gave me a microphone. I started out literally just talking. Sometimes in the early days, I'd have a room full of people, and sometimes it would be just me and one other person. Even if that other person didn't even speak English, I would talk about the collection, because I just loved it. I really enjoy what I do and I've always felt very blessed to be able to do what I loved to do.

Then it got to a stage where there were so many people coming to the shows, I needed a bigger venue because we were adding categories. We had accessories buyers that needed to come to the show as well. Then we moved to a bigger venue and then it became a show. But I called it a presentation for as long as I could, because I was really scared.

You are a major fixture now on the New York Fashion Week calendar with a beautiful show. Beautifully led by Thierry Dreyfus, who is here tonight. The collections are carefully edited. They are very controlled shows, and a very difficult ticket to get.

Well, thank you. Thank you very much.

Are you terrified each season about how to follow up and keep that momentum going?

I am, and sometimes I think I really wish that I could sit back and enjoy, and live in the moment more. But I am terrified and I want to better myself. Not that I ever want to prove anything to anybody other than myself, but I am very ambitious. There's lots of things that I want to do. It's nervewracking and it doesn't get any easier.

I can't even remember who I asked—it might have been Marc Jacobs—I said, "Does it get any easier? Am I going to feel like this every season?" He said, "Yeah," and I do. I mean, I'm very hands-on with everything that I do.

Do you go to the design studio every day?

Every day, yes. I'm there every day.

Describe who your customer is.

My customer is a woman that loves fashion, appreciates luxury, and someone that wants to feel empowered. I love to empower women. I want to make a woman feel like the best version of herself; that's why I do what I do. My customer travels a lot.

She's me, really. I mean, I have to say, I'm designing clothes for me as well.

I've opened a store in London and what's great about that is that I'm really getting to know my customer more and more. I like to work with my retail partners and do lots of in-store events where I am literally getting to know my customer. I want to know what she wants in a collection, what she wants in a pre-collection.

Tell us about the store because I hear rave reviews about it. Everybody, including Donna Karan, leaves you notes about how great the store is.

You know, I'm very, very proud of the store. It's on Dover Street in London, which has always been my favorite street in London.

Is it across the street from Dover Street Market?

How great is that? It's right across the street from Dover Street Market, which is very exciting. It's a big store. I worked with Farshid Moussavi, who is an architect. She had never worked in the retail space before. She's a strong woman, she loves fashion, she's got a very good eye, and I really knew what I wanted. It's a real collaboration between the two of us, and it's beautiful. It feels like a different shopping experience.

Before we opened the store, we started an e-com site. We did it the other way around the way that most people do it. I like to think outside of the box and do things differently. What I loved about working on the e-com site was actually all of the packaging. If somebody can't come to my store, then their brand experience is going to be online. Things like the packaging are very important. How my customer feels when she gets that Victoria Beckham box. Those little details are things that I love, and I appreciate, and that's what my customer likes

as well.

What's the percentage of your business from e-commerce versus retail?

Retail is bigger. I don't know what the exact percentage is, but e-com is doing really, really well. I shoot a lot of the content myself. You really do see the brand through my eyes, whether you're in the store or on e-com.

Will you be opening more stores?

We will. The second store is going to be in Hong Kong. Asia is my fastest growing market. Hong Kong will be next.

Will New York be on the docket?

Hopefully very soon after that. That is the plan for this year and for next year, to really focus on retail.

Where in New York are your clothes available for people who want to see them?

We have Barneys, Bergdorf Goodman, Neiman Marcus, and Net-A-Porter as well.

Do you consider yourself a workaholic?

Yeah, I am.

As your fashion career was blossoming and you're working like crazy, you also gave birth to your daughter, Harper. Was that a dream come true, to have a little girl?

Yes. It really was. You know, I was told when I went for my scan that I was having another boy. When I was pregnant with Harper, I felt so lucky to be pregnant. Whether Harper was going to be a boy or a girl, I felt very blessed. It was a really lovely surprise.

Was it a surprise when she was born?

I knew just before I had her that she was going to be a girl.

Is she treated like the princess with all her brothers?

None of the kids have ever been spoiled, other than the way that we love them and kiss them lots. They're not spoiled children and Harper hasn't been treated any differently to the boys.

I read your kids are very grounded and very normal. Brooklyn works at a café; is that true?

He does. He has been working for two-and-a-half years at a café down the road, where he does the washing up on a Saturday and a Sunday. I think that's good. I had a Saturday job when I was younger. I don't see why it should be any different for our kids. And he loves it, he enjoys it. It's not that he puts up a fight.

The paparazzi is not outside watching him do that?

No, and he loves it, and it's good. It gives him a little bit of cash as well for when he's going out with his friends.

Romeo was in a Burberry campaign. Was that fun for him?

He was, yeah. It was really good fun. When Christopher Bailey phoned me and asked if Romeo would do it. I was nervous because I've never wanted the children to do anything like that. But I asked Romeo. I said, "Do you want to do it?" He was very excited and he had so much fun. You could see it in the pictures, he was laughing and he was smiling. He really,

to have each other. We're lucky to have each other to support. I couldn't do what I do without his support.

When you're traveling, how many times a day do you call or text?

We speak a lot because we always make sure that one of us is at home with the children. Quite a few times on the phone.

That's very special. What is next on your proverbial bucket list? Something crazy that you still want to do.

What do I want to do? I'd like to collaborate with someone, and I would like to reach more people. I'd like to offer clothes to people that either can't or don't want to pay designer prices. I would like to do that at some point.

I think people would like the idea of that.

I would love to do something like that. Like I keep saying, I really want to make women feel great and feel empowered. Even if they either can't or don't want to pay designer prices, I still want to make them feel great and I still want to reach out to that customer.

Have you not been approached by those mass retailers?

We have in the past. It's just figuring out who to do it with, and when to do it. It's definitely something in the future that I would love to do.

I could say that would be flying out of stores. Let's try and make sure that that happens! There are a couple of questions here from the audience, so let's see. How do you differentiate your brand from the crowded marketplace?

I think what I'm offering is different to what is out there; that's why I decided to do what I do, because I couldn't find what I personally wanted. I think it feels different.

I think we've answered this, but how do you handle it all: career, family, and marriage? She handles it extraordinarily well. I think that's worth a round of applause.

I don't know, but that's very kind. Thank you.

I mean, sometimes I just want to scream and say, "I don't know how you're meant to do it all." I'm sure there's lots of working mums out in the audience. It's tough when you're trying to juggle everything, but we do it. I have a good team of people around me that help manage my schedule so that I can be at all the school plays, but then also be at the office on time. Be at the parents' meetings and the football matches, but do what I have to do professionally as well so. There's a lot of people that help me make it possible. I'm not doing any of this on my own.

It takes a village.

It really does. It really does.

Have your kids seen *Spice World*? And if so, what are their thoughts?

I've watched it with them. They laughed. They found it quite funny. One of them was obsessed with the Spice Bus.

Do you think any of them will go and have musical careers?

I don't know. They're all very sporty, but then they're also very musical. They love to sing and dance. They're really happy kids. There's always a lot of laughter in the house, and footballs being kicked around, and lights being smashed, and all kinds of things. I don't know if any of them would go into the music industry, but they certainly enjoy music.

This is the last question, and we're kind of right on time tonight. What would you consider your greatest fashion achievement?

Oh, goodness. I really don't know. I mean, it was quite incredible when I won the British Fashion Awards. That was an incredible moment, because who would have thought? It was in England, and my parents were there, and my team was with me. That was quite incredible because I am always, like I keep saying, dreaming big. But if you'd have said to everybody that was in the room that night, from the fashion industry, that I would be up there winning that award, nobody would have believed it.

I saw you Monday night at the CFDA awards. Maybe we'll add on that list, the international award from this organization.

I mean, that would be incredible. Maybe I'll put that on my vision board.

You seem to accomplish the things that you set your mind to.

That's definitely the way that I lead my life: creative visualization, and dreaming big, and being positive, and focusing and working hard. All those things are things that I try to do every single day.

Well, I dreamed very big to get you here.

Well, I hope that I did not bore anyone. I've been talking for quite a long time. Thank you so much.

SINCE FASHION ICONS

In 2017, Victoria was appointed an Officer of the Order of the British Empire for her services to the global fashion industry. The award was presented by Prince William, Duke of Cambridge. In 2019, Victoria launched Victoria Beckham Beauty, a cosmetics brand rooted in cruelty-free practices, clean formulations, and inclusivity. Because of her family's investments in the Inter Miami CF soccer club, she now splits her time between homes in Miami and London. Follow Victoria on Instagram: @victoriabeckham

STAN HERMAN

Where do I start? This should be the easiest Fashion Icons interview, but could very well be one of the toughest. Stan Herman and I worked together for ten years at the CFDA, and we were basically attached at the hip. Well, maybe my hip and his elbow. Some people called us the odd couple, but whatever we were called, and we were called a lot of things, we accomplished a great deal together.

We became friends, real friends, and have been now for thirty years, and neighbors on a magical lake that I am eternally grateful for him introducing me to. Stan can identify every tree, bird, turtle, goose and gander on our lake, probably because he feeds them all. He is the dog whisperer. If anyone has lost a dog in the Hamptons, it's probably at Stan's house.

Stan is a designer who has dressed more people in America than all of my previous guests combined. He is the "King of Uniforms." You see his work on a daily basis: every time you receive a FedEx package, every time you take a JetBlue flight, every time you spot a staff member while walking through Central Park, and for years when you ordered a Big Mac at McDonald's.

Stan is a community activist and an opera connoisseur. He melts at the sound of a string quartet, especially if it's Schubert or Mozart, which was the name of his beautiful standard poodle.

He is a mentor to many, including me, and the longest-term president of the CFDA. He loves students of fashion, and made it possible for students and teachers at FIT, Parsons, and Pratt to be here tonight, along with so many of his pals. Pals like Marylou Luther, who wrote the first article ever about him, and they've been friends ever since. Like Bernadette Peters, Terrence McNally, and Edie Windsor, who took her case for the Defense of Marriage Act to the US Supreme Court and won! He hangs with a good crowd.

Stan has been in this audience for almost every one of my Fashion Icon interviews. I always wait to get his thumbs-up when they are over. But he always kind of gave me that look, and nudge, of "When am I going to be up there?"

Well, Stan, tonight is the night, and I would be remiss if I didn't say, "be careful what you wish for." Ladies and gentlemen, let's give a very warm welcome to my friend Stan Herman.

STAN HERMAN: It's not going to get better than that. Oh, my, OK. Thanks.

FERN MALLIS: I need you to water my plants this weekend.

I know. She just said that to me backstage.

Can we go back to the beginning? You were born on September 17, 1928. How young are you?

Eighty-seven [STANDS UP AND RAISES HIS HAND]. Fern is telling me to sit down but I have to tell you if you're an opera singer, what you do if you're baritone and the applause comes like that, you place your hand over your heart. If you're a tenor, you go, "Me? Who, me?" And if you're a soprano, you extend your arms. I'm doing the soprano. Thank you so much.

How old do you feel?

How old do I feel? How old do I look? I feel, seriously, sometimes I feel quite old. Sometimes I look in the mirror and I say, "Where did all that go to? But then there are other times that I feel very good about myself. I'm one of those lucky people that has lived long enough and I really like my life.

We'll talk about it. Don't tell it all right now.

I feel older. But there's a young heart beating there, and there's a will to like people. I like people. I like touching them, as you know. I like feeling them. I like sex.

Kind of sounds boring now to say you were born in Brooklyn Jewish Hospital.

I was. There isn't such a thing anymore, is there?

I don't know, but I was born there also. You're a Virgo. I know that you're somewhat of an astrologer yourself. Our favorite astrologer in the world, James Haigney, is in the audience. But you've said that Virgo is your least favorite sign.

Well, it is. I once opened a company called Virgo Design that went down in the tank so quickly I can't begin to tell you. We all hated each other by the end of the evening. I had to hire an Aries, like you are, to get it all together.

Virgos can be, well, you could probably tell me, but I'm going to say: service-oriented, critical, perfectionists, and negatively and overly critical, which is true if you ever sat next to him at a fashion show. He's very critical.

Hard on themselves. Have a purity of vision and attention to detail. Really messy or neat. Never satisfied, indecisive, fault-finding. Can miss the big picture because of the focus on details. You also have Cancer rising and your moon is in the fifth house in Scorpio, which rules the house of performance, theater, and entertainment.

Also Cancer rising keeps you surrounded by family. Always having family or friends around and staying in touch with contacts from the past. Do you agree or disagree with all of that?

I agree with almost everything. I am very Virgo. You know, I guess people's signs by physical features. I walk up to somebody and say, "You're a Scorpio."

But how do you learn that? Tell us what some of those features are that define signs.

Well, there are four elements. But there's earth, fire, water, and air. I think people are full of water in their face.

What does water in your face look like?

There's a slight puffiness. You could be as thin as a stick but there's just a slight puffiness in the face. Earth signs tend to look like me.

Do I have an Aries face?

No. You must have a very, very important rising sign. James, what rising sign does she have?

Gemini.

You're a Gemini. Oh, I think you look much more air than you do, that's air.

Back to planet Earth. Your parents, Sydney Herman and Helen Tannenbaum, they moved a year after you were born to Passaic, New Jersey. Why?

Well, you know, those times were different. There were so many immigrants in New York, first and second generation. My father's family came from Vienna, Austria, and moved to Passaic, New Jersey. It was a small town but like all small towns at that time there was a core. There were churches, synagogues, and a library. A downtown that you went to, a soda fountain that you went to.

I think they wanted to get out of the nexus of Brooklyn. We went there, and I lived right in the shadow of New York. Very much in the shadow of New York.

When people ask you if you're from New York or New Jersey...

I say I was born in New York. I tell cab drivers that all the time.

Your mom, Helen, she died at thirty-six. From what?

Endocarditis. She had a heart problem, which they couldn't treat then. My mother died at thirty-six. And my father died at 105. Isn't that extraordinary? I find that extraordinary.

My brother Harvey, who is here, right, remembers her quite well. More than I do. I think I blocked her out. Although the things that she did, the way she dressed me… they put me in tap dance shoes when I was four. They did all the things that I think the genes were telling them.

Piano lessons? Dance lessons?

She loved making her own clothing. She was pretty. She tended to get a little heavy but she was very pretty. I have a diary that she wrote many, many years ago that my aunt gave me, which was so frustrating because she was, like many women at that time, completely flummoxed by the idea that she couldn't go to college. That her brothers did. She only had two brothers. She wanted to play tennis. I got the tennis gene from her.

From left to right: Stan Herman at age four; Stan with his mother Helen and brother Harvey Herman in 1939.

Mitchell, Harvey, and Stan Herman celebrate their father Sidney's 100th birthday in 2004.

Your dad who passed at 105, was still driving, riding horses, and working at one hundred. Wasn't he?

He stopped the horses at ninety-three, but he was one of those extraordinary people. My other brother Mitchell is here, too. I think my dad was born erect. I don't think he ever sat any other way but like this. He had a great body from when you ride horses all your life; there's a posture that I think you take on. I was lucky, really lucky, to have a father of 105 to talk to on a personal level. To go back over times with him.

You spoke to him all the time.

All the time. I called him every day. We were very much like clones. I used to say all the time, "Sydney, we're identical except I'm a faggot. What are you?"

What did your dad do when you were growing up?

He was a pickle man to start with. I bought pickles today at Bryant Park, very good pickles.

Pickles in Bryant Park?

Yes. Very good pickle guy in Bryant Park. My father was a pickle man who eventually moved back to Passaic, New Jersey, with the family and went into fabrics.

He owned silk stores. We used to call all fabrics silk. He had a chain of stores called Herman Silk Shop. In Passaic they ruled the roost. They were in Pennsylvania. Actually he had the silk shop in the basement of Macy's, on the corner of 34th Street. Yes, I have pictures of it to this day.

Sydney remarried rather quickly though after your mother passed away. Was that disturbing to you and your brothers?

One year.

It was freaky. We didn't quite know what was happening. It was a very difficult time for me. It was just when I was bar mitzvahed. I became a man, and she just didn't quite fit into my way of thinking. She tried, but I could be a tough guy.

Are there some funny bar mitzvah stories?

I had the grandest bar mitzvah in our garage. It was the fabric. We put this big chandelier up and it was pre-Studio 54. It was really great. I was wonderful at my bar mitzvah. I did all the prayers. I shoved the rabbi aside. I took over.

You are very close with your brothers, Harvey and Mitchell.

I am. We talk all the time. We are together.

The three of you talk about cars incessantly, for hours on end. Where does the car thing come from?

I don't know where it came from, but I am a car nut. When car magazines from Britain come, I'm in heaven. I go through every page. I always thought of cars like fashion because every season there's a change.

My greatest desire was to design a car, and I lost out to Oleg Cassini. I tried and they picked Oleg. He wasn't the wise choice, but they picked him.

The other person that got the first car design was Bill Blass. Bill designed the interiors for, I think it was Lincoln Continental. But he didn't design the car.

You remember when we went out to General Motors? They took us into this design lab so I just freaked out. I mean, I freaked out.

It's so extraordinary: the feel of a car, the way each part links to each other. I just love the look of it and still do. I bought the first Range Rover in America. The first. Dino De Laurentiis took the second. It was before they were legal. I still have a Range Rover.

… And he's at the Ranger dealership every weekend because something is not working.

I talked her into getting a Land Rover. Yours was fine, right?

I got rid of it. You went to Passaic High School, and you were voted best dressed?

I was voted best dressed.

Which is unusual for a boy to be voted best dressed in high school.

No. That was always a part of the whole thing. I was very disappointed.

There were four guys who really hung out together, and I wanted to be considered best friends. But I was taken off the four. They gave three of them best friends, and they gave me best dressed. That really bothered the hell out of me when I look at that, you know, we're talking about sixty, seventy years ago. Is that amazing? Just amazing.

I was voted best dressed in my high school, too.

How did you feel about it?

It was a very nice honor.

You know why I was voted best dressed? Harvey and I talked about it all the time. My father went into the vest and jacket business and he decided that there shouldn't be any collars on the jackets. Remember those cardigans? I had so many cardigans in my life. I mean, every color of the rainbow. I thought they were awful. I thought I looked like a waiter, but everybody else thought I looked great. So I got that award.

You went to the University of Cincinnati and got a BFA in 1949. How and why did you

choose Cincinnati?

Well, it was, I guess, important to know that this was 1946, and it was right after World War II. And there were so many people coming back, so many guys coming back who had to get into school. The GI Bill was flourishing and I didn't want to stay in New York. I was a little frightened of my sexuality at the time.

I looked for a city, rather than a campus, where there was a symphony orchestra, where there was some culture and suddenly Cincinnati popped up. It was what I needed. I had a wonderful time and I became president of my fraternity, Sigma Alpha Mu.

Is that the beginning of your political career?

Yes. Very much so, very much so.

Now you're in college and you had a summer job at Vogue Patterns?

That's right. I forgot that.

This is one of our similarities. I had a summer job at Simplicity.

Really? Well, you know, do you know how designers looked at Vogue Patterns? They used to come to work with hats and gloves and would sit, take off their gloves. All they did was sketch all day but keep their hats on. It was just an amazing time. The building was on 40th and Fifth Avenue, which is now down the block from where I am on the top floor. My father got me that job because he sold a lot of Vogue patterns and fabric.

Then you won a scholarship to Traphagen School of Design. It was to introduce students from Cincinnati to the school.

All over the Midwest, all over everywhere. We were introduced to New York, the sophisticated New York. That was a big thing in my life because that changed how I entered the fashion business.

Then you met John-Frederics, who was known as Mr. John, and took a job in Philadelphia for several months before you were drafted into the army.

He got me the job in Philadelphia. It was a very, very difficult time for me. I really wasn't prepared and I was very nervous. I would be on the train going down to Philadelphia and I must have been so nervous. It was pre-antiperspirant, pre-Ban. I remember coming to work one day and there was an envelope on my desk and it was from the models and they all said to me in this little sweet note, "We love you, you're adorable, but you smell." I'll never forget it as long as I live. I wear so much perfume now you wouldn't believe it.

John-Frederics was the hat designer in the 1940s and 1950s. That was the opening of the key to my life in fashion because at that time the fashion business was so tiny that you had to find a keyhole and find your entrance. If you didn't find that keyhole, not the big splash but that keyhole, you didn't make it.

You found the keyhole but then you had to go into the army during the Korean War. Did you see combat?

I saw lots of beer in Germany. No. I was sent to Germany instead, and that too proved to be an extraordinary part of my life. I had never seen mountains like that. I was just a boy from

Photos from Stan Herman's army tour of duty in the Bavarian Alps in 1952.

New York, New Jersey. When I opened my eyes one night, and I saw the Alps, I said, "This is where my heart is."

I actually forced my way into staying in the Intelligence Corps there. I stayed in the Alps for almost a year.

What did you do for the other two years in the army?

Well, most of it was learning. Thank you for asking that, Fern. I was in the army when the army was integrated. When I went in, there were Blacks and there were whites at Fort Dix. I remember the moment when we were integrated and Blacks and whites came together.

They said to me I had to do the cadence call for this group of Black soldiers. I said, "I can't do the cadence call for them." And I did and, boy, was I good. I mean, I really did.

Whatever, it's a—I'm going to sing later.

He's going to sing us out of here. Was it in the army that you realized you were gay?

I probably knew the gene was there. But it was in the army that everything sort of fell into place. I've said this before and I'll say it again. The day in my life that I don't walk into a room and I don't feel the sexual pleasure of seeing somebody, male, female, that I love, then I'm going to hang up my shoes. I think sex is just there for the taking and you just have to use it properly.

When I went into the army, I remember I went to a special course in Dachau, and I came back and all my mail was there from the previous two or three weeks. I looked through the screen and there was this man I had never seen before. He handed me my mail and he said, "Where have you been?"

That started the whole thing. We became very close. We were not sexual friends but we became very close and he taught me the ropes and I became very good at it.

Let's leave it at that. In 1953 you came out of the army and that would actually become an important year in your life. You got your first real job with Fira Benenson, known as the Countess of Illinska. Your job was to keep her vodka cold in a crystal decanter.

It's true. She was one of those women who had all the intellectual Jewish women from the "our crowd" group of upper Park Avenue. She made these very stiff-looking dresses that look like you were wearing wallpaper.

I actually took the job from a guy named John Moore, who was Norman Norell's lover at the time. I was more package handler than anything, but it was my first job. My part of the job was to run down 57th Street (we were at Sixth Avenue) to 33 East 57th Street to get the chilled martini with lemon ready for the countess every time she came home. She never offered me one.

She was a wonderful lady. Also a good designer, not a great designer. But she had a terrible habit of talking like this [HAND COVERING HIS FACE] because she had a nose job. I couldn't understand anything she was saying. She would say things to me like, "I don't like that sleeve you draped," and I had no idea what she was saying to me at all. We became very close friends.

Stan Herman and his one-time boss Oleg Cassini in 2005.

Was she your first boss? Or was your first real boss Oleg Cassini?

Well, he was my friend. I did sketches. Oleg Cassini at that time was known as the table top designer. He did everything up here [PLACING HIS HANDS ON HIS CHEST].

He never cared what happened below that but it was up here. I worked from his house on 61st Street. I would go in every day. His mother would check on me. She was across the street. She checked on whether I was in at nine or ten or eleven and she would clock me.

Oleg was a very famous ladies' man at the time. On the left of my desk, believe it or not, there was a silver frame with a beautiful picture of Princess Grace of Monaco, whom he was having an affair with at that time. On my right was another picture, but this was in gold, of Gene Tierney, his wife. I got so bored; he never came in to see anything. And I would sketch and I would say, "This is for you, Gene. This is for you, Grace. This is for you, Gene. This is for you, Grace."

This went on for months. The piles were this high. I told him about that many years later when we became good friends. He had no memory of it whatsoever.

You also lived in a rooming house on 86th Street between Fifth and Madison for thirty-eight dollars a month. In 1953 you also met a very close friend, Arnold Scaasi. Tell us about meeting him: his name, his convertible. Was he already known as a designer?

For those young designers out there, he's a wonderful test run because Arnold, at the age of twenty-two or twenty-three, was already very famous in New York. He was born to the manner. I came from Cincinnati, Ohio, having come from the army and I was in awe of him.

He got me my first apartment across the street from where his studio was on 84th Street. Then eventually I moved into the apartment that he used as his studio. We were not lovers, but I stayed there at night and he stayed there during the day.

He sponsored my singing career, believe it or not. He just died, as everybody knows. Arnold was not an easy person. He was difficult in many, many, many ways but when you have a

friend for over sixty years, some odd years, those things wash off you. You feel responsible for them.

The last night I was in his house for dinner, with Parker [Ladd], it was like being back in time, served with all the utensils with the servers in white linen, in New York, with all the mirrored walls. He knew how to live.

I really enjoyed Arnold, and I know how difficult he was. You know how difficult he was. Everywhere he went he left residue.

People crying.

But not to me. He was different with me. I knew how to treat Arnold.

And was it your aunt who helped him change his name?

That's the truth. Arnold would say, no. But he was at my home for Passover dinner and he was in a quandary because he was not able to get an ad with General Motors for their Cadillac. And they said they wouldn't use a Jewish name…

… It was Arnold Isaacs.

It was Arnold Isaacs at that time. My aunt Florence, my brothers will attest to it. We played Scrabble with the letters in his name and she said, "Why don't you spell it backward?"

So, Arnold Isaacs became Arnold Scaasi. I know that because I tried my name backward and it was not right.

Then you worked for Herbert Sondheim for a year. What was his business, besides being Stephen Sondheim's father?

It was mostly in the fifties on Seventh Avenue; they were very parochial, a small campus of better clothing. There were three buildings. There was 530, 550, 512 was the suit business, and 498 was the upstart young business.

Sondheim was typical of the "no name" designer. My boss came from the same town as Bill Blass. The same state as Norman Norell, and he was a very good designer. He hired me as his assistant. I went through the assistant thing for years and years and years in New York. The way it worked was you started as a sketcher, and you went from a sketcher maybe to a draper, and then you eventually got a third design room, and maybe a second design room, and then a first design room.

My big moment was for a company called Martini Design, which was owned by two men named Sylvan Rich and Jerry Silverman.

Also that year, on July 25, 1953, you say at 5:30 in the afternoon, another thing happened that would change your life: you met Gene Horowitz. Tell us how you met. What was Gene like?

This is a real great movie, because I don't know how many people out there ever met the love of their life and they knew it the second they saw them. Well, that's what happened to me.

I was, again, quite promiscuous at the time and, I was at a party that was being given by John-Frederics. People like Jerry Silverman, they're all there, and this guy was coming in from California. We're supposed to have this big thing that night, and he didn't arrive. They said, "Let's go to a bar until he comes." We went to a bar called the William Tell and it was July 25, 1953, at 5:30 in the afternoon.

I walked into that bar, and there was a guy sitting there all burned to a crisp from Jacob Riis Park sun, and a tweed jacket that was so overdressed; I don't know where the hell he got a tweed jacket. It just hit me. Obviously it worked both ways. I motioned to him, and I said, "Go in the back."

This is the time before you could go into a gay bar. You couldn't touch anybody, you just didn't do that. There certainly wasn't dancing. There wasn't anything like that, but you could nudge, you could move up against somebody, you could walk down the street and maybe rub up against the guy or the woman.

I said to him, "I'm busy tonight, but I'll be finished by about two. Would you call me?" I gave him my number. When I touched him, I just felt *that*" [MAKES ELECTRIC SPARK NOISE].

When I got back to my apartment, I didn't have a phone. It was in the hallway and the phone rang, and he came up, and we were together for forty years.

Gene was a great guy. Also in 1953, you both went out to the Hamptons for the first time. It was very different place than it is today.

Describe what you bought and how you got there and what that means to you?

Well, I almost wanted to ask you the same thing, because Fern has been lucky enough to dip into the lore of that lake. I went out, it was a year that Gene and I split, we actually split the first year because he turned to me one day and he said to me, "You're not ready for this. I am, but you're not. When you're ready, it'll happen."

We split and that summer I had a little thing with the man out in Bridgehampton, and my tailor at Martini and Sylvan, who was my boss, used to rent a place out there. I didn't know anything about it, I didn't know anything about the Hamptons. I went out to visit them and Sylvan was in the green camp that you have been in. Fern was there for six years.

I looked at this lake and I said, "My God, this is heaven." I remembered we paid $250 a month for it. Then when Gene and I got back together again I said, "This is the place that we have to develop." I'm still there.

It looks a little different. I have a house that's much nicer. We had no hot water in our house. We took baths in the lake, this is in Southampton. We took baths in the lake. We had an outhouse, actually.

But we had this beautiful piece of property, and I bought enough property next to it so that I'm protected. I still run out there every weekend. Fern came into it naturally. Was it the first year that we knew each other? She had a wonderful dog. She took this little green camp and made it into something that could have been photographed for any magazine.

I took out all the crap he had in there.

That place had bones. Jerry [Jerome] Robbins lived in that place. There's some really great people that lived in that place. Let me tell you they had real big bones, she took the bones out.

I decorated the bones. Now it is a very special place on the lake and Bronson Van Wyck

Page 178: Stan Herman's partner Gene Horowitz and dog Mozart in the Hamptons. This page: Stan and Gene with close friend and civil rights activist Edie Windsor.

is here, who also just moved next door on the lake. And his dog named Cat is always at Stan's house.

Do I love his dog. I really do, and she loves me.

With Gene you left the Upper East Side and you moved to the West Village? And then you settled in Murray Hill.

Gene suddenly died in 1991, after you were inseparable for forty years. If he had lived, would you have gotten married?

Well, I will say that right in this audience tonight is the woman who would have allowed it: Edie Windsor. Do you know Edie Windsor?

Those of you out there who are quite young, look at the person next to you. You never know what that person is going to be like in forty or fifty years. Edie and I were young kids; we've known each other from a very young age. Here she ends up in *Windsor v. the United States of America*. She made marriage possible for me, for people like myself.

I think we would have. Gene did not want to emulate heterosexuals at all. He was pretty tricky. I think brighter than I was, and much more political and almost radical. I don't know, it's been a long time. But I would have wanted to and certainly just from the idea of when I die, my estate is willed. I think most people have that option. That's a wonderful option.

Would you have had children? Would that have interested you?

I love children, people don't think I do, but I love children. I don't know. Those are such hard questions to answer. In fact, *The Advocate* once wrote a very long piece on the two of us, and on our relationship, as we never hid who we were.

I'll give you an interesting time, Fern. In the 1960s, when we were together, I was asked to be on a television show: *The David Susskind Show*. I actually was interviewed for a different show with him. It was on just designers. They thought I was funny or something, so they said we have another show for you that we'd like you to be on.

David Susskind pulled me into the back room and he said, "We know that you're a homosexual, but would you talk about it?"

This is 1968, and I said, "Sure."

Then I went home and I spoke to Gene, and he was a teacher. He said to me. "I think it's wonderful that you're going to do it, but it's going to be tricky. One of your biggest accounts is McDonald's."

… And the show's subject was "Famous Sons of Jewish Mothers." The other people on the show were: Mel Brooks, George Segal, David Steinberg, and Dan Greenberg.

It is incredible you can still pull it up on YouTube; it's still great. I wore a knit suit that I made for myself. Have you ever had a knit suit in your life? I started out in the show, my crotch was up to here [MOTIONING TO HIS CROTCH], and by the time the show was over it was down to here [MOTIONING TO HIS KNEES].

I walked off that stage, and it looked like I had my pants down. It was hysterical. But that show is worth seeing. Mel Brooks was extraordinary. They played it every New Year's Eve for ten years.

On that show, I complained that my mother took the locks off the bathroom and I couldn't masturbate because I had to keep one hand there. Evelyn, my stepmother, was so upset, she kept saying, "Why do you keep saying that over and over again every year?"

But you really didn't talk about being gay on that show?

No, they didn't ask. I was so nervous because I thought he was going to ask about it. Who was the guy, who was the comedian? David Steinberg.

I had heard through the grapevine that he was having an affair with somebody—a man. I thought to myself, now it might not have been true at all. I said, "But if he doesn't say any-

Stan Herman posing nude with model Naty Abascal for Mr. Mort in 1968.

thing, I'm not going to say anything." David [Susskind] never got around to it.

At one point, I got on the floor and sang to Mel Brooks, which was really very sweet. It was really special.

You talked about that, Jerry Silverman?

Does anybody remember Jerry Silverman at all? You know, there was a moment in New York in the 1970s when the fashion business became political. We were never very political. Actually I was appointed to a community board by Mayor Lindsay. I was on the Midtown Manhattan community board for twenty-five years—a long, long time. Again, lost my train of thought. Anyway, he was very close to the mayor. Pauline Trigère was like the mistress of fashion, all related to Gracie Mansion.

… And you freelanced for her, and she never paid you?

She didn't. She became my great pal, but she didn't pay me. She gave me a mannequin figure as payment. She never used the sketches. I was sort of conned into it.

That goes back to Arnold Scaasi. I had this dress form. This butch guy who liked car magazines had a dress form. Arnold and I had to leave my apartment and Arnold decided to put me in his big Buick convertible, with the top down. We looked for an apartment for me, or at least a hotel. Every time we got to the hotel, he kept saying, with this mannequin in the back seat, "My friend wants a place big enough for his mannequin."

Do you still have that mannequin?

I do. It sits in my studio, it's a size six Wolf form, and it was given to me by Pauline Trigère.

That's great. In 1959–61, you became unhappy as a designer and you wanted a career on Broadway, and you took singing lessons? And Arnold Scaasi helped.

Who's laughing? Arnold actually paid me five hundred dollars a month. When I had my first audition, he came to it. It was for a show called *Girl Crazy* by Rodgers and Hart. I had sheet music for a song called "Breathless," which had a range of about four notes and I had the chutzpah to go to an audition. Arnold came and sat in the back. My accompanist, who was the house accompanist at that time, was John Kander.

He still remembers it. He kept saying, "Four notes, that's it?"

I sang and I came offstage and Arnold said, "I thought you could sing, I couldn't hear a thing." Actually, at his memorial service at St. Bart's just a month ago, I did sing the "Kol Nidre" for him, which was very nice. I might sing it tonight.

But you did get a part in *La Plume de Ma Tante*, which I know my mother had the *Playbill* for. It's in my garage.

Really? Well, I wasn't ready to go onto Broadway. But there was something about me, that sort of, I don't know. When I went on the stage it was there and so they cast me in the second lead in *La Plume de Ma Tante*. I was under a guy named Robert Clary. I guess that's a name that most people wouldn't know now. He was big star at the time, and he had been in Auschwitz, a Holocaust victim and he had this big stamp on his hand.

He hated me. He couldn't stand me, and we played all these scenes together on the stage.

Clockwise from below: Stan Herman's Mr. Mort trompe l'oeil dress on a bust form gifted by designer Pauline Trigère. Fern Mallis, Todd Oldham, and Angel Dormer gifted the dress to Stan after finding it at a New York City flea market; Stan's sketch for the Mr. Mort dress; Ali MacGraw wearing Mr. Mort in 1970's *Love Story*; Stan's sketch for the Mr. Mort logo.

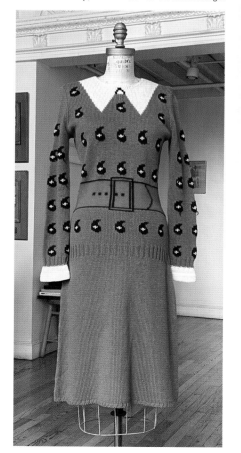

One was where we were in a pissoir in Paris together and I had to jump on his shoulders. What he did to me, every night, was indescribable; he would kill me. He finally got me out of the show.

At that point I decided that I wanted to really learn how to sing. I discovered a guy who was a Svengali and he said I couldn't sing for three years, if I was studying with him. He rebalanced the voice, so I ended up singing opera. I think Ruth Finley is here. She saw me in one of those performances.

During the day you designed for Junior Forum?

Yes, while I was in the show, I was with this company called Junior Forum. I had no idea it was owned by the Mafia, and we were a sensation.

Women's Wear Daily said, "A star has been born."

Absolutely. It was a different *Women's Wear Daily* then. The reporting didn't have all the gloss that we have now, nor the power. But they said, "A star was born."

I was cast in a show called *Parade* with Anna Maria Alberghetti and I was supposed to go away on the road with it in a second lead, and then understudy. I made a decision to stay in New York with Gene. I couldn't do that anymore.

The Junior Forum line was so successful that Mr. Mort, which was a very hot label, asked me to come to them, and that started the real trajectory of my fashion business.

Anne Klein and I were the hot designers at that point. Remember Anne Klein? The real Anne Klein? Anne Klein could clink scotch with me better than anybody I know. We would have scotch at Bill's restaurant every night, three and four nights a week. We would sit and talk about the world and about fashion. There was a moment when she looked at me and she said, "I've got it. I know what to do. I'm going to do pants and pieces. Women don't want to wear dresses. They want to wear tops and bottoms. They can buy different sizes, and every season, the colors will coordinate and they'll never be jarring. They'll go around and around in a circle, and I will dress women."

She said, "You should do the same." Boy, was I wrong, I never did it. She did it. She was, I think, the woman who started American fashion as we know it. I'm not saying the most exciting fashion, but the most exciting concept.

It's amazing to think back that there was a time when people weren't doing tops and bottoms.

They were not. Originally they were doing tops and bottoms. Then they put them together and called it a dress. But you know in the 1950s, 1960s, and even part of the 1970s, they called it the dress business. They don't call it the dress business anymore. They used to call it the schmatta business.

They still call it that.

Fern and I were in a great film called *Schmatta*. If you haven't seen it, it's a really great film.

It was a documentary commissioned by Sheila Nevins for HBO.

Tell us about the Mr. Mort dress worn by Ali MacGraw in *Love Story* in 1967.

She's still my friend. She's still my lady.

… And years later Estelle Getty would wear your chenille robe on *The Golden Girls*.

I have done more chenille robes for movies. You could tell a chenille robe because it sheds. I watched Estelle Getty shed everywhere. But it's comfortable, isn't it?

Around that time you finally got into the CFDA, after several attempts. You were going to start up another organization to compete with them.

Right, they wouldn't let me in. Because the CFDA was a different organization at that time. It was a very small, tight group and only the so-called better designers were in it. They weren't ready for the onslaught of young designers, and there were lots like Leo Narducci, Don Simonelli, Gayle Kirkpatrick, Chester Weinberg. Well, Chester was in the CFDA. Chester was an old man before he was young.

But we got all these guys together, including the guy who did menswear out in the Hamptons, and we said, "We are going to form our own organization; we don't need them." Every time the CFDA would take one of them in, they would drop it. They would drop me, so it was not a winning situation. I did eventually get in and the rest is history.

Then you had done a TV pilot for McCall's home sewing show. Whatever happened to the home sewing business? That was the biggest thing.

Well, that's when I started. My father had the silk shop. My idea of heaven was at the end of the day, before the lights went out, to go down and close the Vogue [pattern book], and close the Advance [pattern book], and close the Simplicity [pattern book]. People actually came in and they would ask my father what color they wanted for their dress. People did sew. At one point we tried to do a sewing show, but I was a terrible sewer. I just couldn't lie about it. I said to them, "When the camera comes, use somebody else's hands because I can't

This page: Stan Herman, Arnold Scassi, Liz Smith, Marylou Luther, Peter Rogers, and Parker Ladd at Scassi's home for the CFDA new members party in 2006. Next page: Stan and model Renee Hunter presenting his collection at the Osaka World's Fair in 1969.

sew this thing."

I did do something called "Fashion in a Box" where you put all the clothes in a box. I was, at that point, at a company called Russ Togs. We actually sold this "Fashion in a Box." My brother Harvey did the advertising for the cover of it.

In 1968 you worked with a young editor at *Vogue* named Kezia Keeble. She told you to design pants under dresses and gave you an unknown French designer to copy. The original label was Sonia Rykiel. What happened?

Well, there are actually two different stories. Kezia was my woman. She was—she's legendary. She started KCD [Keeble Cavaco & Duka Public Relations], for those who are young enough not to remember her. She was one of those extraordinary people in this business. She thought I was very talented, and she would very often come and say, "You know, you should do this," or "You should do that."

She showed me some Indian dolls, with the tunic tops and the pants. Skirts at that time had gotten so short. I think Bebe Winkler might be here, the woman who I fitted on. Skirts were up to here. We decided one day to put pants underneath the dresses. It was the most extraordinary thing that happened to me. The buyers came and hated it. But the same year, the same time, Yves Saint Laurent did it in Paris.

Mildred Custin, president of Bonwit Teller, called me from Paris and said, "I want all those things that we passed up as windows." It was Paris who put the imprimatur on it, and it made my company at that point.

In 1969, you and Rudi Gernreich took a trip to Japan for the Osaka World's Fair. The show was sponsored by Mikimoto Pearls. The other designers were Chester Weinberg, Count Sarmi, Gayle Kirkpatrick, and Victor Joris.

It was a wonderful four weeks. Rudi came from the West Coast. We all flew in from New York, and we met Rudi in Honolulu. We were supposed to be doing a big fashion show at the fair. Everybody had trunks full of clothes, accessories, the whole bit, shipped before us, and shipped after us. When we got to Honolulu, Rudi came and he had this little bag, a little satchel. I said, "Where are your clothes?"

He said, "They're in here." He had all his knit dresses wrapped up with little ballet slippers. He stole the whole show. He was extraordinary. He said to me, "You know, Herman, I think you could inherit my mantle." I thought, "Oh, my God."

I also had a very hard time talking to him because he had a terrible toupee, just terrible. It was always slightly askew. But believe it or not, two years later, I inherited his factory in Menominee, Michigan. I tried to save the factory that he did all those phenomenal knits in for years and years and years. He refused to get off the double-knit bandwagon and the company that owned it was dying. I spent two winters up in Menominee, Michigan. It is cold. I tried desperately to keep it going but it didn't work.

June of 1969 was the first time I met you, when I was a *Mademoiselle* magazine guest editor. I got to interview you, Mr. Mort.

Why did you choose me?

Because you were the hot designer at the time. Five groups of four guest editors; we all went to different people. We went to designers, a poet, a writer, all different disciplines, and you were the designer that was selected.

I remember. I always felt that with the cyclical nature of our business, there was a ten-year period for a designer who really could make it. I think they've broken that barrier now, people today like Diane von Furstenberg, Tommy Hilfiger, and Ralph Lauren, their businesses are fortified against the kind of cycle that we had in the 1970s and the 1980s. But so many people just disappeared; their businesses just went "poof!"

Well, in the 1970s, you were working with Geraldine Stutz at Henri Bendel. She set up designers to have their own studios and boutiques that she sold at Bendel's, but also wholesaled to other companies.

Some of the designers that you shared spaces with there were Giorgio di Sant'Angelo, Stephen Burrows, and John Kloss, and Joel Schumacher was the visual merchandiser and windows designer. Tell us a little bit about that?

Well, Bendel at that point was the "fashion store" with the boutique concept. After Mr. Mort closed, and it was not a nice closing, Geraldine called me and she said, "We love your clothes up here. We sell them very well."

I found out later on they were selling [my dresses] to all the hookers on 59th Street. But there was one great dress, a marvelous dress, that was down to the knees and everybody was shortening it right below the crotch..

I went up there and we actually made clothes for other stores. We sold to Saks Fifth Avenue, and it was produced by Bendel. Nobody even remembers that.

It sounds like a broken record, but it didn't last very long because I think I took it too seriously.

The clothes were great, but they didn't have the ability to produce such a diversified line. Stephen Burrows was the wonder up there. He used two fabrics. They were all basically the same things in different colors, and they had a ball with that.

By Geraldine's request, you had lunch with Ralph Lauren at his studio on West 55th Street. He discussed with you the possibility of going into business together. But what did you say?

"Me? What do I need you for? No. No. No" [LAUGHTER]. She was concerned that Ralph didn't know how to make a dress. He was just going into the women's business and she said, "Why aren't you up there and talking to him about it?"

It was 55th, right above the Italian Pavilion, which is now Michael's. I went, and there was Ralph in his undershirt. I thought to myself, "He's in his undershirt." He showed me his clothes. They were so beautiful. The colors were beautiful. The prints were beautiful, but they were clunky looking. He said it himself; he had never really done dresses.

Then he said let's have lunch, and I thought he was going to put a jacket on, but he went downstairs in his undershirt. I kept thinking, what am I wearing a tie for? This is ridiculous. But we had a wonderful lunch. We talked about the possibility, but I was so full of myself at that time. Ralph really always knew what he was doing. Some of us don't. We think we do, but Ralph always knew what he was doing.

In 1975 you rented your own studio on Bryant Park, a space that used to be Irving Penn's studio.

It's 80 West 40th Street. People should really walk by that. It's a landmark building.

Anyone remember the illustrator named Leyendecker? Leyendecker was in my studio, Irving Penn was in my studio. I remember the first time Lauren Hutton came up, she said, "Oh, my God, was I nude in this studio?"

Opposite: First Lady Hillary Clinton hosting Stan Herman and Ralph Lauren at the White House in honor of their work leading Fashion Targets Breast Cancer in 1994. This page: Stan's windows at Bonwit Teller.

It's a great studio. It's a great building. It was an apartment house. Louis Sullivan was involved with it. There was a great murder on the top floor. I love the building.

It's one of the reasons we were in Bryant Park in the tents. It was called Needle Park at that time. I was the Head of Parks on Community Board Five at that time so I knew it very vividly. It made me feel very comfortable being there.

OK. But while you were in that studio early on, you also had a student from Parsons that impressed you and apprenticed in your office?

He wasn't from Parsons. He was still in high school. I got him myself, and other people got him into Parsons.

His name?

Marc Jacobs. Marc had his first job with me. He was sixteen and it was so interesting for me to be hiring young apprentices still in high school. As… what do you call it when you don't pay them?

Interns.

Interns. Thank you. You pay them now, thank God.

But I had one student and my studio was very open. It's not that I was throwing my sexuality around, but I just talked openly about who I was and what I wasn't. In fact, when you interviewed Marc on the stage, he even said that, which freaked me out. He said the reason he remembers the studio is because he felt welcomed as a person, as a gay person. When I looked at Marc's sketches, I just, I couldn't believe it. He only worked with me for a short time but he was definitely there, and the talent was there.

In the 1970s, 1980s, your freelanced out of that studio, doing many of your big uniform jobs: TWA, United, US Airways, McDonald's for fifteen years, Royal Caribbean Cruise Lines, Humana Hospitals.

Tell us a little bit about the uniform business and how that was perceived by the industry. Did you get respect for doing uniforms?

Having been in the hot center of the business in the 1960s and early 1970s, and then losing your big business, and going into a freelance position, it's tricky. I've been able to work it, but it's very tricky. In the early 1970s, I got a call from Doyle Dane Bernbach, who represented them. The president of Avis wanted a new uniform.

I took myself out to Garden City. I met him and I thought, "Gee, that's a fun idea."

I took it seriously. I mean, they were in red, head to toe. Could anything be worse? I put them in red and gray and suddenly everybody thought I was a genius in that business. From there on I decided I could do that. I became a part of Hart Schaffner Marx, and next did TWA.

The TWA uniform is quite extraordinary. We did a blouse for TWA. It was all a haberdashery with a repeating "TWA, TWA, TWA" print. You could hardly see it. We mapped it out, and then we printed 36,000 yards. When I got the first yardage through, there was no space between the TWAs.

Can you picture it? Spell "TWA, TWA, TWA." You read it as the first four letters, and then

the next four letters…

On 36,000 yards. I mean, it was extraordinary.

They're still figuring it out [LAUGHTER].

McDonald's is really quite a fascinating story, because I competed for the McDonald's business and I lost to a knit company. I can't remember their name, but they convinced McDonald's that they could make knit uniforms.

I wrote a letter to the president of McDonald's; it was Ray Kroc at the time. I said, "You guys are crazy. I mean, that will never work. That's going to stretch." Besides which, it was like a ticker tape: "McDonald's, McDonald's, McDonald's," all over the damn thing. It was hysterical. It just kept growing and growing and growing and growing.

I was at the Beverly Hills Hotel around the pool, and you know everybody wants to get a call around the Beverly Hills Hotel pool. I didn't want to get a call, but I kept getting these calls from McDonald's, "We apologize. We want you to come back. We want you to come back." That was for fifteen years. I should have taken their stock. I should not have gotten paid.

By 1975, you won your third Coty Award for loungewear, the same year as Halston. Then your career kind of flatlined.

It did. I don't consider myself a garmento, but I think that's a part of my deep DNA. It's such a maligned thing and I come from a different time. I'm talking about somebody who walked on Seventh Avenue when every corner had an egg cream for you. Where the tailors came out of their buildings—530 and 550 and 512 and 500—and talked about politics in the sunlight. There was no restaurant to eat in. When Norman Norell would take his phalanx of boys up to Schrafft's, and you wanted so desperately to be one of those boys, but never became one.

The industry itself was so tiny. Really small. Where every business operated behind closed doors, and nobody knew anybody. I mean, there was one point when I had a showroom right next to where Donna Karan's mother worked. We would talk about her daughter, who she thought was going to be the greatest designer in the world. It was such a different time than it is now.

Sometimes it's hard for me to put things in perspective when people talk about garmentos, or talk about the fashion business. That's why I'm on the Garment Center board for thirty-two years. That's why I'm on the Bryant Park board for thirty-two years. I think I'm the only designer that I know of who has become political in that way. I do it very quietly. I don't brag about it. I just do it. I believe in the Garment District. I believe in my life, and I think there's very little of it left right now.

But then you continued on doing more uniforms: MGM Grand in Las Vegas, Amtrak's Acela, and JetBlue.

When Acela first started, I did Amtrak. I was doing Amtrak and JetBlue at the same time. Amtrak had so much history. They were being bogged down by everybody who knew what they wanted to look like.

From left to right: Stan Herman's sketch for the TWA uniform that caused a stir when the fabric printer did not leave enough room between the TWA logos; Stan's uniform designs for the TWA Hotel at John F. Kennedy Airport in 2019.

JetBlue was new. There were only five people working there when they came to my studio. They called themselves Taxi, believe it or not. That was what they were going to call themselves. I thought, oh, my God, I have to do a yellow uniform. Jesus, I don't know how I got the yellow uniform. But then we did a black uniform because they wanted to be so chic. We did the black with white. They named themselves JetBlue. I got screwed. But I've been doing that since their beginning.

But Amtrak was hard. There's so much history there. Uniforms can be quite fascinating..

We're up to about 1990. We're now in the full-blown AIDS crisis and you were very involved in that, from the beginning, with Larry Kramer and Terrence McNally, and everybody who was trying to move the envelope there and do something. But also at that time, CFDA was being pushed a little bit by DIFFA to do something important for the fashion industry, and the first Seventh on Sale was created.

It was the first big AIDS benefit that the fashion industry did and it was chaired by Donna, Ralph, Calvin, Carolyne Roehm, and Anna Wintour in November 1990.

The AIDS crisis was so extraordinary because our industry was really hit by it, and we didn't react in the beginning. We just didn't. We kept saying we were going to do something, and everybody wanted to do something better than the next person. We could never come to any agreement.

When we did finally do our first AIDS benefit, we had no idea how extraordinary it was going to be. How much money we were going to raise. The confluence at that time: you came, and I came to the CFDA. Here we were, for the first time that I can remember, and I've been around a long time, that the CFDA actually did something and raised money. We had $5 million, and we didn't even know what we were doing with it.

At that point, the executive director's contract was not renewed. CFDA president

Carolyne Roehm stepped down. You and Monika Tilley, who is here tonight…

Monika and Patricia [Underwood]—Patricia is here, too.

… Became the search committee.

… And that's when you came into my life. Absolutely.

But first I'll talk about Monika and Patricia, who were very important in my life. There were three angels. The third is Mary Ann Restivo, who is no longer with us. They kept putting a bug in my ear that I could possibly be president. I didn't have any idea that I was going to be president.

In fact, there was somebody named Eleanor Lambert [the founder of CFDA] who said that I "was not to the manner born." It was very tricky for me.

I got the job first as executive director.

You did. Then I realized that if she got the job, then I could be the president. We had a hard time finding anybody to be president. We really did. Everybody wanted the executive director job. I don't know how many people we interviewed. But Fern came in at the end and she just was great. It made all of us realize that now, with what we have done with AIDS, and with her background, we could build a pedestal that became the CFDA, rather than the little fraternity that it was before that.

And that was a very heady time for both you and me.

It's wonderful. It was wonderful.

When you threw your hat in the ring and were selected as president, did you feel that that was a new validation for your career at this stage in your life?

First of all, everything happened at once. Gene died, and the CFDA became my lover.

… And I became your date. We were each other's plus-one.

I became the head of an organization out in Southampton on the East End called East End Gay Organization [EEGO]. We produced, I don't know, three or four big parties called "Take-

Opposite: Fern Mallis and Stan Herman are New York Fashion Week front row fixtures, like at this Nicole Miller show in 2006. This page: Stan catching up with Bill Cunningham while wearing a "Save the Garment District" shirt.

Off." I became politicized in a way that I never had before.

I think that happened to a lot of gay men during the AIDS crisis, and Fern was extremely polit-icized at that point. It was the horror of what was happening at the moment; it inspired a lot of people to do things they may never have done before.

That's true. That could be a whole night's interview. In the early 1990s you started to work with QVC. You'd often be in the room next door to your friend Joan Rivers.

We were great pals.

… And created this whole chenille business, which we found out sheds. Even when you did that, people were pooh-poohing designers going on QVC. Now they are lined up to get on there.

It was considered backdoor fashion. I was backdoor fashion. I was doing loungewear and uniforms, and not ready-to-wear anymore. Somebody came to me and said, "You know, there are a lot of women who watch QVC who stay home, and they wear bathrobes and they wear things like that."

I felt that's a sweet idea. I went down and I tell you I fell in love with it. I just fell in love with it and we were amazing, and for instance we sometimes sold 100,000 pieces in a day.

It was extraordinary, but now it's even more extraordinary. If you sold $2,000 a minute or $4,000 a minute, it was extraordinary. Now, when you go in prime time, you sell $25,000 a minute. The other day I was on, and it was incredible. I sold $20,000 worth of merchandise in a minute. In twelve minutes we sold $275,000 worth of merchandise. But the week before, I tanked. I tanked so badly with my favorite piece, so you just don't know.

You go out there and the cameras are on and all the guys in the back are not looking at you and what you do. They look at the numbers, how much per second, how much per minute, and it's getting tougher and tougher. I'm lucky I have a built-in customer, and I love the cam-era, as you can see. I like being onstage.

During our ten years together at the CFDA, we changed the office, the logo, the agenda, the spirit, and democratized lots of things. We did CFDA Awards galas. Nine out of our ten years, they were at Lincoln Center.

We had the pleasure of honoring Princess Diana, Yves Saint Laurent, Gianni Versace, Elsa Peretti, Audrey Hepburn, and all sorts of fabulous people, with sponsorships from Dom Perignon and Hearst Corporation. But I think you want to tell the story of a call you got from a candidate who's running for president: Donald Trump.

Oh, my God. Can I tell that story?

It was the year that Princess Diana came here to give an award to Elizabeth Tilberis, editor in chief of *Harper's Bazaar*, who was just one of the most beloved women in our business. It was a very tricky day because everybody wanted to be on the receiving line. We were very much involved with the Hearst Corporation at that point, and I just couldn't stand all that. Who's going to be first, who's going to be second, who's going to be third.

Fern and I decided that there would be an after-party with Susanne Bartsch as the host.

Remember Susanne Bartsch? We were all there, dancing up a storm, and Susanne, when she puts her act together, she's about six feet tall, and I'm 5'4" on a good day. We were dancing and she said, "Dip me."

I said, "Dip you? What? Are you crazy? I'll drop you."

She said, "No, you won't drop me, you'll hold me."

… And I dropped her, and I fell on top of her. Bill Cunningham photographed it and it was in the society section of the *Times* the next week: "Stan Herman on top of… "

That Monday I was in my office and the phone rang and it was Donald Trump. He said to me, "Stan, how was it being on top of Princess Di?"

I said, "What?"

He said, "Wasn't that Princess Di?"

I said, "No, that was Susanne Bartsch."

I thought it was hysterical. But I found out later on that he did have a very big thing about Princess Di. He loved Princess Di.

He once offered us Central Park for New York Fashion Week, right?

He was very creative and wanted very much to have Fashion Week in his venues and any place that he owned. He was always offering space, whether it was the Wollman

Previous spread: Stan Herman meeting Diana, Princess of Wales, with Katharine Graham and *Vogue*'s Anna Wintour nearby. This page: Stan and Bernadette Peters celebrating his 2006 CFDA Lifetime Achievement Award.

[ice skating] Rink or buildings he was building on the West Side.

We were very polite and enjoyed having the negotiations but always said, "I don't think our industry wants to go to Trump Pavilion, or Trump Tent, or Trump anything."

We went to a party at the tower. If I remember, it wasn't even finished inside. He took me to the corner, and he said, "I'll give you the whole park."

But we did create 7th on Sixth. You were very instrumental in negotiating our contracts with Dan Biederman for Bryant Park because of your role there. But we also did Fashion Targets Breast Cancer and took all the CFDA members to the White House a couple of times. We did several more Seventh on Sale AIDS benefits in San Francisco and New York. Then we sold 7th on Sixth to IMG.

Right. That was a fascinating moment because the CFDA started 7th on Sixth and we didn't hire many people. We were a very small crew. I'm president of the CFDA, president of 7th on Sixth, which is a nonpaying title, and we were beginning to lose money. Most of the effort, including Fern's, was going toward Fashion Week and not the CFDA. We just had to sell it.

When you run a board, sometimes they're very interested, and sometimes if it's running very smoothly, they don't really care, until something goes wrong. I knew that if we didn't sell we were going to be in deep shit.

Chuck Bennett from IMG Fashion was like, "Well, how much do you want, Herman?" and we sold it.

It was hard to sell sponsorships for CFDAs Awards gala, for all of the initiatives we were creating, as well as creating sponsorships for the tents. Fashion Week didn't embrace every designer in the CFDA; there were lots of people who didn't put on shows. They were jealous that the shows got a lot of attention. We both wore two hats. It was a groundbreaking decision in 2000.

You went on to join IMG, and I stayed on as the CFDA's president. I had no idea that I would be president of the CFDA for sixteen years. I thought it would be two years.

... And then Steven Kolb, who's here.

Well, I've got plenty of Steven Kolb stories to tell.

Steven, who's doing a great job at the CFDA, and whom I knew from my DIFFA days; they're doing great things now.

When we were looking at people for the job, everybody thought that the job was like $500,000 a year. Anna Wintour was sending me people, and I was saying, "I can't afford those people. I just can't afford those people."

When Steven walked in, I looked at his square-toe shoes and I said, "He's the guy." I said, "He doesn't make that much money." But boy, was that a wise choice. It wasn't just me. It was Diane and Joseph Abboud, who was on the committee who selected him. Lisa Smilor was one of the people who brought him in, and that's history.

In 2006 you were also presented with the CFDA's Lifetime Achievement Award. Bernadette Peters, who is also here, sang "Fever" for you.

Let me tell you about Bernadette Peters. I mean, we're a perfect couple. We're the same size. She is a spectacular human being. I think I'm a singer and sometimes people open their mouth and you can't recognize that voice. That voice is just so recognizable. She opens her mouth and it's just Bernadette Peters.

Everybody should have that in their life.

What is your relationship like with Diane von Furstenberg at the CFDA?

When it was time for me to leave, I wasn't even sure I was leaving. But everybody else began to think it's time for you to leave, Herman, and they were right. I took on another year, instead

Opposite: Stan Herman at the *50 Years of the CFDA* exhibition at the FIT Museum with Herbert Kasper, Diane Von Furstenberg, Donna Karan, Oscar de la Renta, Tory Burch, Yeohlee Teng, Mary McFadden, Patricia Underwood, and Philip Crangi in 2012. This page: Stan at the 2018 CFDA Awards with Fern Mallis and Jeffrey Banks.

Donna Karan hosting Stan Herman's surprise ninetieth birthday celebration at Urban Zen West Village in 2018 (also pictured: Bernadette Peters).

of two years. At that point, I thought that it should be Joseph Abboud. He was very much an active member. But Diane is formidable, and everything about her is formidable. A lot of people on the board were not sure that she would be the right person.

I tried to stay above the fray. I tried to be nonpolitical, and I am a political animal. At the end, about a week before we went to vote, I admit that I made a lot of strategic phone calls and Diane won handily, and the rest is history.

I mean, perhaps we built the pedestal and she took it into the next generation and beyond. It was just perfect timing. The crew they have there now—I mean Fern, how many people did we have? Four.

In the beginning, six, and about ten when I left.

What do we have now? About thirty. It's run like a clock. The offices are beautiful. I'm so impressed every time I go down there. Diane couldn't have been better, it's just been perfect.

You stayed on the new admissions committee to stay in touch with the young designers?

Which I gave up this year, because Reed Krakoff is doing it now. He's more in touch with it. I go down and do a little thing when the new designers come in. I talk to them about the history. The problem is that so many designers don't know the history. I mean, I mention names sometimes, like Rudi Gernreich or John Kloss… we don't remember those people.

When I mentioned Anne Fogarty before, I'm just happy that some people did remember her. The other day I was talking about Pauline Trigère, and nobody remembers. When I'm gone, nobody's going to know Stan Herman, but there should be some sort of history. If you're in the business, you should know about the business, and I think that's something that should happen.

Are there any young designers out today that you are impressed by?

The only thing I feel about young designers is I have sympathy for them, pity for them, because the business is so sharp edged. It's so elbow oriented. They become successful so quickly. There are lots of real talents. I don't know if they're being allowed to develop in a way that we were when we were younger.

I mean, I've spent years as a second and third and fourth designer, and I got better because of it. I think, very often these days, and you can see it in the attrition, some of them just go by the boards too quickly because they are very talented. They don't keep their eye on what they're doing.

The one thing I keep telling everyone is that you must have an alter ego. You must have somebody who takes the business aspect off of what you do. Because I think if I had had that in my life, at Mr. Mort, I could have been maybe the biggest thing that ever happened. I could never find the alter ego that could run the business in a way that would build it. That's what young designers have to do today because it's tough. The demands of the stores are extraordinary. Demands of the profit margin are so extraordinary. It's taken the guts out of creativity. We talk about it all the time at the board meetings.

Is there anything that you wanted to accomplish at the CFDA that you didn't?

At the CFDA? I think Diane has done what had to be accomplished. Sometimes I miss the camaraderie of a smaller organization, but that's just my feeling. We have 502 members now. That's a lot of members to keep happy. But it's powerful. Power is the big word of the twenty-first century. If you're plugged into power now, things seem to work for you.

Is there something in your life that you still haven't accomplished that you want to?

I haven't sung at the Metropolitan Opera yet. I said before I have a very, very good life. I still work. I still have the fear of failure that I think most creative people do have. I don't know what I would do if I stopped working.

I have a very long written memoir that's not published yet. I wrote it myself. It's quite beautiful. It tells no dirty stories. Maybe I have to do that. Maybe if I finished that and really got it done, and went to the right person to lead me in the direction, but look… here I am at the 92nd Street Y talking to all these people. I feel great about it.

Do you have a favorite outfit you've designed over the years?

Mr. Mort was known for let-out pleats. I had a white dress that haunts me all my life, and a wrapped linen dress that also haunts me. I did it on the bias. Linen on the bias, which was thirty-six inches, and that brown linen wrap dress is probably the best dress I ever did, and it sold, and sold, and sold.

What would you change in your life, and why?

You're looking at a content guy.

… And, last but not least, because it's a question from your friend Monika Tilley. Where do you think fashion is going or should we call it women's apparel?

Monika calls me all the time to ask me that same question.

I wish I had the answer to it. I don't think I have the time, but the one thing I would like more in fashion right now is to nurture the creative spirit. If we can nurture that spirit, it will dictate the direction it's going, instead of, you know, force-feeding the plant. I think we have to let it nourish itself. That would be my answer to it.

On that note, we've gone long over our time.

We did?

And Stan, thank you.

Thank you. Thank you, everybody.

SINCE FASHION ICONS

In 2018, Stan's surprise ninetieth birthday party, hosted by Donna Karan at her Urban Zen West Village space, brought together his friends from the worlds of fashion, entertainment, and New York City politics. In 2019, Stan's re-created designs took center stage at the opening of the TWA Hotel at New York's John F. Kennedy Airport. Stan continues to appear on QVC to sell his successful loungewear collections. He also finished writing his memoir, so stay tuned for its publication. He splits his time between New York's Murray Hill neighborhood and his beautiful lakefront compound in Southampton. Follow Stan on Instagram: @mr_stan_herman

ANGELA AND ROSITA MISSONI

Tonight is a dream come true for me. For as long as I can remember I've loved all things Missoni.

My first Missoni purchase was at the original Barneys on 17th Street, where Americans were introduced to so many of the great European brands. I bought a Missoni bikini, and when I got home to take it on my next fabulous beach vacation I read the label and it said, "dry clean only."

I thought, "OMG, can I wear this in the water?"

One of my biggest regrets is a decision I made when I joined the CFDA. I decided to only wear American designers, and I did so for over ten years. I gave away all my Missonis except for a lone sweater and my scarves. I can still remember everything I gave away, and it drives me crazy.

But enough about me. Missoni is a company that has stayed focused on knitwear for over sixty years. Their clothes are instantly recognizable. No one has come close to copying their trademark pattern. They are timeless, happy clothes.

Behind these gorgeous knits is a beautiful, warm, and loving family working together and having fun as a tight-knit family, no pun intended. The family, headed by Rosita and her late husband, Tai, set a high bar for quality and creativity from their countryside design studio and factory in northern Italy. Their long and loving relationship produced three talented children, who have produced a new generation of Missoni grandchildren. Together, the three generations of Missonis keep this company and its legacy going forward, hopefully forever.

Ladies and gentlemen, let's give a very warm welcome to the iconic Rosita Missoni and her daughter, Angela Missoni.

ROSITA MISSONI: Thank you.

FERN MALLIS: Welcome, and thank you for being here. In these interviews, I always start at the very beginning. This is the first time that I have two had people on the stage, and a mother and daughter, no less.

Rosita, you were born November 20, 1931. That makes you how old?

RM: Eighty-four.

Not too bad. You are a Scorpio. Do you believe in or follow astrology?

RM: I have a Scorpio ascendant also.

Some of the characteristics I read about Scorpios are: passionate, exacting, reflective, secretive, steadfast, and stubborn. They crave alone time. Their mantra is, "I don't need to control everything. I am free and peaceful." Do you agree with this?

RM: I think so.

Angela, do you think that describes her?

ANGELA MISSONI: Yes.

She has a strong opinion.

Tell us about where you were born and what your parents were like?

RM: I was born in Golasecca, which is a village just fifty kilometers from Milan. I was the first child of an industrial family. Everybody was working in a factory at that time. My grandparents were working on embroidering fabrics, done with beautiful multicolored yarns for shawls, kimonos, and all that kind of stuff. When there was the big crisis in 1929, a lot of their products were going to the east and to the Mediterranean but they couldn't export anymore. So, my grandmother started cutting garments, but she was not a pattern cutter.

She realized that something had to change, and it just so happened that a cousin of a friend was a very good pattern cutter in Milan. She had a fire in her atelier. My grandmother saw this lady crying, desperate. They were not insured. She was asking, "What are we going to do now?" My grandmother said, "Don't worry, I can give you a job."

The woman was living in Milan and they already had the factory in Golasecca. My grandmother said, "Why don't you come, and with our fabrics, you can cut clothes: jackets, pajamas, or whatever."

She asked to think about it and said, "But I have a husband."

"What does your husband do?" asked my grandmother. She said, "He's an accountant."

My grandmother said, "OK. Don't worry. We will give you a house. He will work as an accountant, and you can do the pattern cutting."

Then she came back saying "Yes, I can come. But I want to receive fashion magazines from all over the world." My grandmother, she said, OK, fine.

This lady came, and she is the one that dressed me when I was a little child. My wedding dress was also made by her. I grew up among fashion magazines, pattern cutting, and bits

This page: Rosita Missoni growing up in Golasecca, Italy. Opposite, from left to right: Tai Missoni at age seven; Tai in the 1940s.

and pieces of embroidery.

AM: How many fashion magazines were there in the world at the time?

RM: Oh, many. By 1930, there was already *Vogue*, and since then many, many.

In my village, if the ladies were working, they were working in our factory. The men were waiters, most of them, and they were working all over the world, including France. So my grandmother received the magazines from France and New York, and she paid the families of the waiters working in Paris and in New York. It was her way of helping.

You grew up very early on with many fashion magazines?

RM: Yes, and since I was very weak when I was a child, very often I was in bed, cutting out fashion magazines. The 1930s have always been my world, my dominion, the period of fashion that I love most. Because I think I knew it by heart by cutting out magazines.

Did you work in the factory as a young child?

RM: Well, when I came back after college, yes. But it was also our playground. Since we had big spaces, we could skate.

Skate in the factory? Were you expected to take over the family business?

RM: Yes, I started to follow my father. He was working in sales and I used to follow him to places like Rome, to sell.

When you were seventeen years old, what brought you to London with the Swiss Sisters of the Holy Cross?

RM: Because I had studied languages, French and English, at the end of my studies, our sisters offered us the opportunity to go and spend the summer in London. Of course, my family agreed, and I went there. It was June 1948.

In July, the very first Olympic Games after World War II were in London. Our college was in Hampstead. One Sunday a friend of mine called me and she said, "Rosita, we are in London because we have an athlete, Ottavio [Tai] Missoni, who is part of Italian the team in the 400-meter

hurdles and also the 400-meter relay."

Our sisters were very clever and very brilliant. They took us to all the parks, and castles, and museums, and to Stratford-upon-Avon, and then to Oxford, and Cambridge and so on. There was also one day at Wembley, the stadium for the Olympic Games where all the track and field events were going on. It was a very cheap seat. We were next to the flame, which was at that time very modern. It was right by the passage with all the athletes.

So, we go there, and we were watching the athletes coming out, and we see this Italian, and he had on the numbers "331." Three hundred thirty-one.

But before you noticed the number, you noticed how tall and handsome he was?

RM: … Tall and handsome, of course! But for me, "331" makes seven, and seven has always been a good number in my family. My grandfather used to give us, every Sunday, seven lire. The windows in the factory were seven by seven.

It was meant to be.

RM: I thought, "Who's going to win?" On that day, Missoni won. I didn't know anything about track and field at that moment, but I could see he had fantastic style. His run was much better than the others.

AM: … And faster.

RM: Of course he won the heat, and for me, he was a winner. When he came back and we were watching him, he started drinking water and spitting everywhere. I thought, "Oh, my God, he is so…"

AM: … Disgusting.

RM: It really was. I didn't have a good impression anymore. Anyway, then I learned that when they finished a run, they are totally dried out and they need to drink.

A week after, I received a call in my boarding house from my friends. The father of this girl-friend of mine was the president of the club for which Tai was running. They had come to see their athlete in London, and said, "Well, what are you doing on Sunday?"

I said, "Well, I'm probably visiting a castle or something like that."

They said, "Can we come to pick you up, and we can go to Brighton?"

They came with the car. I enter the car and we stop in Piccadilly. They said, "We have two of our athletes coming with us on this trip."

We stopped in Piccadilly and I saw Tai coming out as a normal person, not as an athlete, with a fantastic uniform: a double-breasted, electric blue jacket, gray flannel trousers, and black moccasins, a very elegant blue and white tie, with the coat of arms of Italy on the jacket. I saw these two guys coming out.

Of course, Tozi, who was a security guard in real life, was an enormous giant, but Tai was particularly handsome and smiling. Later on, I realized that we were in Piccadilly, and there is a column in Piccadilly and on top of the column there is a Cupid.

Share with us what you wear around your neck every day. A little charm of Cupid.

RM: It was something that I received a couple of years ago from an antiques dealer who found it for me, knowing that I had a story about the Cupid in Piccadilly Circus. He gave it to me, and since that day I wear it every day.

I love that story.

RM: Also my great-grandchild, Margherita's child, who is two-and-a-half years old now, every time he wants to look at it he says, "Cupido! Cupido!"

Well, he's going to be somebody's Cupid soon. Was it love at first sight?

RM: For me it was not love at first sight.

He had to convince you?

RM: No. But, when I came home, I was sixteen at that time and…

AM: … And he was twenty-seven.

RM: When I heard he was twenty-seven, I said, "It's Methuselah for me." I will never reach him. I looked at him, and he had some gray hair already on his temples.

At that time, Tai was living in Milan. We were planning to celebrate my seventeenth birthday and the end of college. I don't know how I dared to ask my girlfriend, Ivana, "Do you think that if we invite Ottavio Missoni, he will come?"

… And he came! He came. We had a fantastic party with all my family, cousins, family friends, and so on. He made a beautiful drawing in my souvenir book, with… how do you call the bird that brings the children?

A stork.

RM: The stork had a ribbon reading "1931" [the year Rosita was born]. Then "1948," a celebration with champagne. Then at the bottom, "2048," with this tiny mother with a lot of family and the very tall handsome gentleman.

Do you still have that book?

RM: Yes. It is still in my book collection. Of course.

Beautiful. He and his teammates launched one of the first athleisure collections of tracksuits. They did them with zippers on the legs because you said he was too lazy to take his shoes off.

RM: Yes. With a friend of his, Jojo. They used to travel from Milan to Trieste once a month to go and see their mothers.

He's good Italian boy.

RM: Jojo, the friend, was very tall and he regularly took his jackets to his mother to sew buttons back on, because riding on the tram [HOLDING UP HER HAND AS IF TO HOLD A TRAIN'S OVERHEAD RAILING] in Milan, he lost all his buttons. On one trip, he said to his mother, "Mama, this will be the last time you have to sew back my buttons, because I am buying a car."

His mother slept on this big news, thinking, "My son has some money set aside." She was a woman alone, a widow. She had a sister, also a widow. She said to her son the next morning, "Listen, I am very happy to sew your buttons back on every time you come home. Instead of buying a car, buy a knitting machine for me and your aunt so we will have an opportunity to

Page 212: Tai and Rosita Missoni met when he competed in the 1948 London Olympics. This page: Tai can be spotted in this London Olympics advertisement by his jersey number: 331. Page 218: Tai and Rosita's wedding in Golasecca, Italy, 1953.

earn our own keep." He did not dare to say no to his mother. He bought the knitting machine. He got very interested in watching the yarn going back and forth, and the texture coming out, and so on.

The next time, he invited Tai to come and see what he bought his mother. She is knitting. Both of them became very interested in this. Tai says, "Listen, I can buy a second one for your aunt." They built their first atelier with two knitting machines for the mother and the aunt. Then there were two presidents, watching the two ladies working. Tai used to say, "Always let the women work, because they do it very well. I will just be the president."

That was the beginning of the Missoni family knitting experience.

RM: That was the beginning of our knitting. They did track and field suits because that was their sport. They made fantastic things. They started putting in zippers, and the top parts were real ribbed knits. It was all very nice.

When we married, there were eight machines.

AM: Then you split the company?

RM: Four of the machines came with us to Gallarate, where we started our first atelier.

Extraordinary to think how a business like that could start.

RM: I was trained in fashion, and of course as soon as I could, I started making little dresses. I was also fascinated by knitting.

You had all those pictures from those fashion magazines, so you knew what you wanted to make. When you started the business, you called it Maglificio Jolly, Jolly Knitwear Factory? Where did that name come from?

RM: "Jolly Joker." I thought it was a good luck trademark.

AM: To this day, she really believes in luck, like with the number seven.

He was running the business and you became the designer. That's how it all started, basically?

RM: The business was not a business. For the moment, we were trying it. But we had friends. We were making little sweaters for Biki. Luis de Hidalgo, who was a friend of Tai and the director of Biki. At that time, he was the couturier who was dressing Maria Callas, so he was very popular in Milan. He used to order from us, for her boutiques, six sweaters at a time. It was not much, but it gave us a foot in fashion. It was important anyway, that connection.

The person directing the boutique of Biki was then offered the job to go and open the first office of style for La Rinascente [a group of high-end Italian boutiques].

That's when you had your big order. You married in 1953. In 1954, you gave birth to your first son, Vittorio. Two years later to Luca. Two years later to Angela. How happy were you when you had a daughter after two sons?

RM: I was sure that there would be three boys because she was bigger. Her heart was stronger. Angela was much bigger than the boys. I had just given birth to this baby when I heard the nurses say, "È una bimba!" Which means, it's a girl. I was jumping on the bed because I was so happy. I had prepared my boys to play *The Three Musketeers*.

Angela, you were born on December 26, 1958. Almost a Christmas baby. This makes you how old?

AM: Fifty-seven now.

You're a Capricorn. Do you care about your astrological sign? What I read was that Capricorns are the most practical sign, with their feet firmly planted on the ground. They are loving, sympathetic, sensual, faithful, instinctive, charitable, and they can overreact and be moody. Your mantra is, "I am successful and content."

AM: Moody, no. Overreact, yes.

What are your earliest memories of your parents and growing up with them working?

AM: I witnessed our first fashion show in a theater in Milan. It must have been 1965. It was at Teatro Gerolamo. I was seven years old. Since then, I have witnessed every single show.

There was one two years later held in a swimming pool in Milan. It was a collection we made with Emmanuelle Khanh. They had inflatable chairs going from one side to the other. Emmanuelle's husband was a designer, Quasar Khanh. He designed the first inflatable chair. He also designed an inflatable house structure that was in the middle of the swimming pool. All of a sudden the house collapsed. At the end, all the girls were in the water, and it became a big party. That's how the party started. I remember that I was at the entrance, and I was always next to my mom. I remember Anna Piaggi arriving with a dress, half black and half white, and saying, "Rosita, look what I'm wearing."

She was wearing a vintage Missoni.

RM: Yes.

… And she was extraordinary.

RM: Exactly.

Your mother said that, growing up, she would play in the factory. Growing up, did you go to the factory to watch and see whatever they were doing?

AM: Home or the factory, they were the same.

That was your playground?

AM: Yes, absolutely.

You collected a lot of Bambis?

AM: That's a recent thing. I'm a flea market freak. Not flea markets, but secondhand shops. Since maybe eight to ten years ago, you could find the good stuff. Now, it's harder and harder. I started collecting things and made up stories for them. I started collecting abandoned objects to give them a family. It's kind of an adoption. So those Bambis became a part of the…

… Part of the family.

AM: Yes, exactly.

Back to the businesses. As you said, La Rinascente was really your first big order. They ordered 500 striped shirtdresses.

RM: That was La Rinascente, in 1958.

… And they featured Missoni in their windows?

RM: They featured Missoni on eighteen mannequins in the windows. In two different styles; one was a shirtdress with two vertical stripes. One was a smaller print we called the "mattress stripe" because it was wild.

They seemed very daring in terms of the print and the color, but really they were dark brown and beige with a purple stripe, and gray and black with an orange stripe. Now, they wouldn't be considered…

AM: … Extravagant.

RM: Whoever made up the windows put some handkerchiefs in the brighter stripe color, and they looked like… [MOTIONING COVERING HER EYES]

Oh, like blindfolds?

RM: After we finished our day of work, it was nearly eight o'clock at night and it was a very foggy evening in Milan. It was dark. There was nobody around.

La Rinascente had their windows facing the Duomo. The buyer of La Rinascente called us to say, "Come and see. You have a full window, full of your dresses."

We got there, and we are watching as a man goes by. He was dressed in jeans. At that time, jeans meant that you were a worker. He stopped in front of the window and he said,

Clockwise from top: The 1966 Missoni fashion show at Teatro Gerolamo in Milan; The 1967 Missoni fashion show at the Solari pool in Milan; Another view of the 1966 Missoni fashion show.

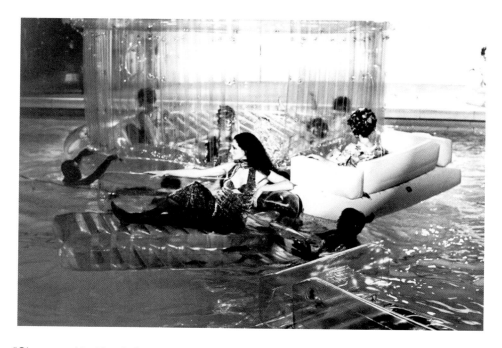

"Oh, poor girls. Thank God that they made them blind, because if they could see the way they look…"

This was the first comment, to our first windows. That delivery of 500 dresses, we cheated a bit with La Rinascente, because our label was still Maglificio Jolly…

You were still Maglificio Jolly when that order was placed?

RM: Yes, and we had planned to change it. We put a tiny label that read, "Missoni." We shipped the garments without telling them that we put our name on them. They were furious because they wanted to keep the name of their phenomenal producer a secret.

AM: They didn't want people to know who their supplier was.

RM: They said, "Oh, no, you have to change them."

It was such a success. It was a shirtdress open in the front, with these stripes. We had two big sketches by a fantastic illustrator. They called the dresses "Milano Sympathy" and sold them for 9,500 lire, which is very cheap. But they were a big, big, big success.

It sold out in a few days. It was a new thing in ready-to-wear. Customers could try the dresses on without going into the changing rooms. It was a whole new way of selling.

After that order, you then changed the name entirely to Missoni?

RM: Yes. La Rinascente was very pleased and we continued to work together for many years.

Can either of you explain what the raschel machine is, and how it has created your famous zigzag pattern?

RM: Yes. That was also because of La Rinascente. One day a buyer said, "Listen, there is a factory in Gallarate that makes beautiful knits. But they only make white and black." They used to make shawls. White because they could be dyed in different colors, and black because they were sent to the south of Italy where once a woman was a widow, they wear a shawl for their whole life.

We went to see this factory and I asked this person, "Do you have some archives?" And they opened their books for me. For me, it was like we discovered a treasure. I realized they had these unique knitting machines.

Our knitting machines allowed us to use six colors, and not more, at that time. Their machines had warp and weft, like for textiles, but also hooks, like a knitting machine. We made black-and-white dresses for them at that moment, which were very good sellers. In the meantime, I took Tai to see what we could make with these machines, and he started doing his stripes and zigzag. We now could have zigzags, which of course became…

… Your signature. Is there any color that you're hesitant to use? That you don't like?

RM: No, but it was difficult to have a pattern designed by Tai without purple in it. He loved purple. But you know, actors in Italy hate purple because it is not a good superstition.

AM: It is bad luck.

RM: Yes, it is considered bad luck. We made the costumes for *Lucia di Lammermoor*, and we created a black cavalier for Luciano Pavarotti. He did not care if his gigantic black cape had some purple in it. It was not black, black. It was a black and purple cavalier.

AM: He did not care, but the audience whistled at him, at Teatro alla Scala. You know when they whistle at you in the theater, you are making mistakes.

RM: He had not been to La Scala for many years. He was at the Metropolitan Opera here in New York.

They gave him a hard time.

RM: Of course. In Milan, they felt his voice was off. That was fun because it was 1983, the year that my granddaughter Margherita Missoni was born. Margherita met him, in Pavarotti's

Opposite: Models on floating pool furniture designed by Quasar Khahn for the 1967 Missoni fashion show in Milan. This page: The original 1958 Maglificio Jolly advertisement for the Missonis' first collection at La Rinascente.

dressing room.

That's a nice memory.

RM: Yes. We were the designers for the costumes. At the end we were supposed to come out, after the applause. First the singers, then the maestro, and then at the end, the designers all came out onstage. That was the rehearsal.

At the premiere, Pavarotti got very little applause. I didn't realize it. All the gentlemen started whistling and booing. It was so terrible. Then an order goes out that after the applause, we would all have to go out at the same time, chained one to the other. With the singers, all of us…

To counterbalance the booing…

RM: That was an impression to see, this theater full of people. The light goes on, and all together, I was trembling a bit. Tai turned and said to me, "See, they are using us try to get the applause. They should have just let us whistle."

To hear all the boos from the theater was quite an experience. But it was a success anyway.

Any other take on it for you, Angela?

AM: I am not sure I was there. I was there at the first rehearsal. I was not there because I had Margherita, who was only one and a half months old.

Tell us about your Sumirago property, where your husband said, "Let's build a factory, and let's build it in a place where we'd like to go on weekends."

RM: Exactly.

It was a wise decision. You also said that he liked to sleep late.

RM: Of course, yes.

We found out that there was a place nearby our factory, where most of the knitters working for us were coming from. The women had to go and work in other places, not in that village. We could take part in a special law if we increased the work available for women in that village. If we built the factory there, we could receive help from the government.

We went. The fantastic thing was that this place was beautiful. It was on a hill. It had beautiful views of the Alps. I could see from my house where I was born. I was born facing the Monte Rosa. My mother used to wake me up at seven o'clock, saying, "Look at the Monte Rosa." I loved to sleep.

But anyway, I'm used to waking up at seven o'clock. Tai said, "There's no point to wake up at seven o'clock. I am awake only at noon. One thing is to wake up, the other thing is to be awake. So if I wake up at noon, so what?"

If you are still not awake, what's the point?

RM: What is the point?

But we built the factory there. We think that this was the best thing we could have done in our life, because we built a beautiful factory around a huge natural park. It is all woods, with oaks, pine trees, and chestnut trees. We built a very nice factory, with beautiful views of this mountain, which is still there. It has become even more beautiful.

Then you built a house shortly thereafter?

RM: Then four years after we built the house. We had to start building the factory in 1968 because this law that made us decide to build there was ending in 1968. The factory had to be ready to work by 1968. So that's what we did.

It has been the best thing we could have done, because to make creative people work, it's important to be in a nice place.

… To be in someplace beautiful.

RM: I think, yes. In the beginning, we still had our apartment in Gallarate, which was a very nice apartment. Not the first one, but the second one. The first one was a hundred-square-meter apartment near the highway. It was just the start. After six or seven years, we moved and we had the biggest place in town. Then in 1968, we started working where we are now.

That is still where the family business and home is?

RM: Exactly.

What was it like for you growing up there, Angela?

AM: Basically, I grew up first in Gallarate. But we were used to going on the weekend to the country. When I say country, it was twenty minutes away, to where my grandparents lived.

Then we moved to Sumirago when I was fourteen, and I was mad. I was mad, mad, mad because I didn't want to move. It was in the middle of the country. I was going to school in Varese, but then they asked me to come back home and I didn't want to move. At the beginning, I was a bit upset. But then I had my motorbike, so I could move around on my own.

I never lived in a city. I've never been in a city more than fifteen days in a row. I moved out of my parents' home when I was eighteen or nineteen. I moved into a house very nearby. I always lived around that area, with the view of the big mountain, that I see from my office now. I see it from my new house. I mean, it is a kind of drug.

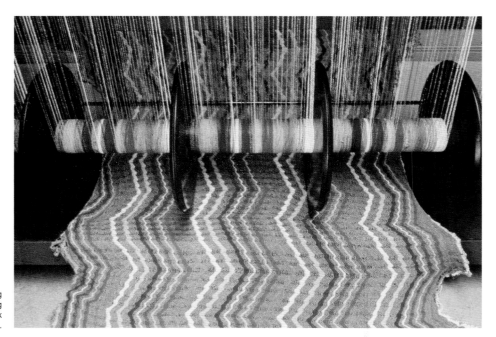

Missoni knitting machines creating their hallmark zig-zag pattern.

Rosita and Angela Missoni on holiday on Isola di San Clemente, Italy.

When you were growing up, did you realize your parents were famous?

AM: You know, fashion was not the way it is today. I knew that they were special. I knew that they were different from the parents of the other pupils going to school with me. I knew that in the house there were always special people. I might not have known that my parents were special, but I knew that the people coming to the house were very special.

They were special by association.

AM: It was really a mix of people. Some visitors were very important people in sports, or politics, or actors from the theater, or journalists in fashion. They would talk about various things.

Were all your clothes Missoni growing up?

AM: Yes, almost. My mother would design them for me. I still have those dresses. Margherita was wearing them, and then they are passed on.

It's a vintage archive in your home.

AM: Yes, of course.

Rosita, you were delivering a camera for someone to the Plaza Hotel in New York. Is that how you met the designer and stylist Emmanuelle Khanh?

RM: No. I was invited by my parents to New York in 1965, for the inauguration of the *Michelangelo*, which was a big Italian ship. We left from Genoa on the ship, and then we went back by plane. We were staying at the Plaza. It was me and my cousin, both invited by our parents because my uncle was the mayor of the village of Golasecca. They wanted to meet all the waiters who had left the village. There was one who was at the 21 Club. He wanted to come and greet all his citizens.

We made that trip on the *Michelangelo*. In Paris, I knew an American couple who owned the

Villager. They had invited me, knowing that I was coming to New York, to visit their factories and their stores in Philadelphia.

I am staying at the Plaza, and I came back one evening around 7:30 p.m. There is a message for me from Madame Emmanuelle Khanh. I knew who she was because I was a reader. She was a young French stylist. She was very good. She invited me for a glass of wine in her room.

She had brought from Paris a camera that an American had left in the apartment of a common friend. Knowing that I was going to Philadelphia, she asked me to take the camera to Philadelphia. I was hoping that Emmanuelle had called me because she knew that we were making nice sweaters. It was not that at all.

I went to the Villager. I could not imagine a store of clothes that huge. At that time, the Villager was very popular. They had little spots in the main stores, selling town and country clothes. I think only women's clothes, but very nice. I saw hundreds of clothes hanging in displays, enormous.

I met Emmanuelle Khanh, we talked, and we exchanged our cards. Then later on, we had been invited by La Rinascente because Pierre Cardin had opened this boutique in La Rinascente. We had met him with Luis de Hidalgo, our friend. We received an offer to go and talk to Pierre Cardin.

To the Pierre Cardin company in Paris?

RM: Yes, the company because they had seen what we were doing for La Rinascente. We went to Paris, Tai and I, full of hope. We got there, and we go on our visit. We don't see Pierre Cardin, but we met with one of his commercial team members.

We said, "Yes, we would be very pleased to do something." Then they said, "We have seen what you are doing. They are very nice products. We like it very much."

I asked, "When shall we have the meetings to decide the line or what we are going to do together?"

They said, "Just prepare your collection. When you're ready, you call us. We will choose ten pieces, and we will allow you to sell them with the Cardin label. Then you give us 10 percent." I left. I was crying. I was so disappointed.

I remembered that I had the address of Emmanuelle Khanh with me. I called Emmanuelle and said, "You remember we met in New York."

She said, "Of course, of course. What are you doing in Paris? Why don't you come over and have a cup of tea with us?"

They were very near the Hotel Lutetia, where we were staying. I said, "We were here to do something because I would be very pleased to work in France, which is the country of fashion." In a certain way, our approach to knitwear was very modern. I was dressed in one of my dresses, a raschel one.

Emmanuelle said, "It's very nice. Why don't we do something together?"

We said, "Yes! Why not?"

We decided in two hours without any lawyers and things like that. We did a collection together. This was the collection that we showed at Teatro Gerolamo. It was very nice. She was a very young designer.

How long did you collaborate with her?

RM: We made four collections together. Then she got pregnant with her second child and she could not travel anymore. I did not want to work with her husband. He was not the right collaborator.

At that show in 1966, you also had a model who was Giorgio Armani's sister?

RM: Yes. That show that we presented with Emmanuelle. Paco Rabanne came with his jewelry.

AM: … And his accessories. His accessories are great. We used them after for Carnival. All the masks, the mirrors, the earrings. Me and my brothers were at Carnival dressed with the Paco Rabanne accessories.

RM: We didn't have shoes, so we decided we would have all the girls go…

AM: Barefoot?

RM: Not barefoot. They did not have shoes, but they had stockings.

At that time, with his sister in the show, Mr. Armani worked at La Rinascente. He wasn't even designing for them, right?

RM: No, at that time, he was in charge of the windows of La Rinascente.

That's how far back this incredible legacy goes. Mr. Armani was designing windows for a department store in Milan while the Missonis were doing their shows. Then your second fashion show you did was presented in Florence.

AM: No, the second was the swimming pool.

But there was one where everyone was braless, and you got a lot of flak for that?

RM: Yes, exactly. At that time in Florence, you had to choose sixteen outfits to show on the runway. They gave you the models. The sixteen models were chosen by them.

AM: So the hair and makeup was the same for everybody.

RM: Yes. We tried to do hats, little caps, so we did not have to make a special hairdo. Everything was so homemade.

But anyway, they tried on the clothes, made of a very sheer Lurex. We tried them on the models, and their underwear was not appropriate because they were wearing white panties and a white bra. They said they were already wearing body stockings.

I said, "Well, they could keep their panties on, but at least the bra, you have to take them away." When they went onstage, even if we had pockets on the breast, they were transparent. There was one girl, who was a beautiful model. She was the sister of, you know…

AM: Antonio Lopez?

RM: Antonio Lopez. She was beautiful. She was, like, made of marble. She was admired by the public. But they thought that you could see her breast through the sheer fabric. They said in the headlines, "Missoni has done a 'Crazy Horse' collection."

AM: It was marked as a scandal in Florence.

The 1972 Missoni fashion show in Palazzo Pitti, Florence, Italy.

RM: They said they did not want us back. The following winter, Yves Saint Laurent did the New Look. We did not do it on purpose but…

… You were ahead of your time? Then you decided to show in Milan. Your husband said, "It's near our airport; why don't we show in Milan?"

RM: Exactly.

The fashion critic from the *New York Times*, Bernadine Morris, wrote that there's a good reason to go to Milan, and it was to see you.

RM: Exactly.

Could you tell us about meeting *Vogue*'s Diana Vreeland? She was a huge fan right away and introduced you to lots of people.

RM: This was 1967 maybe. Consuelo Crespi was the American *Vogue* editor in Italy. She was a beauty. She called me and she said, "Rosita, Diana Vreeland is coming."

At that time, the fashion collections in Italy were presented in Rome. She said, "Put some of your clothes in a bag and come down, because Diana Vreeland is here and I want to show her your dresses."

I went down and I took my model. She was a nice girl. She had studied at La Scala to become a ballerina, so she moved very nicely. When we arrive at the Grand Hotel, Consuelo greets us. She said, "No, I don't need the model because I will wear them myself," and she did the modeling for me and for Diana Vreeland.

Diana Vreeland was in the sitting room, next to the bedroom of the suite. When Consuelo was ready, she opened the door. Diana Vreeland comes in and she says, "Who said that the rainbow has seven colors? There are many shades."

When she came back to New York, she started writing me that we had to come to New York. She would like to introduce us to all the fashion coordinators of the different stores.

Did you all get the line that Diana Vreeland said? "Who said the rainbow has seven colors? There are many shades," and that was to describe the clothes she saw from you.

RM: Yes. Exactly. We decided to come to New York, and we had the suite at the Plaza. The same suite that I was in with my two cousins and friend, when we were invited for drinks by Emmanuelle Khanh. Which I thought was a good sign, because I felt like I was at home.

In this little sitting room, Diana Vreeland came with all the editors. It was crowded. There were fourteen or fifteen ladies, all of them editors. I had to change the model by myself. I had my PR assistant, Joanna, who was traveling with us. Our room was filled with flowers, all sent by *Vogue*.

Vogue sent all the flowers?

RM: Yes, our little suite at the Plaza was filled. I thought that this was the American way to greet foreigners.

AM: Like everybody would greet us like that.

RM: They are so nice, the Americans [LAUGHTER].

So anyway, she comes and we are showing with one model. They receive a call from the desk. They said, "There is a gentleman from Neiman Marcus downstairs."

I said, "We have an appointment with Neiman Marcus for tomorrow."

This gentleman comes up and Joanna opens the door and she says, "Rosita. The gentleman has the Légion d'Honneur." It was Stanley.

Stanley Marcus?

RM: In person! Diana Vreeland called him, saying, "There are some Italians you have to meet," and he came.

When Diana Vreeland calls Stanley Marcus, he shows up.

RM: Yes. Then when she walked out with all her ladies, she pointed to my husband and me, and she said, "These people are geniuses."

Which was for us, I mean…

This page: Rosita and Tai Missoni accepting the 1973 Neiman Marcus Fashion Award from Stanley Marcus. Page 231: Rosita and Angela Missoni cooking in their family kitchen in Sumirago, Italy. Pages 234–235: Rosita and Tai at the end of the 1982 Missoni fashion show in Milan.

It's an extraordinary compliment. Then you got the big award from Neiman Marcus a couple years after that.

RM: In 1973, we got the Neiman Marcus Award.

How important was America to your business?

RM: It opened up a new customer. Bloomingdale's, Saks Fifth Avenue. Marvin Traub at Bloomingdale's, we called him our godfather. He wanted us to do everything. We made a bed and bath collection.

Marvin made an introduction to Fieldcrest for you?

RM: He came with the people from Fieldcrest, and they said, "When are you sending your lawyers to talk about the agreement?"

… And my husband said, "Lawyers? We don't have lawyers. The lawyer is just me and Rosita."

That's a nice way to do business. Around that time, Angela, you were about fifteen years old and you told your mother that you did not want to work. You wanted to have children and get married early. Was that a reaction to watching her working so hard?

AM: No. I had thought this way since a very early age. I knew I would have children young. At fifteen, I said to my mom, "You know, I think I'm going to have a child at eighteen." I think she fainted.

What was your relationship like with your brothers growing up? Were they protective of you?

RM: Not really [LAUGHING].

AM: Vittorio protected me from Luca. Luca is the middle brother. That explains itself.

RM: I was the youngest child. I was always trying to keep up with them because they knew how to ski better, they knew how to do everything better. I was the youngest, so I was always late. I always tried to…

RM: … Compete.

AM: … Compete up there with them.

Some other milestones in your business were your first store in Milan in 1976. You had already had a boutique in Bloomingdale's since 1970.

AM: … And in Paris. Paris was way before.

In 1978, you mounted a twenty-five-year retrospective of Missoni designs, and it came over here and it was displayed at the Whitney Museum in New York.

RM: Yes, of course.

That must have been an extraordinary experience, having a show here?

RM: Yes, absolutely.

Right after that you debuted your men's collection. In 1981, it was also the beginning of Missoni Home?

RM: The men's collection started a little earlier than that. We were producing small collections, for accounts like Browns in London.

AM: Yes, a few pieces.

RM: ... And we had to dress Tai and the children. We showed on the runway a couple of men's looks.

Was Home a natural extension for you?

RM: For Home, we did four years with Fieldcrest. It was just bed and bath. At that point, my brothers had an old factory that was making loungewear. They then turned it into bedspreads, rugs, and bath also. They said, "Why don't you work with us instead? Why do you need to go and work in the States?"

We decided to start working with my brothers, with my family company. Little by little, we introduced rugs and new patchwork.

AM: When we moved into the new house in 1972, she covered the furniture with Missoni fabric that they were doing our sweaters with.

RM: With them, we were also producing textiles for the home. It was very nice. Too many things, in too long a life.

We're only in 1982! We have a lot of years to catch up with. Angela, in 1982, at age twenty-three you married an event producer, Marco Maccapani. Then, quickly thereafter, you had Margherita in 1983, Francesco in 1985, and Theresa in 1988. So that was your dream: to have your family.

AM: ... And divorced in 1991. But we are still very good friends with each other.

At that point, you started to assist your mother in the business, designing childrenswear and accessories for the licenses.

AM: I was in and out during the first years. I never saw myself taking over in the company. I never had that thought. I was pregnant. I was doing different projects outside of the company. Everything related to the well-being of my children.

When I was pregnant with Margherita, I did a project with a children's playground. When I was pregnant with Francesco, I did a project with an organic chicken farm. It was really ahead of its time. It was more than thirty years ago.

When I was pregnant with Theresa, I went to my father, which I would only do when I had something very special to tell him. I told him, "I would never work for the company. I realize that this is not my thing."

He said, "What would you like to do?" I said, "I think I'm going to design jewelry."

He said, "But, you know, this company, whatever project you have, it's like a big umbrella. You can develop that under this umbrella, but on your own. You don't need to work with your mom every single day."

I had a good relationship with my mom, but my dad was working with my mom for many years, and he knew that I had to go and walk on my own. She was very strong and opinionated. I needed to find my own path.

Jewelry was that path?

AM: I did not start the jewelry at this point. I started with the children's line for Missoni. Then I started to do a few licenses. Then after three or four years, I said, "In fact, I like fashion."

I realized that I knew how to translate Missoni. It was so natural to translate Missoni. But I wanted to do fashion for women. I started my own line, Angela Missoni. I started with solids, and only textures and shapes.

I could see that I was kind of a late bloomer. I was a silent child. I was an observer. They did not have many expectations for me because I wasn't showing a particular creativity. My brothers were better at doing everything. They were creative. I was, like, always keeping back, but listening and watching, watching and listening.

They did not expect me to be creative. In fact, I could see that my mom was surprised that, in every collection I was doing, I could handle the collection from the beginning to the end. To do the show and prepare the girls and shoot my little campaigns. She was my first customer because she was not allowed to do solids, and she loved solids, and she would buy them from me.

After three seasons, I started to add patterns. A little pattern here, a little there. By the fourth or fifth collection, after my show, my mom came over and she said that she liked what I was doing. She could witness it, because I was working in the same factory. Then she said, "You know, have you ever thought of doing the main line?"

I said, "No." In fact, I never had that thought because I was doing something separate.

She said, "I think you should, because what you're doing, it's what I would like Missoni to be today. You know, I'm tired. I have many things I want to do. In fashion, you have to do it when you're young, when you're passionate, and when you have the strength to fight with the commercial side of it." I realized that she was kind of trapped in a zigzag cage.

A zigzag cage?

AM: Yes. I started by doing the editing of the looks for the shows. Then I realized that there were always new things flourishing in the collection, but they were submerged by all the history of Missoni. In the beginning, when they were asking me, "How did you do it?" I said, "I'm just cleaning." I started to pull out the essence of Missoni, to redefine the image, and to sharpen it again.

You have done an extraordinary job.

AM: In 1995, I hired Mario Testino and Carine Roitfeld to do the campaign for Missoni. We worked together for seven years. I think that is when I realized I had a good eye, because that was exactly the same moment when they started working with Gucci. That's how I started.

After two years, in October 1997, I was on a catwalk, and I'm still here. Next year, it will be twenty years. There's more than one generation of customers that only knows what I've done. This has made an impression on me.

How proud are you, Rosita, of what Angela has accomplished?

RM: Absolutely. I'm there. I can see it. We live our life in a factory. We see how they follow her with passion. This is something very, very special. I don't think there are many places where the contact with the workers is so intense. She is very much loved.

AM: We have a very unique factory. I think it's very rare today to have a design team that works in a factory. Today, design teams work in one place, and then you have a factory somewhere that does something. They never see the full process. We still have the full process from head to toe, from beginning to end. It's very interesting. It's very special. The point is that we are still very artisanal.

Was it under your guidance that the M Missoni line was created?

AM: Absolutely. Missoni was lucky to have Margherita in it, because Margherita did not have a project at Missoni yet. It happened when she was eighteen, and she had a natural allure and talent. She started wearing the clothes that I was making. She made them believable.

She became the ambassador?

AM: She became a natural ambassador.

Was she also designing accessories and beachwear?

AM: Yes. She had stayed for a few years in New York. When she came back from New York at twenty-five, she said, "Mom, I think I've done enough there. I think I realize I don't want to live my life there. I want to have children and have them grow up the way I did. I think it's about time that I come to Italy, otherwise I will never come back."

She did one year in Rome. At that time she was studying acting. She said, "You know, I realize I don't have anything anymore to prove to myself."

I said, "Wow, at twenty-six? Good for you, because it took me longer."

She said, "I'd like to try to help the company." I started to give her the accessories. Then I gave her the Margherita collection that I started ten years earlier.

She had a nice collaboration with Converse.

AM: She worked on that. She worked on the Target project. Also my younger daughter Theresa. A very different character from Margherita, but she is very talented; she often helps in all the special projects that we do.

Tell us a story about the craziness of the Target collaboration, which broke their website and just about broke the internet. It was gone in a minute.

AM: I think that Target already had problems with their website. It wasn't just because of us, right?

They came to us a few years before. It was the beginning of their collaborations and we couldn't trust them yet. Then when I saw the way they were treating the other labels, the way they were marketing them, it was very high-end, quality marketing.

Then I put it to the family and to our commercial team because not everybody in Europe, in Italy, understood exactly what this collaboration would mean. They just saw Target as a lower tier retailer.

There were like 400 products?

AM: It was huge, because it was the first time they were doing a full lifestyle collaboration. Then I realized how much that people in the States love Missoni. But there was a generation that loved Missoni, without even knowing that there was Missoni, right? It was a good

moment to let them know that it was us.

Would you ever do something like that again?

AM: Yes, why not? We did it in Australia, one and a half years ago, with Target Australia.

Did it fly off the shelves?

AM: Yes. It was very successful.

Do you want to touch on the tragedy that struck the family, when Vittorio's plane disappeared?

AM: Disappeared, yes. We have never found him.

RM: The plane, they found it.

There's never been any closure?

AM: No. That was a very strange feeling, right? Because then my father passed away a few months later.

Tai passed away four months later?

AM: There was a lot of news coming in then. I realized I never even wrote back to many people who were writing to me, because you never know what to say. In a way, we're still searching for Vittorio. I flew to and I traveled around South America, up and down.

When you go to a country like Venezuela or Colombia, and you meet with people, you hear so many stories. Weird stories, and everything is believable. It is like anything can happen. For a while, we really hoped that we could find him. For almost one year.

Anyway, then in the middle of this, you had to do a collection, you had to take care of your family…

You are now the focal point for the family because you have the biggest table in your house?

AM: I'm the one who has the largest table.

The biggest table, that is where everything happens?

RM: It was a table that I bought because I liked it. But it was too big for my house. But I bought it anyway. Then it was perfect for her room.

Any advice to anybody out here about how to run a family business?

AM: I didn't know any other way. I know the good and the bad. It's like if you work with partners, you have to deal with your partners. You know, the funny thing is that if you find a partner, usually, you have tried to find someone who had the same ideas.

What is always surprising is that brothers and sisters, who grow up in the same space, with the same parents, can think so differently. Somebody really needs to explain this to me. How could it be so different, their point of view?

But anyway, you make it work. I know sometimes I felt during those years that Missoni was moving like an elephant, very slowly. Or just doing one step ahead, two steps back. Two steps ahead, and one step back. But as you said, I am a Capricorn, and I would never back down. You put me down, and boom, I'm up again. I realized that I'm driven, no matter what. I'm like a builder, and I would just go for it. I'm like that.

FOTO GIUSEPPE PINO

Page 236: Angela and Tai Missoni walking down the runway at the 2011 Missoni fashion show in Milan. This page, clockwise from top: The Missoni family in a 1990s ad; Tai and Rosita Missoni and their grandchildren; Angela and her children Margherita, Francesco, and Teresa Missoni-Maccapani.

How are the next generation of the Missoni children going to be part of the company?

AM: Now, Margherita is home with her two children and is designing a line on her own for children. Theresa is working on another project that will be out next year, also clothing. I'm very happy that they're building their own experience, a little bit outside of the family. But I'm very happy if they have a project to come back to.

Some of your brother's children are involved, too?

AM: Yes. I have two nephews who work in the company, on the commercial side. Basically, it seems like the passion for fashion comes through the women's direction in a family.

I'm going to ask you this one audience question: what is your favorite pasta shape?

AM: Spaghetti. Big spaghetti. Vermicelli.

Rosita, and yours?

RM: I think spaghetti. It is the thing that you can turn in many different ways. If you have to buy a pasta, buy that one.

You haven't made a zigzag pasta yet?

RM: No. But then, pasta, it's a fantastic element in a kitchen.

You both are fantastic elements. What you have done is incredible. Thank you.

SINCE FASHION ICONS

In 2021, Angela stepped down as creative director of Missoni, succeeded by her protégé, Alberto Caliri. She continues to serve as president, while Rosita still designs the home collection. The next generation of Missonis are stepping up to the plate; all of Angela's nephews play leadership roles in the company. The family entered the world of high-end real estate with the Missoni Baia development in Miami. The Missonis live and work together in Sumirago, Italy, even hosting Stanley Tucci for a family meal featured on his CNN series *Stanley Tucci: Searching for Italy.* Follow Angela on Instagram: @missbrunello

IRIS APFEL

At ninety-six years old, the self-proclaimed "world's oldest teenager" and "geriatric star-let" is busier than anyone in this auditorium. She makes the Kardashians look like they're asleep. Tickets to this evening sold out in record time.

Iris has had one of the most colorful and fabulous lives imaginable, and it's one that she never planned. In her exotic life, she acquired an enviable collection of clothes and accessories that fill several rooms in her homes in New York City and Palm Beach, several museums, and at one time all of Bergdorf Goodman's Fifth Avenue windows in celebration of her book Iris Apfel: Accidental Icon.

Tonight you will hear how Iris developed her famous sense of style and confidence at a very early age. She believes more is more, and less is a bore, and that color can raise the dead. You really know you've made it when you become a Barbie doll. Iris in her eighties started a whole new career out of just being Iris.

She is anything but an "accidental icon." She is proof positive that if you want to stay young, you have to think young; and to be interesting, you have to be interested. She is not fond of the fashion industry's obsession with youth, and wonders where all the dresses with sleeves are. In her own words, "Seventy-year-old ladies don't have eighteen-year-old bodies, and eighteen-year-olds don't have a seventy-year-old's dollars."

How could you not love someone whose drug of choice is caviar, and favorite drink is a chilled Tito's vodka with a few drops of Angostura bitters?

Ladies and gentlemen, let's welcome the one and only Iris Apfel [APPLAUSE].

IRIS APFEL: We must be doing something right.

FERN MALLIS: I'll say. That was a marvelous reception for you, and well deserved.

Thank you so much. It's just wonderful to be here and thank you so much for coming. I really, really appreciate it. OK, let's go.

As I told you, I always start at the very beginning. We're not going to go to everything in your life, because we'll be here a little bit too long. But let's start since you are the longest living Fashion Icon I've interviewed.

I'm the oldest person wherever I go.

That's probably true. You were born Iris Barrel on August 29, 1921, in Astoria, Queens?

Right. I think I was born in a hospital in Manhattan, but we lived in Astoria. My grandparents were settlers. They came from Manhattan, because Grandpa got sick, and the doctor said, "If you want to have an old age of any kind, you'd better get the hell out of this island and go to the country."

Queens?

… And Queens was the country. There was no bridge at the time. I don't think the Queensboro was built until about 1911. He had to hire a boatman and get a boat, and they kind of paddled across. They lived on a little farm. They had a half-interest in the nanny goat.

I don't think I'm going to need to ask any questions tonight. We're going to go back to when you were born, in August. You're a Virgo? Do you believe in astrology?

Well, most of the Virgos I met have the same personality quirks that I do. I don't know much about anything else. I just know what they tell me.

They tell you that you're strong minded? You're loyal to a fault to your friends?

That's true.

You're confident. To capture a Virgo's attention, you need traits like ambition, confidence, and most importantly, intelligence. You're bossy, but only to get things done. Perfectionist?

Oh, terrible, terrible.

A conservative approach to life?

Conservative? Only in some areas.

… And you can be harsh. You call a spade a spade, and you don't sugarcoat your opinions?

Oh, no, goodness, no. I should sometimes, but I don't.

And some of the famous Virgos are Michael Jackson, Tim Burton, Warren Buffett, Beyoncé, and many great designers, including Tom Ford, Karl Lagerfeld, Stella McCartney, and Olivier Rousteing.

Oh, I'm in good company.

Tell us about your parents, Sam and Sadye. What did they do? Dad had a mirror business?

Well, my dad, he had a lot of different things. The family had a mirror business. First of all, my

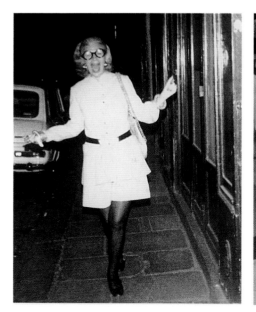

This page, from left to right: A candid of a young Iris Apfel; Iris's parents, Sam and Sadye Barrel. Opposite: Iris's 2005 Metropolitan Museum of Art Costume Institute exhibition *Rara Avis*.

father was a graduate lawyer and a graduate accountant but he never practiced either. He had an import business when I was a young child and he'd spend many months a year in Europe, and come back with all sorts of treasures. It was pre-Hitler, and Germany was going to the dogs, and that's where he spent most of his time.

He used to tell stories about how the [deutsche mark] was falling. He would go to the bank and he had to go eventually with a wheelbarrow, because they gave him so many marks. Money was just flying; it meant nothing. People were giving things in exchange for what they wanted. He got some of the most beautiful porcelain and linens and all kinds of stuff about which he knew nothing, but he had innate great taste.

He bought things and he brought home enough stuff over the years to do a trousseau for all of his sisters, and load up our house. I guess he gave me the bug.

It was pretty terrific. He brought back all kinds of other things, too, because one of the areas he worked in was very expensive, high-end toys—stuffed animals. I had teddy bears ranging from this size, to human size, well, not human size…

Teddy bear size?

… Teddy bear size, bear size. Anyhow, it was pretty swell. I had all kinds of dolls and stuff like that, and then he went into other things.

You still collect all those things: animals, toys, trains…

I love animals. Since I don't have enough time to devote to the live ones, I substitute and I'm loaded. I invest all of my stuffed animals with a life of their own. We have a pretty wild existence. For instance, Kermit lives in Palm Beach, and in case you don't know it, Kermit is a lush. I have a big bar, and if any of you have seen any of my exhibitions, you've seen the beautiful life-size ostrich, carved of wood. You open her—her name is Gussy—you open Gussy's wing and her belly is full of booze. She lives with me in Palm Beach. Kermit lives with her in Palm Beach, he hangs around her neck. When people aren't looking, he imbibes.

So he's usually crocked.

It must be very lively conversation with you and all your toys and pets?

Oh, yes. We have wonderful intellectual chats.

You have said that your mother worshipped at the altar of the accessory?

She taught me a lot of things. I was a child of the Depression. My mother had great taste and we weren't poor, but we didn't have extra money. She taught me that if you want to be well dressed, you should start with a basic wardrobe. Buy a few good, simple, well-cut pieces, the best you can afford. Perhaps take gray flannel or black, and if you had a nice pair of trousers, a skirt, a sweater, a dress, then you could start to buy accessories, and accessories are extremely transformative.

You can make a hundred outfits if you know how to put them together by changing the accessories with the same basic pieces. I've done several shows at museums, showing people how you can go from early in the morning at your office to a cocktail party at night with the same outfit by just changing your shoes, a belt, a necklace, earrings. It's incredible what you can do.

She was a whiz. I never found anybody that could do so much with a scarf as she. She was a remarkable lady. In November she'll be gone for almost twenty years. She died one month past her hundredth birthday. She not only graduated college, but she went to law school. She did not graduate because she became pregnant with me, and she gave up and spent a few years at home. Then eventually went back into business.

She just answered all the questions on this page for me that I haven't asked yet.

Oh, I talk too much.

No, you are perfect.

When you go from basic day to night, the way you just described with changing just your accessories, the way you do it, though, you probably need to carry a suitcase with you to change everything up?

Oh, you're so right. I mean, it's so hard for me to travel. My accessories take up much more space than my clothes.

How many suitcases do you take back and forth, like when you go to Florida to your house in Palm Beach?

I don't do it all in one swoop. There is another train, big enough to carry it. I have it down to a science now. I box things. I have a trucking service. You know, I send a load down at the beginning of the season and take it back at the end.

Do you have collections that you leave down in Florida?

Some things, but I always leave the wrong things there. Now I try to take home as many as I can. Then they just sit there because they don't go out very much anymore.

But what the heck, they need to get out occasionally.

You can put them on the bears and the frogs.

Oh, yes, all my animals are dressed.

Iris, how important were your grandparents when you were growing up?

Very important. We kind of lived on the compound and Grandma was in charge. She did all the cooking, and she supervised the house. She was fabulous. My grandpa, he had a lot of style.

Well, Grandma and Grandpa had this kind of *Fiddler on the Roof* existence. They lived in the shtetl. Grandma was fifteen when she married Grandpa, who was sixteen. They were not married quite a year, and she became pregnant. He was conscripted by the Russian army and he did not want to go, so he ran away. He came to America.

He did not know where he was going. He had no money. He told her that when he got established, he would get her a ticket. Now, can you imagine a young girl of that age, pregnant, with a husband who she did not know where he was, or if he was ever coming back. I don't know how she did it. But she did it.

Finally, Mother was born and when she was three months old there was a big party in the shtetl. This guy came on horseback with a little letter. Grandma opened it and it was a ticket from Grandpa, telling her she had to go immediately to Hamburg. A boat was coming. He had gotten her a ticket to come to America.

She lived in this little teeny-weeny town. She spoke nothing but Russian and Yiddish. She had to go to a foreign country, with a new baby, all by herself. She got on the train and they went to Hamburg and the boat was late. She lived in some stinking rat hole for two weeks until the boat came. She had a ticket in steerage.

I could never understand why, when Daddy used to make all these trips to Europe on the most elegant boats, you know, the *Leviathan*, and all those great boats, we would all go and have a party, but she would get as far as the dock, and then she refused to get on the ship. She could not put a foot on a boat. I did not understand it until I went to opening night at Ellis Island. It had a new facility and they showed archival footage of a steerage voyage. It was so absolutely horrendous. I was catatonic. I just could not move at the end of it. They had to come and pull me out of my seat. It was so overwhelming.

Anyway, she comes to a new country, all by herself. Does not know a soul, hardly knows her husband. I don't know how those people did it, and then you look at the kids today… Oh, my God.

It is extraordinary when you think of the comparisons to today. It's what has made you as strong as you are. It is *Fiddler on the Roof*.

Oh, I guess nothing just happens.

Tell us about your early subway trips. When you were younger. You would buy a token for five cents to go to the city, and you went to Greenwich Village to some basement shop.

Pages 248–249: Iris and Carl Apfel and friends. This page: Iris and Carl's world travels. Page 254: Iris and Carl share a kiss in 2014.

I'm trying to remember now. I had quite a few. Well, anyway, it was the first time I could pay for my own vacation. I went to Lake George. And that's where I met Carl.

Was it love at first sight?

Oh, no. No. No. I went up with a friend and the friend knew Carl. They knew one another. Carl was very busy with a very attractive young lady whose father had a beautiful boat. They were on the boat all day long. I did not know, but he told my friend he thought I was very attractive if I'd only go and get my nose fixed. Immediately I was not enchanted with Carl.

I do not believe in unnecessary plastic surgeries, I guess you all know because I'm always shooting my mouth off about that. If God gave you a nose like Pinocchio, you have to do something about it. I think plastic surgeons are a blessing. If you had an accident or fire or you have to do something. But just to carve yourself up to try to look a few years younger or you know, tilt your nose a certain way, I don't believe in it.

Anyway, enough said.

But I guess Carl got over your nose because you then started to…

Well, I guess so. Maybe something happened to his eyes.

What business was Carl in when you met him?

He was working with his father, who had a very interesting art studio. They were sort of sub-contractors for advertising agencies, and they had accounts like Revlon and some of the department stores. They would furnish the artwork and the photography.

I remember once he had a job on the outside. It was to do a catalog for a furrier. He was supposed to do it with the fur buyer of one of the big department stores. She was a big lush and she'd go off on a toot every once in a while. She was on a major toot, and Carl came home and he was absolutely frantic. We were just married. He was frantic. He didn't know what to do because the catalog was due the next day.

I remember staying up all night, and I wrote it for him. Oh, I'll never forget, it was in the summer, it was so hot, and I remember my grandmother had made cold borscht. I kept drinking that all night to stay awake [LAUGHS].

We're going to backtrack a tiny bit. Your first date with Carl was on Columbus Day in 1948. On Thanksgiving, he proposed. On Christmas, you got blinged. And then you got married on Washington's birthday, all in 1948?

Right, exactly, and then our honeymoon was over St. Patrick's Day. Everything happened on a holiday.

Can you describe your wedding dress?

Well, being very practical, I thought it was silly to spend a fortune on it. I did not want the wedding anyway; I thought I'd rather elope. But grandparents always want a nice wedding. We had a very pretty little wedding.

We had it at the Waldorf Astoria. It was a pink wedding, one of the first pink weddings. I had a pink lace dress. I designed it and had it made. It was quite beautiful. It was a strapless dress with a full skirt, and it had a capelet. I thought I'd be able to wear that for formal affairs, because I thought it was a sin to spend all that money and put your dress in a box and never wear it again.

That's true. What are some of your top secrets for a long and happy marriage?

Well, we were together for sixty-eight years. I think, first, a sense of humor. You must have a sense of humor, not a ha-ha sense. But you must be able to laugh at yourself and not take yourself too seriously.

I think you have to give one another space. You must realize that you're two people, and you don't combine just because you're married. You don't combine yourself into one and have to do the same things and like the same things. I mean, Carl was a real football fanatic. I hated football like poison. I used to say the best thing about getting married was I didn't have to freeze my butt off at any more games. If he wanted to go, I let him go. I didn't say, you can't go because I'm not going. Then there were things that I love, like antiquing, which he hated. I would go into an antiques shop and he would stand outside and fret like a spoiled child. But eventually, I would do some things that he liked, and he would do some things that I liked, so it worked out.

I think you have to have curiosity to keep things fresh. I don't know, we just liked each other. I mean, just getting married for sexual attraction is pretty silly.

How did you start Old World Weavers?

I started Old World Weavers because when I want something, I'm like a dog with a bone. I was doing a beautiful house on Long Island and I needed a fabric. I wanted a fabric that did not exist. I searched high and low. I went all over the city. I went everywhere, and I could not find it.

Finally, one day, I ran into this young lady, who I had gone to school with, whose father was a wonderful, absolutely extraordinary weaver. He had come from the south of Italy with a few handlooms and settled in Paterson, New Jersey, which was a sort of small silk center. Anyway, he had started a small mill in Long Island City. He was weaving for Scalamandré and Schumacher, all the big houses.

She said to me, "If you're looking for something special, why don't you go and see Papa? Maybe if he likes it, he'll help you."

I brought the sketch. And I went to see him. And he said he liked it and he would make it for me.

In those days, we could do a few yards at a time. I made the fabric, and it was a big success. Then he said, "Have you got any more designs?"

I said, "No, but I could get some."

I brought some, and we made a little collection and he liked them very much. And I had special fabrics for my clients that nobody else could get. He said to me one day, "You know, I'm sick and tired of weaving fabrics for other firms. I'd like to go into the wholesale fabric business myself. Would you and your husband be interested? Carl could do the business, you could do the designing, and I'll run the mill?"

This page, from left to right: Iris Apfel shopping in a souk; Iris and Carl Apfel visiting a mill. Next page: Iris surrounded by her wardrobe at her Upper East Side home.

I spoke to Carl and he liked the idea. The only problem was we did not have enough money. But we decided that we would take a chance, and we did. It worked very nicely, but then the union stepped in, and they made it miserable. We just couldn't do anything.

We decided we would keep trying with the mill and supplement it by going to Europe to see if we could buy over there. It was really difficult because Major Brunschwig [of Brunschwig & Fils] was a French war hero and he had the whole fabric market tied up. He represented every good fabric house in France.

All of the other mills wanted huge quantities, which we couldn't afford. If you bought one pattern, you'd have to buy it in four colors, six pieces, which was impossible. We kept running around and knocking on doors and coming up with schemes. And finally, we worked out a deal where I would give them a design and say, "If you weave this for me, I will give you the rights to sell it everywhere except the United States." My designs were good, so they bought into it. That's how we started.

Extraordinary. You also went through Europe, researching old period textiles that you wanted to re-create.

I loved to do that. I would go to all the museums, all the flea markets. In those days, right after the war, what you could find in flea markets was just… I mean the flea markets today are just nothing.

There were tons and tons and tons of period fabrics. I love to scrounge. I think I was a hunter-gatherer. I find little bits of things. We decided not to do any contemporary or any new designs. I did only replicas and tried to have them woven as closely as possible to the original fabric. That took us on a lot of travels because there's not one mill that can make all kinds of weaves and textures.

But it was very, very interesting. I learned a lot. We went to museums, we went to archives, we went to all kinds of places looking for designs. It was very, very exciting.

You eventually opened up a showroom in a town house on 57th Street with clients like Greta Garbo, Estée Lauder, Marjorie Merriweather Post.

Mrs. Merriweather Post was just fabulous.

We couldn't afford anything except the very top floor, and it was a four-story walk-up and there were the high ceilings. The ladies would totter up in their high heels, exhausted. Mrs. Post's feet always hurt because when she was a little girl, her father made Postum [grain-based coffee substitute]. She used to go door to door in the cold winters selling it, and her feet were often frostbitten. It left a mark, so she wore sneakers. She didn't care. When she came to New York, she was always dressed up with sneakers. She would just jump up the stairs.

She was one of our best customers. She was just wonderful. We did all the fabrics for her home, Hillwood. It's now a museum. It is in the estate section of Washington, DC. She had a camp in the Adirondacks, and she had Mar-a-Lago in Palm Beach.

Anyway, there's a famous story to tell. We were working on Hillwood and early one morning the phone rang, and I answered. She said, "This is Marjorie Merriweather Post. I must immediately speak to Mr. Apfel."

I said, "May I ask what this is about?"

"Well, last night, the draperies were installed and I want to talk to him about it," and I thought, oh, my God, something awful happened.

Carl got on the phone and she said, "Mr. Apfel, I am now sitting on top of an eighteen-foot ladder, inspecting the beautiful installation of my gorgeous fabrics. I need to know, because you made beautiful swags and festoons, and you made beautiful fringes to trim the width. I have a ruler in my hand. I'm trying to figure out how many little silk balls should I expect to find in a running yard?"

I mean, it's handmade. Carl thought a minute and then he said, "Mrs. Post, every morning I eat your Raisin Bran. Would you please tell me how many raisins I'm supposed to have in a tablespoon" [LAUGHTER]?

She said, "Touché, Mr. Apfel. I'm a silly old lady. I can't help that that's the way my mind works. I'd better get down off this ladder before I break my neck. The fabrics are gorgeous. I love the draperies. Sorry to bother you. Bye-bye."

Carl had that kind of sense of humor. That's what was so nice.

Clearly a fabulous response. How did you get to working at the White House? Do you have any particular stories you'd like to share, from Truman to Clinton?

We're really not supposed to, because it's not right. We work on the fabrics. We never design them.

When you do a historic restoration, if it's to be historically correct, it's to be as close as humanly possible to the original. It could be the most hideous thing in the world, you are not allowed to improve it.

Of course, the White House was quite beautiful. There were wonderful inventories. We were able to go into the archives. For instance, when the Metropolitan Museum celebrated their anniversary in 1976, we did a lot of fabrics for the restoration and we went to their warehouses, and we were able to peel off some of the original fabrics that had been merci-fully left underneath the coverings. Then we were able to reproduce them exactly. That's the kind of thing we did.

I mean, sometimes we'd have to go to a small mill in the South of France. Sometimes we had to go to Italy. Sometimes we had to go all over the world to get to the right kind of looms. It was very exciting.

Did you meet each of these Presidents and First Ladies when you worked there?

Yes. Yes. Strangely enough, the First Lady I got to know best was the only First Lady who was really interested in the house: Mrs. [Pat] Nixon.

Major work was done during his administration. While she knew very little about restoration, she was passionately interested. She used to nag the interior architect to please let her come shopping. She used to come every time we looked for fabrics. The whole Secret Service and everybody would come. Poor thing, we used to let her play. She really didn't know much at all because I think she was sort of originally a J.C. Penney's customer. I remember Nixon once said, "My wife wears a nice Republican cloth coat."

Anyway, she would pick fabrics, always everything wrong. We would let her take a bag full of samples back home, because we knew what we were going to do. Invariably, the next morn-ing she would call and say, "Oh, Mrs. Apfel, as usual, I picked everything that was wrong. Can you come Thursday for lunch?"

We used to go back and forth to Washington, DC. Those were the days when there was rationing of heat and everything. The White House was, like, at sixty degrees; it was always freezing. We always got cold salmon and cold soup for lunch. Anyway, she was a very, very lovely person.

Do you want to elaborate on what Jackie Kennedy did?

Kennedy, she never did the house. She had nothing to do with it because there is a Fine Arts Commission, and the Fine Arts Commission takes care of it all. Jacqueline, she even said it herself in one of the interviews. That was just a lot of PR. It sounded good.

You, though, were called the first lady of the cloth.

Well, anyway, I tried, I think fabric is wonderful and I don't see how a computer can design it.

On all of these trips when you were traveling to find the fabrics, to find the mills, you would always make side trips to find the jewelry, the accessories, all the things that you started to collect. Were you shipping tons of things home all the time?

Oh, my God, yes. You never saw a collection of luggage like we used to have, because we would buy them on the road. We had everything. We had painted trunks. We had, oh, my God, wherever we were, we bought the local luggage store's trunks. It was wonderful.

Then for my decorating business, I would make two trips to Europe every year to buy. My customers didn't like standard equipment. I did not like going to showrooms and having everybody's house look alike. I used to go and buy antiques. I used to send home two forty-foot containers a year, and there was always room for a few pieces of jewelry.

With all of that traveling, was there a favorite place that you always liked to go to the best?

Well, there are so many, for different reasons. But I guess the overall country that I just love is Italy. I love everything Italian.

We used to love the Middle East. We were crazy about the Middle East. It was exotic, and I have a theory: when the place is spotlessly clean, like Switzerland, it is very boring. When the place is dirty and messed up, it's exciting and that's what we liked. We liked the exotic.

I'm with you there. Do you have any travel or packing advice for people?

Today, the biggest advice I'll tell you is "stay home."

If you knew what traveling was like in the old days, when you went on the great ships, and now you have to travel through an airport, you're being treated like a barnyard animal.

It's not for me. I go, but I sure don't like it.

In the 1950s during these trips to Paris, you also managed to visit a few couture houses: Lanvin, Nina Ricci, Christian Dior.

Well, I was lucky in that I was in Paris twice a year, just around when the couture shows were finished. It struck me that maybe there would be some runway samples that they might want to sell. Nobody seemed to know about doing an archive in those days.

I researched and found the firms that had mannequins that were more or less my size, like Dior and Nina Ricci. I would go and ask if they had anything that they wanted to part with, and they always did. I bought them at prices I could afford, even in those days. I began to collect; that was one of the cleverest things I ever did.

One of many. But did you keep any of those? Do you still have them?

Oh, yes. I mean, the museums have some, and there are some I can't bear to part with. They will go to museums, but after I go. I used to wear them because Carl and I used to go out a lot in the 1970s and 1980s; we wore black tie like four nights a week. I used to wear them,

From left to right: Iris Apfel trying on jewelry; Iris at Estée Lauder's Palm Beach home.

and now I just take them out and pet them once in a while.

You were also an Olympic shopper at the original Loehmann's in Brooklyn. Can you tell us about the back room with the Norman Norell and Pauline Trigère pieces.

Well, I had only heard about it. I didn't know too much about Loehmann's, but I had heard the name. Very shortly after I was married and I was launching my decorating career, I had a client in Brooklyn who wanted to interview me and we made a date.

I got all mixed up with the subway system. Do you remember Thomas Wolfe and his short stories? He did one called "Only the Dead Know Brooklyn." I found that out to be true. I got lost in this Brooklyn subway system, and I emerged in this pouring rainstorm. It was beautiful when I entered, but it was raining the proverbial dogs and cats, and I didn't know where the heck I was.

It turned out I was on Bedford Avenue and I started to walk. I did not know where I was going. All of a sudden, I see this window and I said, "Oh, where am I?"

It was a long, thin window and it had a beautiful, real Tiffany glass screen at one end. Over it was draped a Norell dress and at the other end was a Trigère outfit, and I said, "Where am I? Did I die and go to heaven?" I thought I'd walk in, and it turned out to be Loehmann's.

I walked into this huge, cavernous space and I see ladies running around in various shades of undress, and disgruntled husbands lining the wall, grumbling, "Hurry up, let's get out of here."

I looked at the racks and I thought, what was all the fuss about? It was low-end stuff and not appealing at all. I must have looked upset because some nice lady, I bless her to this day, came over and said, "What's wrong?"

I said, "I heard so much about Loehmann's and all the beautiful clothes and I don't see one." She said, "Oh, you're not in the right place. You have to go to this part of the store and walk up the stairs and then ask for the back room," and I did. Then I thought, oh, my God, I mean all the great designers that I used to drool over when I read *Vogue* every month. I never thought I'd be able to own one and they were ridiculously low prices. I thought, oh my goodness and I didn't have any time or any money with me. I don't think I had a credit card in those days. I said, "I've got to come back."

I got the job with this person and every time I went to Brooklyn, I would come either early and stop there, or go later on my way back. You couldn't exchange or return anything, and very often I didn't have time to try things on. But being a fabric person, the textiles on the clothes were so exquisite in those days, and I'd say "Well, at this price, if it doesn't fit me I can make pillows." I didn't make many pillows.

Anyway, I kept going and I accumulated some of the most beautiful things—some of them were in my museum show. At prices that were so insane, I mean, you couldn't even buy lunch for that price.

That's true, and Mrs. Loehmann with her little pouch of money. She would stand on the stairway. I grew up going to Loehmann's as a little kid in Brooklyn.

You remember what she looked like? She looked like she's out of Toulouse-Lautrec, didn't she? She had a little topknot, and she wore a high-button blouse and a big skirt. She carried a miser's purse she had stuffed with cash. If it wasn't for Mrs. Loehmann I think some of the biggest names in fashion would have gone out of business. She would bail them out. She would buy their overruns and their samples and everything else. She really saved Seventh Avenue.

She would come and occasionally sit in the back room, and then there was a big space where they had other racks. She would sit on a tall stool, like somebody that was observing a tennis match. She looked at everybody and saw what they were doing, and she used to fixate on me, and she made me very nervous.

One day, she called me over and she said, "Young lady, you're certainly not pretty. Don't let anybody tell you you are. But you're something much better. I watch you every time you are here. You have style." I didn't know what the hell she was talking about. I thought she was some kind of a nut.

I kept going back and buying all these wonderful, wonderful things. There never was a place like that and there never will be again. She was really the grandma of discount shopping, don't you think?

Absolutely, and people did undress in the aisles. The men stayed on one side. Everybody was undressed, trying things on wherever they found them. It was quite remarkable.

Then after she died, her son Charles opened the place in the Bronx. I used to go there until the neighborhood got so dreadful. We were all afraid to go. And then it became too big.

But honestly, it was so nice, because I think I probably was their oldest customer. They invited me to celebrate my ninetieth birthday because we were both ninety at the same time. That was fun. We had a cake.

From the 1950s to the 1990s, your business kept growing. You both kept traveling and collecting, and you finally sold your business to Stark Carpets in 1992. You thought you and Carl would retire, relax, travel. What did you think you were going to do?

I never wanted to relax. Carl wanted to. All his friends were driving him crazy to come to Palm Beach to play golf and all that. I mean, to me, I could not think of anything worse.

We did sell finally. My mother kept saying she would buy me a beautiful house and six dogs. I liked the dogs part of it, but that was all. Anyhow, we sold it, but they said part of the deal was we were to stay on for three years. Then they made it five years. We stayed on for eighteen years, which is just unheard of when you sell a business.

Finally, I was rescued by the Metropolitan Museum of Art.

Tell us about that phone call, when you were eighty-three years old in 2005 and Harold Koda called you?

I got a call asking me if I would like to do a show. A show of my accessories. And I thought, gee, that would be fun. I was very busy, and that shouldn't take very much time, because all I'd have to do was take my stuff and put it in a nice case.

I said, "OK," and then I didn't hear anything from anybody, because a lot of things were going on. Then all of a sudden, I got a telephone call and Harold Koda said he wanted to come to see me. Harold was the head honcho [the curator of the Costume Institute]. Such a shame he retired.

Anyway, he said he was rethinking the project, and to show accessories out of context did not make much sense to him. He thought the public would be much more interested in seeing what I could do with accessories. Could I possibly spare maybe five outfits? He would choose them to be curatorially correct and I could dress them any way I chose. I could accessorize with what they went with originally, or all new things, or any kind of combination I wanted. I said, "Oh, that sounds like fun." I didn't know what was going to happen.

I said, "Well, what would you like?"

He said, "Well, I don't know. What have you got?"

I said, "Well, do you want to have a look?"

That opened Pandora's box. They opened every closet, every armoire, every chest of drawers, every box—they even looked under the bed. And they kept "oohing" and "aahing" and I'm kind of cuckoo. Sometimes I go on a shopping spree and I buy things, and I stick them in a closet, and I forget about them. We found something I bought thirty-five years ago with the tags still on.

Anyway, they kept taking this and taking that. They asked if they could come back tomorrow, and they kept coming back. They came back for, like, a week. Then we finally had to go out and buy ten pipe racks. We had to push all the furniture in the apartment to the side and clear off all the tables. They were piling things up and they couldn't decide what they wanted. Being that they were so close, it wasn't a hardship for them to send a truck every day. They hauled away eventually about three hundred outfits.

From five outfits, it went to three hundred?

The show was supposed to be in one gallery. It ended up by taking the whole [Costume] Institute. I think they ended up with about eighty-six outfits. It was an unusual and exciting experience.

... And then it was called *Rara Avis*?

It was called *Rara Avis*, and I kept saying I don't like that title. Harold kept saying that it was just a working title, and they would change it. They never changed it. It means "rare bird" in Latin and some of my very intelligent friends would call me up and ask me what that meant. They said they looked it up in the dictionary and they couldn't find it, and I said of course you couldn't.

Anyhow, it started because Richard Martin, who was a cocurator with Harold, used to call me the rare bird. Then they translated it into Latin, and that stuck.

How did it feel having an exhibition of all your things at the Metropolitan Museum?

Oh, it felt pretty swell. It kind of rejuvenated the institute because it had gotten kind of boring. It had its glory days when Diana Vreeland was there. She did spectacular shows, the

curators went crazy with it because she had no scholarship at all and didn't care, and they'd go nuts. But the shows were really wonderful.

We brought back a little bit of that pizzazz and the fashion students started to come back. Every morning they'd be lying all over the floor. You couldn't walk. They were sketching. Everybody who was anybody came. Thanks to Bill Cunningham, he was just wonderful. He was very upset because they never invited him to the opening.

They were very nervous because the show before was with Karl Lagerfeld. It was a Chanel show and it was such a disaster. The *New York Times* panned it in four different articles, even on the editorial page. They were very nervous because they were breaking the glass ceiling in letting me do a show.

There was an unwritten law, that unless you were in the trade and a fashion designer, or you were dead, a woman couldn't have a show at the Met. That brings a funny story to mind, because they didn't do any publicity about me. They were kind of afraid. One day, my nephew, who would go often with his friends and listen to what people had to say, told me that two ladies were discussing who I was, and nobody knew. They said, "Oh, I don't know, she's probably dead."

He came back, and he told me and I said, "Next time you hear that, tap the lady on the shoulder and say, 'My auntie is very much alive. She's walking around to save funeral expenses.'" Nobody really knew who I was for a while and then all of a sudden, I blossomed. Then everybody said I was an overnight sensation. I said that was true, except my overnight took seventy-two years.

… And the show traveled to the Norton in West Palm Beach, the Nassau County Museum, and ended at the Peabody Essex in Salem, Massachusetts.

That was the most beautiful show, because the galleries were great, with soaring ceilings. I decided that I would give them the collection.

How did you make that decision that they would get it and not the Met or FIT?

Yes, because the Met has so much, they wanted to cherry-pick. I wanted the collection to stay intact. It was unbelievable, because the Peabody Essex had a wonderful collection of very early things. But by about 1940 it kind of tapers off. They had very beautiful clothes that were given, but they were very conservative Bostonian. I mean, no pizzazz at all.

My collection sort of begins at that point. It is not theirs yet. They're holding it. But when I kick off, they will get it. I give them more and more pieces every year because I have no room in my closets.

How did you also then become a visiting professor at the University of Texas at Austin?

That's another crazy story. One day, I got a telephone call while the show was up at the Peabody Essex and it was from a Texas alumna.

She said she saw the show and she flipped. She thought maybe I could be of some help to the school. They had a fashion department and maybe I could do something with them, would I be interested? I said, "Well, I'd like to know what and let's talk about it."

They came to New York and we talked and we decided that we will do something together. We decided that the first thing we were going to do is that Carl and I were going to spend a week and he would do a couple of master classes in textiles and I would do some, and we were going to have a black-tie fundraiser.

I had spent a lot of time in Texas, but I never went to a cattle ranch and I was dying to go. The kicker was that I agreed to come if they took me to one. They said that was no problem because they have a lot of alumni who have ranches.

This is like a very bad soap opera. The morning we were going to have a late flight and I had to go to the dentist to get a tooth finished up and Carl had to go and get an injection or something. I'm in the dentist's chair and he called and said, "They found something wrong with me and I can't come home. They won't let me out of the hospital."

I was frantic. I ran out of the chair. I couldn't for love or money get a taxi. I was at 44th and Fifth and New York Hospital is at, what, 68th and the river, and I ran all the way. I got there and he had some cardiac problem. I thought, oh, my God, what am I going to do? They're expecting us tonight. They have all this planned. They had television setups, and everything. I was so nervous. I said, "They'll never speak to me again."

I called and I explained the situation, and they could not have been nicer. They decided that they would come to New York.

At first, they wanted me just to take them around and introduce them to designers. I said I didn't think that was the way to go. I've been looking the situation over, and so many students get out of school, and they just don't know where to go, they don't know where to turn. They all want to be a designer or a merchandise person, and if they don't get that job they give up. They have to be taught that fashion is a great umbrella and there are all kinds of things they don't teach in school, like licensing, trend forecasting, museums, and all that kind of stuff. I think it would be very interesting if I could do a program and introduce them to all these different facets.

They said, "That's brilliant. Let's do it."

They said, "But we don't know how to do it. Will you do it?"

I said, "Sure."

Then I thought, what the hell am I doing? I don't know anybody in this field. But I did it. It turned out to be such a great program. The kids love it. They all say it's a life-changing experience. They have gotten wonderful internships and great jobs. There is nobody that has turned me down. I mean, everybody we go to: the Met, we go to Bergdorf's, we've gone to Bruce Weber, Swarovski, everything, and it's very exciting.

Last year, with the help of a friend, we got the gift show to let us have some time. I'm always scrounging to get the kids lunch because they don't have any money. They gave us vouchers for lunch. We decided to do a program with the students, telling them, "Each of you is going to open a shop. Here is $200,000, and you are now going to merchandise the store. You walk through this show. You pick any kind of area that you want to and you pick all the merchandise you want. You photograph it, and you write it up: why you picked it and what the shop concept is and everything else."

I think they got two or three credits, and it was very good. Everybody loved it so we're going to do it again this year. But this year, we're going to do a full day. I think this is the eighth year.

You are an educator as well now. That program at the University of Texas at Austin was what got Albert Maysles to find you and do a film.

He didn't come to Texas. Somebody told him about the program, and he thought it was very interesting. He called me up and he said he wanted to do a documentary and I said, "Thank you very much, but I'm not interested." He called me about three or four times, and I

This page: A matching Iris Apfel and Linda Fargo at FGI's Night of Stars in 2017. Opposite: Iris holding her Barbie in 2018. Pages 270–271: Iris's Bergdorf Goodman windows in 2018.

kept refusing.

I said, "What do I need a documentary for? Nobody knows who I am. I have nothing to sell. I don't have any ego problems. I don't need it."

Somehow, I don't remember if I told her or she heard about it, but Linda Fargo called me, she said, "What's wrong with you? How dare you turn down Maysles? People would die just to have him take a still photograph and you're turning down a documentary? You've got to be cuckoo. You have to do it."

I said, "I just turned him down for the fourth time." She said, "Well, call him up."

Fortunately, he called me a fifth time. I agreed to go up to Harlem and we fell in love. We decided to do it. It took forever, because he was very busy, and traveling; and I was very busy, and he was sick. But it happened.

It happened. What was it like having someone follow you around all those years?

Anytime he heard of something he thought was interesting, they would get a little crew together. They were very nice, very unobtrusive. They never got in my way. It was a very pleasant relationship.

Has that documentary changed your life?

Oh, my God. I don't know why people rave so much about it. It's gotten, I don't know, sometimes I call it spoiled apples, but it's Rotten Tomatoes. Anyway, it's got one of the highest ratings, 96 percent, 98 percent, something like that. It's been shown on every airline all over the world. Right now, I'm very large in Uzbekistan. I meet people from all over, and they all seem to know me. It's incredible. It's just ridiculous. Carl and I used to sit and laugh. You

IRIS
APFEL

BERGDORF GOODMAN PRESENTS
ALL THE GOOD
IRIS APFEL

Window Exhibit: Clothing from the personal collection of Iris Apfel
3rd Floor: Discover the specially curated Iris Apfel shop
Iris Apfel's new Harper Collins book *Iris Apfel: ACCIDENTAL ICON*

"I like that little bit of EXOTIC
it stirs my bones!"
— Iris Apfel

BERGDORF GOODMAN CELEBRATES
ALL THINGS
IRIS APFEL

SELECTED CLOTHING COURTESY
THE PEABODY ESSEX MUSEUM
SALEM, MASSACHUSETTS

know, how did this all happen?

Did you ever talk to Bill Cunningham about it? Because he hated that a film was made about his life. He never saw it. He said it made him crazy because he couldn't do his work anymore.

I never really spoke to him much about my film. Toward the end, I got so busy I didn't see Bill as much as I would have liked. I think I'm one of the few people whose dinner invitations he accepted. He came to dinner at my house a couple times.

To me, Bill was a cross between a monk and an elf. The most unusual person I ever met—so innocent and so pure. He was delicious, delightful. I miss him so much. I can't tell you.

I think we all do.

That film led to you becoming a major player in advertising licensing collections, and collaborations with MAC, HSN, Macy's, Swarovski, One Kings Lane, Hunter Douglas, Wearable Tech, Happy Socks, Eye Glasses, and advertising campaigns with Alexis Bittar, Kate Spade, Barneys, and more press coverage than anybody could keep track of.

How did you decide to do all of that?

I didn't decide to do anything. I just… these things happen.

If it sounds interesting, I say OK. I never planned any of this. I should really be out to pasture. Anyway, I like it. I'm a workaholic and these last years, since Carl is gone, I was really, you know, sixty-eight years is a long time and we did everything together. I thought, oh, my God, what's going to become of me? I said, "Well, if I just stop working or sit home, I'll just cry all day long and he wouldn't like that, and it wouldn't do me any good."

I went back to work, and the man upstairs was very good to me and sent me all kinds of interesting new projects. If something looks interesting, I'll try it. The worst thing that can happen is I don't do it well, but at least I try. I've enjoyed it so much.

I've met so many people. The only thing is I just work too much, and it just makes me sick

Opposite: Iris Apfel celebrating her 100th birthday party at Central Park Towers in 2021. This page: Tommy Hilfiger hosting students from Iris's University of Texas at Austin program in 2018.

sometimes. I mean, fortunately, nothing sick, I just get so exhausted. I can't stand up. Which is insanity. So I'm cutting down. But even when I cut down, I do more than most people.

We are kind of at the end and we're running late because this is an extraordinary life. We have a couple of minutes for some audience questions. What is your favorite piece of jewelry? Is there one?

Oh, no, I don't have favorites. I mean, at different times, things appeal to me. No, I don't play favorites.

What has been the thing that's most surprised you in life?

Most surprising thing in my life? It's stuff like sitting on this stage with you. I never expected things like this to happen to me. Everything is a big surprise.

Any thoughts on the legacy you would like to leave?

I'm ninety-six going on ninety-seven, I hope. I don't want to think about legacies.

On that, let us leave on a high note and say Iris, thank you.

[LONG STANDING OVATION]

They are very nice. Wow!

SINCE FASHION ICONS

In 2019, at the age of ninety-seven, Iris signed her first modeling contract with prestigious IMG Models—brokered by her friend Tommy Hilfiger. Iris continues to be an in-demand curator of style, adding to her vast portfolio of existing collaborations: Zenni eyewear, Happy Socks, Judith Leiber, and even home improvement store Lowe's. She launched a coloring book, with the proceeds going to the UT in NYC textiles and apparel program. In August 2021, Iris turned one hundred years old and shows no signs of slowing down. Iris splits her time between New York's Upper East Side and Palm Beach, Florida. Follow Iris on Instagram: @iris.apfel

CHRISTIAN SIRIANO

Christian Siriano is the youngest Fashion Icon I have interviewed. Christian became a household name as the breakout star of Project Runway's season four, and he is, without a doubt, the most successful contestant from that program to date. Tim Gunn has said, "In thirty years of teaching, working, and launching careers, I had never met a fashion prodigy until I met Christian."

He celebrated his tenth anniversary in business by opening a fabulous new boutique, The Curated NYC, just off Fifth Avenue, and was named one of Time magazine's 100 Most Influential People. He always knew pink, fuchsia, and florals were the norm and he is one of a few designers who has ever been parodied on Saturday Night Live.

Christian is always in the right place at the right time, and on the right side of the issues. He completely disrupted the fashion business with his passionate embrace of diversity and inclusivity. He made headlines by answering a tweet from SNL's Leslie Jones with "I'll do it." Every designer turned down dressing her for the premiere of Ghostbusters, so Leslie took her frustration to Twitter. Christian seized that moment and created a showstopping red dress that became a viral social media phenomenon, one that people are still talking about to this day.

Leslie Jones is now prominent in his front row along with Whoopi Goldberg, Meg Ryan, Laverne Cox, Cardi B, Coco Rocha, Jaimie Alexander, and Olympian Nastia Liukin. Selma Blair walked in his most recent show, along with Ashley Graham and a host of other gorgeous models of every size, color, and ethnicity.

During his busiest season, he also found time to dress twenty-two stars for the Oscars, ten for the Golden Globes, three for the SAG Awards, and two for the Tonys.

Ladies and gentlemen, let's welcome the fabulous and fierce Christian Siriano.

CHRISTIAN SIRIANO: That was the whole interview. That's it, we can all go home [LAUGHTER]. How are you? You look great.

FERN MALLIS: Thank you for my Christian Siriano caftan.

Chic.

I'm happy to be here with you. I think they are all waiting to hear more from you.

I love that photo. It's so beautiful [POINTING AT A PHOTO PROJECTED ON THE SCREEN BEHIND HIM FEATURING ALL OF HIS MUSES].

If you get bored with us, just keep looking at the gorgeous girls up there.

Yeah.

Starting at the beginning, you were born on November 18, 1985?

Oh, we are going back?

Yes, to the beginning. How old are you?

Clockwise from top: Christian Siriano's 2020 fashion show on the lawn of his Westport, Connecticut home (also pictured: Billy Porter); Christian's sketch for his "Vote" dress, created to encourage people to vote in the 2020 US presidential election; First Lady Jill Biden wearing a Christian Siriano dress at the Democratic National Convention in 2020.

What is that? Thirty-two? Thirty-three?

You're a Scorpio? Are you a believer in astrology?

Yeah.

Some of the Scorpio traits that I read about are: strong, focused, brave, balanced, faithful, ambitious, intuitive, dedicated, honest and fair, resourceful, passionate and assertive, determined and decisive, fantastic at management and solving problems, creative and disciplined.

I do all that every day. Times a thousand.

… And the negatives?

There's a lot. Did you edit them? Thank you.

Jealous, secretive.

Always.

Resentful, manipulative.

Interesting.

Violent, distrusting, obsessive, and unyielding. Any of that true?

I mean, it depends on the day…

… And the hour.

… Maybe so. I'm going to think on it.

Food for thought. Some of the famous Scorpios are: Leonardo DiCaprio, your buddy Whoopi Goldberg, Pablo Picasso, Anne Hathaway, Condoleezza Rice, Julia Roberts, Hillary Clinton, Bill Gates, Grace Kelly, Caitlyn Jenner.

Great list. And Grace Kelly.

The Scorpio designers: Calvin Klein, Rick Owens, Emilio Pucci, Edith Head, Roberto Cavalli, Zac Posen, Lilly Pulitzer, and not a designer, but Anna Wintour.

It works. That was so informative. I'm ready to go home.

You were born in Annapolis, Maryland. Your parents are Joye and Peter Siriano. I have to tell you right up front, I love your mother.

My mom only goes to my shows for you. Not for me.

His mother and I have a wonderful relationship at every fashion show. It can't start till

This page: Christian Siriano and sister Shannon Siriano Greenwood growing up in Annapolis, Maryland. Opposite, from left to right: Christian, Shannon, and Joye Siriano; Christian's nephews Oliver and Bruno Greenwood.

we both hug and kiss each other, really.

For real. You hold up the show. It's kind of a problem.

They were both teachers?

Yeah, they were teachers. But very creative people. They wanted to be entrepreneurs in their own way. I think their generation, they felt like they couldn't. But both are very supportive and amazing.

What did they teach?

My mom was a reading specialist for kindergarten to eighth grade. My dad was a guidance counselor. They both taught for forty-three years and then retired. They do their kind of creative things now. My mom spends all my money. It's great.

Tell us what it was like growing up in Maryland. Lots of crab cakes and nautical stripes?

I love a stripe. I love a boat shoe. It was really interesting because in Annapolis we have the Naval Academy. It's quite buttoned up. I found my little world there. I found some really great people who were very eccentric and creative, too. I think that was very helpful.

My sister was also a big influence in my whole life. She was wild and crazy, and a ballet dancer. I think she kind of helped me through that world.

Shannon is four years older than you? You said that because she took risks, she taught you how to do the same?

I mean, every day, she would wear the craziest, ugliest things all the time. I just thought it was so interesting that she was so confident. She would wear huge hats, and platform shoes, and she was in high school. I was like, "Where are you going?"

I always thought that that was so interesting. Now she's a mom and super boring. Not that moms are boring. I just mean she is.

This is being livestreamed.

Oh, I know. I hope she is watching. She knows.

But what I love though is when she comes to New York Fashion Week and visits, she really loves dressing up again like we used to when we were kids. It's really fun. I always love to have that. She's like, the crazier the better. I always think that's just, like, fun to watch.

I also read that when you were kids, your mom had a vintage Elsa Schiaparelli dress with lots of pearls.

My mom actually had a lot of really great clothes. My mom got married in a Diane von Furstenberg dress. She did not get married in a traditional wedding dress. She was quite savvy. She was probably the reason why I even knew who Kate Spade was. She was a big bag lover. She loves fashion in her own way. I think that it definitely helped.

I grew up in a house full of women who loved clothes and were two very different women.

When you were five or six, your mom would take you to see Shannon at the Ballet Theatre of Annapolis, now the Ballet Theatre of Maryland? I read that your mom would bring paper and pencils to keep you busy. You would sketch the costumes. You drew the Sugar Plum Fairy in *The Nutcracker*.

Love a fairy. Love a tutu.

I always went backstage with the costumes and hair and makeup. I knew what a bobby pin was before anything. I was very gay, but that's fine. I loved it. Watching a performance like that, you were in a fantasy world. You're in a dream. To see that as a kid for years was very inspiring. I think it is still inspiring to this day.

When you were there with your sister, you were asked to join the company. You were one of the kids in *The Nutcracker*?

I danced for five years. I was amazing. Actually, I love ballet. It's an amazing sport.

You didn't consider that as a career?

No, I didn't. As it went on, my sister was really, really disciplined. She went to an amazing school called the Kirov Academy, which is a really tough ballet school. When she finished, she was like, "I would never do this again."

… And I was like, "OK, then I'm out."

Let's talk about high school. You went to Broadneck High School for one year, then transferred to Baltimore School for the Arts. You fit right in. What does that mean?

It was amazing. It was the best. It's the most magical place in the entire world. I was just there a few weeks ago, celebrating their graduation. It's just a beautiful place to celebrate creativity and art. Really talented people have gone there, and still go there.

Tell us how you basically changed the entire curriculum in high school to accommodate your desire to be a fashion designer.

Well, listen, you know, I like to be a bit bossy. My senior year, I knew that I wasn't going to be a painter. That wasn't happening. I mean, I was good, but I wasn't that good. My senior year, I just said, "I'm interested in fashion. I want to do something else."

I was very good at persuading the teachers to do what I wanted to do. The dean was very supportive and let me be creative. I kind of just did my own thing. I made my own clothes. Instead of art history, I took a fashion history course that I did on my own; no one else was doing it. I just tried.

… And you graded yourself?

It's all part of it. Whatever; I was just being myself at the time. I was a kid.

I read that Tim Gunn said that they don't usually let college graduates on the show, but he was blown away by whatever you brought?

I brought pretty things, I guess. I hated them, but, you know.

Tell us about the experience of being on the show. What did you learn from that?

I mean, you've seen it. That's, what it is. You sit there, you make a dress, Heidi Klum doesn't know what it is, and you're done. That's what it is. That's all it is.

It's honestly a great experience. It was a wonderful idea. Power to them. It was a place to speak and to show your creative work. I never thought of it as anything else. I just clearly say what I think. You forget that you're there, and that the world can watch it later. Like tonight we're livestreaming, and I'm sure I just said a lot of things I shouldn't have said.

I will say, it's just so beautiful to watch people make something from nothing, from a flat piece of nothing, and turn it into a three-dimensional form in front of your eyes. Forget all the commercial abilities of a TV show, it's still a beautiful thing to watch. That's what I thought was really amazing. It still is amazing.

The finale show was in the Bryant Park NYFW tents. I remember talking to you backstage. How did that feel?

It was great. I showed in the tents two seasons later, which was amazing. I showed at the tents for quite a while, actually. I loved it. It was a great, great, great experience, all through to the end.

… And Victoria Beckham was the guest judge for your *Project Runway* finale?

Christian Siriano and Tim Gunn at *Project Runway*'s season 4 finale party in 2008.

She was. She was also my first customer. I got a nice little check from Victoria. That was great.

… And a check?

Yeah, she bought clothes. It's great. It was really nice. Yeah, she invited me to her home. We shopped. It was nice. Now, she's a very amazing, talented designer herself.

She was here on the stage. Why do you erase your times on *Project Runway* from your biography? Do you think people didn't respect you for coming from that show?

I don't know. I was really young. I was really a kid. I auditioned when I was twenty years old. I was really naive to the world, and I think we all make those interesting decisions then, that shouldn't shape your life or your career.

It's like an actress. If she did one movie that shouldn't shape her entire history in film. That's how I think about it, for sure. I think there's a lot of other designers that have done interesting things early on in their career, that don't shape what they're doing now. I think that's why it's very important to move on from it. There will be things in the next ten years that I will say the same thing about.

Clearly you have moved on, but that really is what put you in the collective consciousness of a lot of people. That one line in your biography, it's kind of jarring that that's not in there.

Someone like me, we kill ourselves every day in this business. I can't imagine even thinking about that because I wish I was on that every day. It was fabulous. I made something, somebody paid for my fabrics, somebody did whatever I wanted, I could make anything. That's not how it is. Now, it's a totally different world. So that's how I think about it.

Then you started your own business? Did you have a financial reward from winning

Models walking at
Christian Siriano's
2012 fashion show.

Project Runway **to start your business?**

I did. I got a nice little check. It was cut in half from taxes, and I went on my way. I showed my first season maybe four months later.

One of the things that I am fascinated by is how do you start a business? What did you do first? Did you get an office? Did you hire people? How do you start?

I don't even know. I had a lot happening. It was really intense, like you said. Amy Poehler from *Saturday Night Live* had just played me, which was crazy. There were so many actresses and people wanting my clothes. That was my biggest issue, and it is an amazing thing. I had people wanting product, but I had no product.

I was a brand already, without being a brand. I almost basically went backward, and had to figure it out really quickly. That was the challenge for me. I was making clothes. I was trying to do what I could do. I had interns. I had a good friend from home that helped make half the collection.

Some other people that work in my office have been with me for almost ten years now, which is pretty great. They started as interns and are now still around.

Several months later, these companies are coming to you about collaborations. Puma was one of the first.

Oh, my God, I remember I did a collaboration with Puma. That's how I met Lady Gaga, when no one knew who Lady Gaga was. I dressed her for her first, like, TV appearance ever. That was really funny because it was actually a Puma project for me. But it was with her, that was really funny. I did tons of things. I worked with LG Electronics. I signed a deal with Payless.

Tell us about the Payless deal.

I have been with them for almost ten years now, which is crazy. We have sold hundreds of millions of shoes. It's unreal. It was a great thing.

Oh, everybody was like, "What are you doing? You're crazy." Because designers just weren't doing mass collaborations yet. That was before Target was doing it. It just wasn't really a thing as much. A few people. Isaac Mizrahi was doing it. But it wasn't glamorous. We made it glamorous.

I have a mea culpa in that, because I was at IMG at that time when you got the Payless deal, and one of our team was pitching them to be a sponsor for NYFW. We all, including me, were like, "We can't have Payless as a sponsor. Mercedes-Benz is on the front of the tents, and American Express, Moët & Chandon. How can we have Payless?"

I know. I know.

Shame on me.

It just was a different thing. Even still now, it's a specific place in my world. But that's what's great about fashion now. What I love is that we like to celebrate people, whatever price point you are. If you have twenty dollars to buy a pair of shoes, that shouldn't hinder what you're getting. I think that that's kind of how I've always looked at my job.

Also, think about this: I was twenty-two years old and this company was like, "Would you like to be a shoe designer for the next four years?" I was like, "Yes, I would." I also needed a check. I needed a job. I thought that it was a great challenge for myself, and it still is.

I mean, Payless is not all cakes and cookies every day. It's a big company. They went bankrupt last year. We're still working through things. I made them a lot of money, though, so listen.

You also very early on picked up Saks Fifth Avenue and Intermix?

Yeah. Saks was my first retailer, which is just crazy.

Which is great.

It was amazing. It was a great experience. Then Neiman's came along.

You played yourself on ABC's *Ugly Betty*.

Oh, I did, that was fun. Nina Garcia was on with me. God, I forgot about that. Fern, you are digging deep. I don't even know where I am.

Then you were in the music video for Estelle's single "No Substitute Love."

Oh, my God. I can hear you laugh [POINTING INTO THE AUDIENCE]. Sorry, Eva works with me, and that's really funny. I looked great in that video, though. It's the worst. Please don't look it up.

Then one of the very first high-profile gigs was dressing Whoopi Goldberg to host the Tonys in 2008?

That was my first major thing. Whoopi wanted me to make her a pirate blouse, whatever that was, and we made our pirate blouse. I just took her to the CFDA awards a couple weeks ago. Full circle.

In fuchsia.

In fuchsia. She looked great.

You've remained friends and have been dressing her for ten years?

I really have. I dressed her just recently for the Oscars. Whoopi has been a big supporter and I love her.

I remember also, from the very beginning, always seeing Christina Hendricks at your show.

Christina and I worked together for years. I dressed her for her first Emmys when *Mad Men* just started. Christina is amazing and has, like, the most gorgeous body in the world. I love making clothes for her.

Let's talk about your passion and commitment to embracing women and models who are not size 0, 2, 4, 6. In this Spring '17 show, you seriously added size inclusivity in your runway casting.

You not only had lots of plus-size girls, but male, transgender, and nonconforming gender models. Tell us how that came about?

I mean, we always had that customer. We've had customers of different sizes since day one. Some of our best customers are size 14 and 16, and always had been. In the beginning of my career, I was doing things that other people would accept more, because I was judged so much in the beginning. Then as it went on, I was like, "Well, I'm over this. I'm going to do

Christian Siriano and his muses celebrating the tenth anniversary of his brand in 2018.

what I want to do."

What was that moment that made you say, "I'm going to do this"?

I don't even know. It just started happening. I just started kind of doing my own thing. I was gaining success without certain things that maybe other designers needed. I think that was why I was able to make those decisions.

It was very frustrating to hear a woman say to us, "You don't have my size," or "You don't have something that I think I could wear." That was very frustrating to hear. I think that would be frustrating for any designer to hear.

You are the first one that embraced that, and not with just one girl walking on the runway.

Because you have to put it in people's faces, because we're in a visual world here. Your attention span is very short. Social media is changing everything. I put it on the runway. I put it on the red carpet. We put it out there in front of you because sometimes it really takes that to, like, get through to people's heads, because we're all stubborn, even myself. Yeah, that's kind of where that came from, I think.

You've said it basically tripled your business?

It makes the business, like, a totally different thing because you're opening up a huge category of people. It's awesome. I love it. It's just a feel-good thing, too. It feels great.

How much of your collection would you say is in that inclusive size range?

Honestly, I would say it's 50 percent of it now. Yeah, it's a lot. But it always kind of was. That's the interesting thing. It's just we really put it out there now.

The reason why it's growing so much is because now other retailers are on board. We got Moda Operandi to change their entire website to go up to size 26. They didn't do that before. Neiman Marcus doesn't even do that. There are a lot of retailers that still don't do that. Maybe they do now, but that was a few seasons ago.

It's still changing right now, which is crazy to me.

That's not easy, grading looks up to inclusive sizes?

No. It is a commitment, let me tell you. Your whole world has to be in it. Your whole team has to be on board. You've got to make sure everyone understands, because it's another process, for sure.

There are so many designers that are truly leaving money on the table by not doing this.

… And leaving making people feel great. I think the point of being a designer is to make people feel good in their clothes. We're not curing cancer here. We're making you look cute in a dress. So if you want to look cute in a dress and you're size 26, why not?

Does your size 26 cost more to make than your size 12?

It does, but we don't charge more for it.

That's extraordinary.

Yes. Everything costs more, for sure, because it's more fabric, it's more fitting, it's more time. But I would think that charging more would not make sense. So we don't.

Good for you.

[TO THE AUDIENCE] Right, Eva, we don't? Thanks. I'm kidding. I know.

Then you did two books. Your first book was *Fear Style: How to Be Your Most Fabulous Self*, filled with very amusing fashion tips.

The worst. Listen, that's the worst book ever written in the entire world. However, I went on *Oprah*. It sold out. Move on.

OK.

She's so mad at me.

That's perfect. I love it. You collaborated with Starbucks?

Yes. I did so many collaborators, Fern. We cannot list them. They are so weird. I did a holiday gift card. It was very beautiful. I was poor. I needed money.

… And you did fashion-themed sponges.

I did. I needed that check really bad. They were really cute, actually.

Do you still have them?

I do have them. Really cute.

You were named the youngest ever "40 Under 40" top entrepreneurs by *Crain's*. At that point, you were in business for only two years and doing $1.2 million. In 2012, the *New York Times* reported that you were doing about $5 million. Do you talk about your number?

Are we talking about money?

You don't have to.

But we don't need to talk about that. Who knows if it's better. I don't know.

What about the collaboration with Disney? That sounded very nice, doing costumes for the fairies in an animated film?

Yes, I did a bunch. It was called *The Pirate Fairy*, which is part of the Tinker Bell franchise.

I love Tinker Bell. Tinker Bell was my favorite.

She's the best. She's cute. She wears a green dress. Who doesn't love her? It was an amazing experience because whenever you are asked to do anything with Disney, and I've done a few partnerships with them, you just do it. It's Disney.

I remember going to Disney, and seeing the animators, and it was so inspiring. That day, they told me the voice of the fairy was Christina Hendricks, which I did not know. It was very full circle. It was really fun.

Tell us about a very special moment in 2016 when the Democratic National Convention [DNC] was on. You turned on the TV and your mother called you?

Yes, my mom told me that the lovely Mrs. Obama was wearing our dress at the DNC; it was so nice. We worked hard on those clothes, let me tell you…

Did you send her several things?

We made a lot of things. We dressed her about four times.

Was that the first time?

We made a lot of things and didn't know what they were for. You don't know; it's very hush-hush.

It wasn't actually the first time we dressed her. The first time was for a funeral. It's not like I was like, "Hey guys, this is looking cute." So that was sad. She looked divine, though, that day. But you couldn't really be like, "Hey, Mom!"

You didn't really want to post that.

I mean, I posted it. But I didn't, really, like, you know, give it its all, like we wanted to. But then she showed up at the DNC; it was an amazing moment. We just didn't know. Even when she walked out, she was so far away. I was like, "Are you sure?"

And that's working with Meredith Koop, Mrs. Obama's stylist. Did she come up and see things? I know she always changes things just a little bit so it's not something on the line.

That was a dress in our collection at the time, a version, I think. I loved working with her. She's amazing.

Then you also dressed another very famous woman: Barbie.

I love Barbie. Barbie is great.

What designer doesn't love Barbie?

I know. She's great. She's really amazing. We did Barbie. Barbie has new body types, which is amazing, finally.

Is there an inclusive-sized Barbie doll?

There is curvy, short, tall, different skin tones. It was amazing. I did them based on iconic red-carpet looks, just to celebrate that. It took them a while, but, you know, it's great.

You've been somewhat vocal on why you wouldn't dress Melania Trump.

Yes. What else you got? I don't need to answer that, do I? But I will.

Honestly, it's kind of like what I'm doing now. I've dressed her before. It's nothing about her personally. I think she is a very chic, elegant woman, trapped in a weird world. But I think it's very, very important for anyone doing anything, to work with people who are following the

same support system and the same beliefs that you're working with.

I wouldn't work with an artist, or a musician, or a singer, or an actress who doesn't support gay people. It's the same thing, and unfortunately, she's in that camp that doesn't support certain people. I'm a young, gay, male fashion designer, so it would be hard to dress someone that is in that world that doesn't believe in that. That's really what it is.

Fair enough. In November of last year you published your second book with Rizzoli: *Dresses to Dream About*.

Yes. Gorgeous. It also sold out. Thank you. We tried. That's all I got.

I was so proud of that book because my first book was so ugly, and horrible, and disastrous. I really just wanted a visual world to show beautiful things that we worked really hard on for the last ten years. It was amazing. I think it turned out really beautiful. I think that for anybody who loves fashion, you get to see how we literally start a dress with a sketch, to the end. I think that's really kind of cool to see.

It's a beautiful coffee table book, even if you don't care. It's pink, it's pretty, it looks cute on the table.

One of the things I always remember is going backstage to your shows before the show started, and there are always one or two dresses that take up half the stage.

Yes, massive tulle dresses, yes.

Massive. You wonder, "How did he get that in here?" It's really a statement.

Yes, and that's why through the whole book there's a range of that. There's even pieces that have never been worn. Michelle's dress is in there. Leslie's dress is in there. It really is like a range of all different things that we've done over the years. I still love those fantasy ballerina ball gowns because that was kind of where I started.

Just three months ago you opened your gorgeous new store, The Curated NYC?

Yes, we decided to try the new world of retail because it's very intense out there right now. I think it was really important to bring it back to the customer a little bit more. I love that it feels kind of like the old atelier style. That you feel something personal. It feels like you're walking into your friend's dream closet. I really wanted that feeling. I think some retail places right now feel very cold and unwelcoming.

You can come in there, and, literally, if you have twenty dollars, get an item. Or if you have $50,000, you come as well. We will accommodate everyone. I hope everyone feels like they get the same treatment because that is the idea there.

This is in the most beautiful mansion just off Fifth Avenue on 54th Street. It used to be the office of Cary Grant, so it has a nice history. I loved watching your Instagram feed as all this dark wood was painted white. It's very white and very fresh.

Very fresh. You just feel like you're in a jewel box. It's like Barbie's Dream House, going back to Barbie. It's nice. We carry other brands.

Tell us about the other brands. That's very clever, because you have other peoples' accessories and clothes.

The idea was a mini department store, but curated by designers. There's no buyer dictating what goes in the store anymore.

You dictate?

I don't, no.

Then who decides what's in there?

Whatever the brand wants to put out, they put out.

They have their spot?

Yes, their space. I mean, I give my opinions. But really, I wanted us all to feel like we could have a place to be open. They can change out their pieces every single day if they wanted to. I think that is very important in retail right now, that we can't be enclosed by a buyer that

Opposite: Christian Siriano with Barbie dolls based on his most memorable runway looks in 2017. This page: The Curated, featuring Christian's inclusive-sized collection with 11 Honoré. Next spread: Behind the scenes at Christian's 2020 fashion show at Gotham Hall.

sits in an office every day and is just looking at numbers. It's really hard for young brands to grow that way. I think that that was why I wanted to try this. We'll see how it goes. We've been literally open less than two months.

… And how is business?

You know, we'll see. I hope it goes good. Anyone want to come in and shop, please?

Are you still opening a café on the roof with Alicia Silverstone?

Yes, we will. Probably next summer. She's real busy, you know. Actresses…

She has an amazing vegan lifestyle brand called the Kind Life. It's like good food, don't get scared, it's amazing home-cooked food. That's the vibe.

But to your point, the store has everything, like fragranced candles…

There's everything. Fern, thank you for selling it.

It's lovely. I came to the opening and Christian was moving around these enormous orchid plants that Heidi sent for the opening.

She did. I'm like, "Honey, those orchids were so much money, you could have bought a dress." I hope she's watching this.

You didn't tell her that though.

I will. I love when I get big flowers like that, though. Every time I'm like, "These flowers were, like, $2,000, can you buy a dress?" But I still like flowers, so if you want to send me them…

You were featured in *Time*'s "100 Most Influential People in the World." The only other designer this year was Virgil Abloh.

Pretty cool. It's me, Oprah, and cool people.

How does that happen?

Yes, they just, like, literally send you an email. It's still a little weird.

How did that make you feel?

It feels really great. It definitely feels like all the hard work and all the craziness are worth something for a minute.

I mean, that is a real validation.

It was really, really nice, yes. To be in that room with those type of people, because it's such amazing types of people from all over the world. That was really wonderful to be a part of. Mine was for reshaping fashion.

Didn't you take Leslie Jones with you?

I did. She screamed all night at J.Lo. It was hilarious. She went to J.Lo's concert in Vegas and screamed so much that J.Lo was like, "I love you; please come and dance with me."

First they put us at a front table. We were so close to her. It was too aggressive. Also, I don't think Jennifer knew that everyone would be so close. Her outfit was a Vegas outfit, so it was very revealing. Leslie was into it.

I was like, "Leslie, should we pull it back?" She was screaming, "No!" Screaming. It was like when she came to my show, she thought she was at the Knicks game, she didn't know. For real. I invited her to that show, and she said, "I've never been to a fashion show before, baby." She

Previous page: Leslie Jones at the premiere of *Ghostbusters* in 2016. This page, clockwise from top: Janelle Monáe leaving the Mark Hotel for the 2019 Met Gala; Coco Rocha and Selma Blair celebrating Christian Siriano's book, *Dresses to Dream About*, in 2017; Alicia Silverstone and Debra Messing at the opening of The Curated.

was screaming so intensely and she was like, "Who's there? I thought it was your friends."
She literally sat across from the *New York Times* and *Vogue*. I don't think she understood. But it made it so amazing because it was just genuine, real realness. Fashion Week can be quite hard for everyone because we're all tired. It was really just a great day.

Were you hysterical backstage?

I thought someone fell at first because she was screaming so intensely. Then I was really nervous because I thought it would be, you know, really disruptive. I thought people would be really annoyed. But then I just think people felt her energy...

... You could not *not* be caught up in her enthusiasm.

... Her amazing energy; it was so beautiful to see. It felt really good.

It was like a Knicks game. It was extraordinary.

It was. I was like, "All right, girl." Please watch it. It's so hilarious. Just for five minutes.

It's hysterical.

What are the cards that you just got?

These are questions from the audience. We'll get to that in about two minutes.

Oh, really?

What is your dream now for Christian Siriano the brand?

I mean, that is a question. The dream is to just keep it going. That is the daily dream, to keep it going, keep it developing, trying new things. We take a lot of risks every single day with what we do. Some work out. Some do not. So, yes.

How important is social media to your business? You have about 900,000 followers. Will you have a party when you hit a million?

I mean, it's fine. It is important, annoyingly. It is all-consuming. I appreciate social media. I appreciate what it does, but I definitely think it's very important that people know that there is a whole other world outside of it. Our biggest customers that we have in the world are not on Instagram. It's not always a real thing, too. People have to think about that.

But it is important, and I understand the importance of it.

I read that you spend a great deal of money on Federal Express?

Listen, FedEx is really the devil.

This is because he is sending so much clothing to stylists and celebrities.

We dressed almost twenty people at the Oscars. Amy Adams isn't paying for her box, so we have to pay for it. You think Lady Gaga is paying for her messenger service? No! I've got to pay for it.

Is there a point where you say, "I can't do any more?"

Yes. We do. You cannot do it all. We physically cannot do it all. We get requests all the time, every single day, all day long. It's awesome. Thank you so much, everyone.

But you just can't. No business could ever sustain that unless you are Christian Dior, because it's so hard. Half the time they do not get worn. It is back and forth, back and forth, back and forth.

What happens with the dresses? Do the celebrities pay to send them back?

It depends. More and more, we are getting a little tougher. Also, when more people wear your things, it's a little easier to be tougher.

Are a lot of these relationships with the stylists or with the celebrities directly?

It's all of the above. It's a mix, yes. I mean, I have great relationships with my friends. Stylists, you know, we have a love-hate relationship with them.

Is there any really fun story you could share about doing a dress with somebody?

Not a fun story. They're all horrible.

They're all horrible?

Yes, they're all the worst. They're never fun. Two of my team members literally just flew to Morocco for a day, to go fit a gown, and they found out the day before. We do crazy things.

You have a good travel agent.

They're all very good at it. The things that go on are really mind-blowing. We've flown around the world to fit things, and fix things, and it's nuts… all for, like, a great five seconds on a red carpet that goes away tomorrow. So sad.

Is there one story that is the most outrageous example of that?

Oh, God, I don't know. I do move on real quick, because it really makes me intense. But actually, that's my really good talent. I actually have an ability to move on very quickly from a bad scenario. I think that's actually what's helped us kind of keep it going because otherwise I definitely would have a breakdown for sure, every day.

How do you like to relax?

I don't know.

Do you binge-watch TV? Do you cook?

I love an antiques store. I love a tchotchke, you know, little things everywhere. I like to chill. I have a beautiful house in Connecticut that I love. It's like my little escape, and that's kind of it. I buy art.

My whole world is this world. Even when it's not, it is. Even when I'm watching TV, I'm like, "Oh, God, I just dressed her, she was annoying." You know, it's like a plague against me. That's the challenge now, when you're really in it.

Is there any advice you would give to young designers?

I have lots of advice. Try to really find out what you love. Meaning, if you are all about evening wear and that's what you love to do, make sure it's the best it can be. Do not try to do a million different versions of that. I think being really focused right now is very important in our business because there are so many brands out there.

We're all competing for the same thing. I think it's important for any young designer to be very focused on what is their full passion.

That leads to one of the questions from the audience. What is the worst piece of advice you've received?

Oh, my God, I get horrible advice every day. Usually the advice is to not do something.

… Like send somebody to Morocco for a day?

Yes. Somebody should have told me not to do that. But it's fine.

I think the worst advice would be when people say, "Don't partner with this person. Don't dress that person." I hate getting that, but I try to not pay attention too much.

OK. Is there someone, dead or alive, who you would like to dress?

I get that question a lot. I actually have had a little bit of a thing where I've never put it out there that I had to dress this person, which is why I think I've been successful in dressing mostly everybody I wanted to dress in my head. I maybe did that early on, but I just don't do that anymore. I'm a big fan of Cate Blanchett and I haven't done anything for her, so that would be nice. But I don't think about it as much. You would be surprised.

Have you thought about creating a men's collection?

I have. I would love to do men's. That will be in the works one day soon, I hope. Oh, God, men are so boring, though. What do they wear? I wear the same thing every day. It's horrible.

But not so much now. The men's market is evolving.

Listen, I would love to. I really, really would. We do men's somewhat in the collection, because our clothes are kind of for everyone. I think if you want to wear that [POINTING AT HIS MODELS IN DRESSES] or this [POINTING TO HIS BLAZER], you should be able to.

Do you feel jealousy or competition from other designers or is it supportive in your business?

It's two things. There are people that are supportive, for sure. There really are. Then there are people that are really not. It's kind of like a full spectrum. There's not a lot of middle.

Again, it is a very intense business. It's really hard to get people to fall in love with your clothes, season after season. We're all competing for the same thing, in the same world. It can be tough, for sure. I'm sure there's so many designers that hate everything I do, but that's OK.

Are there some members of the fashion press that you're still trying to conquer?

This page: Christian Siriano producing face masks in his sample room during the COVID19 pandemic in 2020. Next spread: The season 18 cast of *Project Runway*: Brandon Maxwell, Karlie Kloss, Christian Siriano, Nina Garcia, Elaine Welteroth.

ARTHUR ELGORT

Arthur Elgort is one of those people that makes you smile when you see him. I've known him since my career started at Mademoiselle magazine, where he also started his career. Arthur's work changed the way people relate to fashion photography. As Robin Givhan, the Pulitzer Prize–winning fashion critic of the Washington Post, wrote when Arthur was honored with the CFDA Board of Directors Award in 2011:

"Instead of depicting models as perfect swans with their heads tilted just so, or as haughty mannequins both inaccessible and unbelievable, he turned a journalistic eye on them and their impractical clothes. He caught them in mid-stride, engaged in gossip, or head tossed back in raucous laughter.

For other photographers, models arched their backs and posed. For Elgort, they twirled and leapt. Their haphazard, sometimes awkward, energy made them seem imperfect and alive, endearing and captivating."

He took the models out of the studio. They were on the street and in the cafés, doing what normal people do. Arthur just happened to be there, like an eavesdropper with a camera. He was more of a choreographer, which is appropriate, as his love of dance has been an important influence on his work.

But for Arthur, it's all about family. He said his kids made him more enthusiastic. They are his best subjects. He practices on them. In fact he practices his craft all the time. It's why he loves shooting dancers, because they practice all the time and are always moving.

As Wynton Marsalis, who wrote the foreword to Arthur's book Jazz said, "Elgort's work is executed at the speed of instinct. The range and depth of the feelings in his photographs tell you that he is himself a jazz man, with the same understanding, intention and mythology."

Let's meet the nicest photographer in the business, Arthur Elgort.

ARTHUR ELGORT: I can't see you all, but hello. You know, you can't see the audience from here.

FERN MALLIS: It's better that way.

Really? Because I'll know everybody here.

That's right, and then you'll be making eye contact with them and not with me. You'll be talking to them.

When Arthur insisted on coming out with his bag around his arm, I said, "You're like Aretha Franklin, you need to have the bag with all the money in your line of sight." It's currency for you.

Yes, this is money [HOLDING HIS CAMERA BAG].

Thank you for being here, Arthur. We always start my interviews at the beginning. The

very beginning. We begin on June 8, 1940. That makes you seventy-eight years old.

Do I feel seventy-eight? No, I feel seventy-five.

OK. He's a little bit younger. You are a Gemini. Do you believe in astrology?

No, but my sister does. Once in a while she'll say, "Don't do anything today because it's going to be bad." But that's about it.

Well, that's good. Let me tell you what some of the Gemini strengths are: gentle, affectionate, curious, adaptable, versatile, enthusiastic, soft-spoken.

No.

None of those?

Not loud?

Witty and humorous, intellectual, a wordsmith…

Who is that? I don't even know what it means. I went to PS187 and they didn't teach me that.

Some of the weaknesses of Geminis are: nervous, inconsistent, indecisive, lacks direction, anxious . .

It must be a rising sign that we don't know.

All right. We'll cancel that. We'll have to get your real chart done. Some of the famous Geminis are: Kanye West, Johnny Depp, Marilyn Monroe, Naomi Campbell.

They're crazy, all of them. I mean, nice people, but crazy. Really crazy.

JFK.

I didn't know him well.

Bob Dylan.

I'd like to know Bob Dylan.

Prince, Patti LaBelle, and Gladys Knight.

I like all those.

OK. That feels good. Were you born in Brooklyn or in Washington Heights?

Washington Heights. I forget the address, it was 740-something. I forget the name of it. I went there with my son once and he said, "Where's the doorman, there's no doorman?"

I said, "We don't have a doorman. You open the door yourself."

He said, "That's not good. I like the Eldorado [an Upper West Side building] better." We moved into the Eldorado.

That was a good reason. We're going to cancel Brooklyn, but that comes up in lots and lots of press. I think it's a Wikipedia mistake.

Well, they are wrong. I wouldn't listen to Wikipedia.

Tell us all about your parents: Sophie and Harry. Was it a "When Harry Met Sophie" kind of relationship?

Yes. They met when Sophie was a soda jerk and Harry thought she was cute. He tipped her a lot until he went out with her, and then he didn't have to anymore.

Then he lived with her instead. Then they had Bob, me, and Joan. I'm in the middle.

You're in the middle. I'm a middle child, too. Your dad had a restaurant?

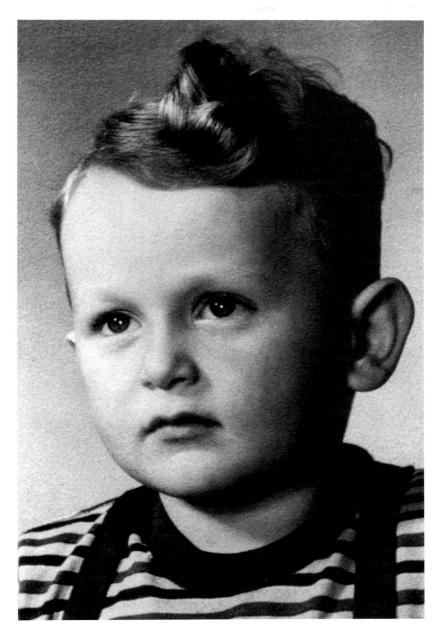

Clockwise from top: Arthur Elgort as a child; Arthur at his bar mitzvah; Arthur and his siblings, Joan and Bob Elgort.

Yes. A sportsman's bar. It was by the old Madison Square Garden. It was on 50th Street. He had a bar, and beautiful steak, and lamb chops that were very good.

Well, for sports guys you need steak.

Not only that, they put in the bone so you could touch it and eat it. What is it called? [tomahawk]

Was your father a foodie or was he was more of the business guy?

He was a business guy and he was called "Harry the Horse." Have you heard that?

No [LAUGHTER].

He was a character in Damon Runyon's play, what do you call that? *Guys and Dolls!*

He was the person whom they named it after. He wasn't in it himself. Grethe [Barrett Holby, Arthur's wife] took him there and saw it onstage.

He really could punch well, because he had a "drunk eye." He knew how to strike! Left hand! [PUNCHING MOTION] And then there! [PUNCHING MOTION] He was very strong.

So, a little acting is in the family genes?

He's a little bit like Ansel [Elgort, Arthur's son]. A little bit. Ansel didn't know him well. I don't think Ansel was born. I'm not sure. I can't see Ansel anywhere. Nothing [WAVING INTO THE AUDIENCE].

He's over there.

There! Oh, I see him. But anyway, that's what happened.

Were you a close-knit family growing up?

No, we never saw Harry because he worked all the time, except Sundays. He would go [WAGGING HIS FINGER], "Don't tell me your name. You're Arthur, right?"

I said, "Yes. Great, you got it!"

Then he said, "I got it. Could you leave me alone now because I'm reading the *New York Times*. He would go like this [CROSSING HIS LEGS], and he would read the *Times*.

I said, "Can I go?"

He said "Yes. But I got your name right?"

From left to right: Arthur Elgort and his mother, Sophie; Arthur with his father, Harry.

Yes, exactly. Julie Ander was terrific and loaned me cameras all the time. She got me interested in graphics.

Where was she a salesman?

It was called Wollman's Camera Store. It was on 60th Street, and close, so I could walk there and come back with a camera… and then I became a photographer.

You were self-taught with your Nikon?

Yes, more or less. But I didn't know how to roll reels yet. I would take them to someone else to roll. But then film was so expensive that I learned how to roll reels. I used to buy bulk film. I didn't buy film in a holder, I bought it. I made my own holder.

That's interesting. I didn't know you could do that. Now, is your little Minolta your favorite camera?

No, not anymore, because it's broken a little bit. I have to get a new one. I like digital ones because if you don't like it [the photo], you can throw it away quickly and you can make believe you never took it. I can go, "No, that was Warren [Elgort, Arthur's son] using my camera," but it was me.

I like digital. But I like big cameras, too. I like 4 x 5 cameras. If someone has any influence here, somebody tell them to make 4 x 5 cameras again. Big cameras and Polaroids. I'm going to talk to Eric about that, because I think he could make a fortune out of it. I'll buy it from you, and I won't ask for a discount, either.

A business opportunity here.

Yes.

But you used your camera really to meet girls, and became the unofficial official photographer at Hunter.

Yes, because there were only two cameras in the school. We didn't have the phones then, what do you call that? Phones that take photos…

iPhones.

Yes, we didn't have that.

You had a girlfriend who was a dancer at school?

Way back. Even before I was taking pictures.

But there are a lot of dancers in your family, because your son Ansel's girlfriend, Violetta Komyshan, is a dancer, too. It all keeps coming full circle.

You also always give people you photograph a print. That was very generous of you.

You should, though. I mean, you took their picture. It's good. You should give them something. Don't you think?

I think that's wonderful. You learned how to develop the prints?

Everything. Everything.

Then how did you start your career when you got out of college?

First I decided I wanted to be a den photographer, but then I realized they had less money than me. They just point. They had spent all their money on a point. I became a fashion photographer instead. A different school, but it's good, and I met pretty girls all the time.

One of your first jobs was with *McCall's* and you took photographs of Clive Barnes, who was the dance critic?

Yes, and I did it twice because the first time wasn't too good. I had him on the couch and he's a kind of a fat guy. I said, "Can I do it again?"

He said, "Sure. Do it again." I waited until the snow happened. He was teaching at NYU. I was in Washington Square Park. I did it there and that was pretty good.

But my break was *Mademoiselle* magazine, because they had the best editors, best photographers I could think of. Gus Peterson, who's dead now, he was a terrific guy.

Were you an assistant to him?

Yes, I worked with him.

… And he was married to Pat Peterson, a great lady also. That was my era at *Mademoiselle* magazine. Just when you started there. I was a guest editor, and I was assigned to Roger Schoening, who was the art director. You were like an up-and-coming photographer.

Yes, and they gave me a chance. The first pictures I did for him were called "Hangouts."

Tell us what that was.

The models, I had picked them out myself. Then it was very normal because *Mademoiselle* was very avant-garde.

It was a great magazine.

Yes. I had to shoot it in an Automat, Horn & Hardart. Then I was in Katz's Delicatessen. Then I was at a place called Eduardo's on Second Avenue. I did Susan Forristal there.

… And so you picked out the locations, all the hangouts, and the models, and you got twelve pages, and the cover?

You know what was funny? They gave the credit to George Barkentin, because he worked more than I did. I took the picture of Bonnie Lysohir, but they wrote George Barkentin. Not only that, they sent him the check.

I said, "That's my picture. I would like that money." I got it.

They corrected it then. That's crazy. I remember as a guest editor, they threw us a huge party in George Barkentin's studio. It was in a great building on Sixth Avenue.

He was a wonderful guy, and his daughter was terrific, too, Pam Barkentin.

Yes, we were all friendly there.

That was a great start for you, and that magazine was great. You didn't really do *Glamour* then, because if you were at *Mademoiselle* you didn't do *Glamour*.

No, in fact, Miki Denhof, who was the art director of *Glamour* said, "I only made one mistake in my life. I didn't choose you. I let you go to *Mademoiselle*, and that was a mistake because you turned out to be good." We were friendly after that. I worked for *Mademoiselle*, which was freer. The other magazine was more money.

Some of the other models that you basically discovered and put on the map: Lisa Taylor,

Clockwise from top: A behind-the-scenes-look at Arthur Elgort and Polly Mellen working with *Vogue* art director Richard Schoening; Susan Hess in Egypt for *Vogue* Italia, 1981; Christy Turlington at La Coupole in Paris for British *Vogue*, 1988. Page 323: Arthur and Christy.

Apollonia van Ravenstein, Patti Hansen, Roseanne Vela.

You got it, and they came out good. I couldn't complain about them.

There's a lot of people here: Michelle Stevens, Karen Bjornson… Oh, there she is! You came late, so you didn't get a good seat [POINTING IN THE AUDIENCE].

Then there was a moment when Grace Mirabella, who was the editor of *Vogue*, asked you to see a girl that she thought you might like and she turned out to be Christie Brinkley.

Yes. But she worked more for *Glamour* than for me.

Why is Christy Turlington your favorite model?

Because she's so beautiful, and she listens, because she had a family that listened. Her father was a pilot and her mother was a stewardess, and they listened. If you have Christy Turlington, you get good seats all the time because she knew all the people at Pan Am. I don't know if it exists anymore. I'm looking for it in the pages and I can't find it.

You said that she flies well.

You got there and she was ready to work, because she flies well.

Right. When you were working at *Mademoiselle*, were you working with Nonnie Moore as the fashion editor?

Yes, but she didn't do sittings. I worked with Deborah Turbeville. She wanted to be a photographer. I don't know what happened, but she lives in a good place called San Miguel de Allende. She was a nice person, but she didn't know how to iron. She would send all the cleaning out to the tailor, and they would bring it back, and then she would shoot it because she couldn't iron.

It's an important skill to have.

But I can't iron, either. I mean, without Eli, our housekeeper, I would be in trouble.

Was Alex Liberman instrumental in your work?

Alexander Liberman was the most important guy I knew at the time. He came to me and said, "You're doing too well at *Mademoiselle*. I want you to throw the job."

That was still one of the magazines in his purview.

But it's not *Vogue*. I said "I've got a better idea, move me to *Vogue*. I'll do *Vogue* instead and screw *Mademoiselle*, right?"

I moved to *Vogue* and I'm still there, well, no, not anymore. I guess I did something wrong, but I don't know what. I don't know still. But anyway, I worked for *Vogue* for a long time and I had a great editor named Grace Coddington. She is in the audience somewhere, we know, and she's the best editor you can have.

As long as you remember, full length first. You have to do full length and, then you can come in. But you have to be quick.

You and Grace traveled the world together?

More or less. We went to China a few times. All the time with good models, usually Christy Turlington, Linda Evangelista, or Carmen Dell'Orefice, and a redhead, somebody named Karen Elson. Grace likes redheaded girls. I don't know why. I haven't figured that out yet. But every time I get a redhead, I send her to Grace.

She's the best editor, and if you can work for Grace Coddington, you got it made. We should have a magazine called Grace Coddington, could we do that? I would buy that magazine.

Was it at *Vogue* when you started working with Christiaan [Houtenbos]?

No, I worked with him at *Mademoiselle* first, and he used to wear a suit.

Christiaan? I don't remember him ever wearing a suit.

No, it's true. He had one suit and he looked good in it. He's very dandy. He used to wear ties. I knew him then. That's a long time ago. I don't think you were born yet.

You've been working together your whole careers.

Yes, but he dropped me, because I was a troublemaker and he got more money from other shoots. Because I didn't make money. I just shoot good pictures. That's not a living.

It's the big ad campaigns that make money. When did you begin working with Christiaan's wife, Marianne [Houtenbos], who is your agent?

They had a place way up in the sky, right across the street from Lincoln Center. I went there and I met Marianne, who was normal, I couldn't believe it. I said, "How did you get Christiaan?" We didn't talk about that. But Marianne has been wonderful. Not only that she is the best art director. The new *Jazz* book is made by Marianne only. I have to give her credit. I did the pictures but I'm not a good art director, and she's mean. She'll say, "This is nice, keep it for yourself. Now show me another one."

She knew how to get the best out of you.

Yes, and she's still with me. She learns some more tricks every day.

When and where did you meet Grethe Barrett Holby?

I met her at a dance. Grethe has a sister named Clotilde Holby who used to be a model. Now she's a book designer, very good, talented, beautiful books. I met Grethe through her, and her boyfriend then. We got along because I could do the Lindy Hop and nobody else was that old and could do the Lindy Hop. Grethe could do a very good Lindy Hop.

This was at Xenon, when you first met?

Yes, and we haven't gone back since.

Do you remember your first date, when you went to see *The Nutcracker*? It was around the holidays.

Yes, yes. We had a wonderful time and before we knew it we were married, and, you know, we had kids. That's what happens.

But I read that your future sister-in-law Clotilde and Jacques Malignon, the photographer, said that you were both snobs because you liked music and dance.

Terrible, yes. We were very snobby.

Now your wife is doing opera and…

… And basketball. [for *Bounce: The Basketball Opera*] You get a basket, you sing, or something like that. It's not only that, but it's very good music, I must say. I didn't produce it.

Well, I know she's working on that because I have talked to her about it. I see her at basketball games all the time.

… And not only that, if you have money send it to Grethe. She needs money for that.

We'll have to create another campaign for that. You got married in 1983 and you were forty-three at the time.

I was old.

You were old?

… But I had a good time.

What took you so long to get married?

Because I was having too much fun. Why get married if you're having fun?

Tell us about how you met and worked with George Balanchine [the cofounder of the New York City Ballet]?

That was Willie [Wilhelmina] Frankfurt. She introduced me to George Balanchine because she knew his secretary, Barbara Organ.

I only showed him "*Vogue*-y" pictures. He didn't like sloppy pictures. I only showed him that, and he said, "Oh, you could be good, so I am going to give you a riddle. I'm going to give you Patty McBride, Nina Fedorova, and Merrill Ashley. If you can do those well, you got the job." I said, "Well, yes, I can do them. Do you want me to do any of the men?"

He said, "Men are not important, they hold the girls up, that's all. They're not important. So we don't worry about that."

That worked for you.

I liked that idea. I liked George, we got along well. In fact, the first time I took Grethe to something, George Balanchine was getting out of the car and I said, "George Balanchine!" and Grethe was, like, "You know George Balanchine?"

I said, "Do I know him? I know him personally, like that" [CROSSING HIS FINGERS].

She said, "I love you now. You must be good if you know George Balanchine."

This page, clockwise from top: Arthur Elgort and his sons, Warren and Ansel Elgort; Arthur and Grethe Barrett Holby with daughter Sophie, son-in-law Eric, and grandchildren Stella and Artie Von Stroh in 2020.

Anyway, what's funny is when I met George Balanchine with Grethe, he never looked at me once. He only looked at Grethe and said, "Oh, you're a dancer. Good legs. You've got a good body; maybe you want to be in my company?"

He didn't look at me at all, so he's not that friendly. He liked women better than men. That happens sometimes.

Well, that would be bonding for you with him. You were also a jazz musician and played the trumpet.

Terrible trumpet player. I mean, so bad. I finally gave it up because it was driving me crazy. I listen to Louis Armstrong still today, and Clifford Brown, that's my favorite. Wynton Marsalis, of course, because he did the foreword in my book and he's also a wonderful guy.

I meant to ask you when we're talking about Balanchine, are you still doing a book on ballet dancers?

Yes, it's at the printer. The printer is called Steidl, which is the best printer, but he never comes out with books on time. If you're still alive when I'm dead, you could get that book. Maybe he'll do it in ten years from now. It could be a collector's item, really.

Tell us about the memorable shoot you did in China for *Vogue*, which was still rather exotic at the time, shooting Nancy Kissinger. Alex Liberman was quoted as saying, "Arthur was the only one who could get the shot on the run."

That's true, and Nancy Kissinger was a wonderful girl and funny as can be. It was still very Chinese then. It was run by, not Mao [Zedong] anymore. They were all…

… Wearing the same things, those blue suit jackets.

Which was good for photographs because everybody looked like Karl Lagerfeld, you know? They looked alike, so it's wonderful to take pictures there, and everybody wore red, no green...

Blue.

Blue. Blue all over the place. So I put them all together, and Nancy Kissinger. You saw her because she was much taller than anybody else. There was a bodyguard there. I think Henry [Kissinger] sent the bodyguard with a gun.

I said, "Don't pull the gun here. You'll be in trouble."

They followed orders.

Nancy Kissinger was so funny because she knew where the bugs were. I would look up and see a plant. She said, "That's not a plant. That's a camera recording."

Nancy Kissinger said, "Now listen to me: we had a wonderful time in China, and we love Beijing, and we love everything about China."

Then we would go in the car, and she always had a crappy car because she didn't want attention. We go in the car, and she would say, "You know, we had to say that. You know that?" She knew what she was doing.

She was married to a diplomat.

Yes, and thank God. Then we stayed in Japan. Anne Kampmann was the editor. I said, "Why don't we take Polly?"

This page, clockwise from top: Arthur Elgort and Grethe Barrett Holby dancing on the deck of their Southampton home on their wedding day in 1983; Grethe and Arthur share a kiss and some bubbly. Page 332: Arthur taking a selfie in 1978. Pages 334–335: Ansel and Warren Elgort, Matthew Avedon, and Stella Tenant for *Vogue*, 2001.

… And Alexander Liberman said, "We finally made peace with China, we don't need another war on our hands." Polly Mellen didn't make the trip.

Anne is so sweet and nice, so we had no trouble. Then we had to meet Nancy Kissinger to make sure we were all right. Her favorite was Christiaan because she liked cool guys. Before you knew it, they were buying screens and sending them there, and there, and there. They were friends.

Let's talk a little bit about your family, which plays a very important role in your life. You got married late, so how soon after you got married did you start having your three children, who were all four years apart?

I think Sophie was three years after? If I'm wrong I'm sorry, Sophie. But she's the oldest girl but she doesn't look old. If you look at her face, I mean, she looks like a teenager to me.

Then Warren came and he was younger than Sophie, and good looking also, and very good at picture taking.

Then Ansel, now he's acting. You never know, it may come out to something, who knows?

You were quoted as saying that they all pay their own rent now, and they've moved on.

Well, they don't pay me anything, but that would be nice if they did. But they could think about it. They're so nice, I must say.

Ansel is the best cook. If it doesn't work out in acting, he could be a very good cook. He has this girl named Violetta, who's a very good cook, too. They make meals. I mean, it's like going to a four-star restaurant. They come a lot to the Hamptons, so I use them. I say, "Make me good fish for a change."

Ansel's career has really taken off and he was nominated for a Golden Globe for *Baby Driver*.

He should have won that. He should have won everything. But there was a guy in there that ruined it for him. I think he's a great actor.

… And coming full circle with Leonard Bernstein, Ansel has just been given the role of a lifetime to play Tony in the upcoming film that Steven Spielberg's going to do of *West Side Story*.

I couldn't even get that! That's pretty good. That didn't happen in a minute. He had to work for that role.

And he's going to sing and dance.

Now? He's coming up to sing and dance now? Should we move back?

No.

We could bring him up here, and he could dance and do all those tricks. We could move back, come on! He'll come up!

We'll do it another time.

OK.

Move your seat up a little, I want you here in the good light. Warren's a filmmaker.

Yes, and a very good one.

Sophie is a great photographer. Do you give her advice?

She doesn't need advice. She's better than me already. But she likes my pictures, because she bought some from me.

She bought some from you?

She didn't buy them. She kind of borrowed them. But she has a beautiful apartment, and Eric, too. They live together.

Her husband.

They have a beautiful baby called Stella, who looks just like Sophie. It's like going to visit Sophie when she was a child. I mean, amazing. But she didn't come to this because she had a previous date. But usually, she's here. We would have her in a carriage here, and she's usually quiet.

She's adorable and anybody who follows Sophie on Instagram will see all the adorable pictures of Stella.

So that keeps you taking baby pictures all the time, which is such an important part of your life. The book that Arthur did about his children is really worth seeing. Every picture in this book is extraordinary. Three gorgeous blond, perfectly beautiful children. They are beautiful photos.

… And we made them ourselves. We didn't buy them. They are not from Russia or something like that.

That book is called *Camera Ready: How to Shoot Your Kids*. Because they were always photographed so much by you, I think that's an important part of their careers. They're very comfortable in front of the camera, and behind the camera; it has helped all three of them.

Ansel especially; he's used to having the cameras there all the time. He's very good at taking … [MOTIONING HIS HANDS IN FRONT OF HIM]

Selfies.

Yes. I can't do selfies at all. I can't figure it out.

I know every time I see Ansel, we give him the camera because he's got the longest arms and he is really good at it. But you take a lot of pictures of yourself, though, in the mirror.

Well, I love myself, so what the hell. If nobody's around and I need a picture taken every day to keep in shape, right? So, I take it myself.

Maybe I'll put a jacket on, or a hat on, or something different, and pray that it comes out, and sometimes it…

… Usually does.

Yeah, not bad.

Let's talk a little bit about social media and iPhones, which you don't carry. But now everyone is a photographer. How do you think that's changed the profession?

Well, you don't need me, you can do it yourself. Which is nice. You can save money.

This page: Arthur and Sophie Elgort on set. Next spread: Kate Moss at Brasserie Lipp for *Vogue* Italia, 1993. Pages 342–343: Lisa Taylor crossing the George Washington Bridge for *Vogue*, 1976.

It's not the same, though. What do you think is going to happen to those billions of photographs people take? They are in iPhones and computers and nobody prints them out. There is something sad about the fact that they're all out there, and no one is printing pictures and making albums.

I have a digital camera. I save it, then I edit it, and I still print it out and give a copy to you. Like, now I have to do Violetta, I have to give her prints because she did photos in a dress that she looked wonderful in, so I have to give the picture to her.

Great.

They will not get it until next weekend. Southampton has the best photo printer. She is called Mary Godfrey, and she's a good printer. She has the right machine. She does wonderful stuff. So I wait for her.

What do you think about how they don't hire models unless they have a huge number of followers on Instagram?

Oh, I don't know. I mean, I find them myself still today. Pretty girls, you just have to give them a chance.

You photographed Melania Trump.

Once, and she was very nice girl. I don't know if she knew what she was marrying into because that guy is crazy, for sure. But Melania Trump is not bad. She just picked the wrong guy.

Did I read he [Donald Trump] owes you money? He didn't pay you for it.

Yes. He was supposed to pay me. I did a picture for him, and he didn't have any money, so I never got paid.

You're on the list of people he owes money to.

Yes, but it was just like a hundred dollars. It wasn't much. But he couldn't pay me, because he didn't have any cash. It's all credit.

Do you still believe in the tips and advice that was in your *Models Manual* book? You said, "Don't cancel a booking once you've said yes."

That's true.

"Learn to act like someone else, but also be yourself."

Yes, that's true.

"Don't bite your nails."

No, it's not good for your nails. I see that right away. I say, "Those are terrible nails, go back and get a … " What do you call it?

Manicure.

Yes, manicure. That's what it's called.

"Be on time."

That's a nice idea. The best at that was Cindy Crawford.

She is always on time.

Amazing. She never was late. In fact, I would come to the studio, and she would be there and say, "Where have you been? I'm ready to shoot." She's a wonderful girl, and her daughter [Kaia Gerber] is pretty good herself. I think she's making some money, too.

I don't know if you're still doing this, a book on nudes and partnering with Karl Lagerfeld?

No, that's not true. I didn't do nudes of Karl Lagerfeld.

No, not…

Not my type, first of all…

… I don't think we want to see Karl Lagerfeld nude.

No, I don't want to see him nude. You know, I would like to see him and André [Leon Talley] together. André and Karl Lagerfeld, you should interview them together on the stage.

Well, I did André, but not Karl.

Well, go and get Karl for sure. Both are nice people.

But I like girls better than boys. I can't help it. Something is the matter with me. I went to a psychiatrist to fix that and they couldn't help me. They said, "You like women better than men." I said, "Yes."

They said, "That's not good."

There's not a book coming out with nude portraits?

Yes, there is, and it's beautiful.

How do you feel in today's climate with #metoo, and several of your professional colleagues being banished?

I'm just taking nude pictures. I'm not sleeping with them or anything, that I know of. I think it's fine. It's a nice book. You have to see it. Steve Hiett did the art direction. It's wonderful.

When is that book going to come out?

I would say in a year.

Well, that'll be a good party.

Yes, and maybe no. I don't think I'll get fired or anything.

Who could fire you?

I don't think anybody can. I think I'm fired already. So it doesn't matter.

Did you have any resistance with any of the models?

No, because I asked them, "Would you like to be in my book? If you do, sign a release. If you don't want to be in it, don't sign the release and we won't put you in the book."

Is there anybody that you still want to photograph that you haven't?

I'd like to go to England and photograph Jean Shrimpton. I know she's old, but she has a hotel in the south of England. She does the cooking, she takes the bags up and everything. I think she's a wonderful person.

I read that you're also doing a book on old and new models? Could you do it for that?

It will happen. I don't think about it too much. I find models on the street.

It's the best place to find them.

I discovered them myself, and then I hope they come out to be Christy Turlington. The person that I think I discovered last was called Karlie Kloss. She was a terrific model and I knew her. She had her dad with her on set because she was fifteen. He asked, "Will Karlie Kloss do well?"

I said, "Not well. Great. I mean, really great. Bring her to New York. She's going to be the next star." I think she did well, and she's the nicest girl also. Have you had her on the stage?

No, I haven't, but she would be a good interview. She's terrific.

Very good. Very nice person.

What would you like your legacy to be?

What does that mean? You mean when I'm dead? No, I don't want to be dead yet. I have to see Sophie get a boy soon. She's working on it.

No pressure.

I need to see everybody do well. So I want to stick around. I'm not ready to die yet.

No, of course not.

Well, you said a legacy.

Like, what would you like people to remember you for? Even while you're alive.

That I like cameras, more or less… and girls.

A guy who likes a camera and girls.

… And girls and cameras together. More or less. It doesn't matter which one, but I like cameras and girls.

In that order?

Kind of. Yeah.

Why do you always have your cameras with you?

I never know when I'll need it. You know, when we have champagne, soon, right? Or maybe they gave that up. We can go out somewhere at the bar, but they used to have champagne here. That's why I wanted to be here. Because they had good champagne here. I think it was called Veuve Clicquot. Do you still have that or not?

Here?

Yes. You did. When I was here for Polly Mellen, they did. But maybe I'm not as important as Polly Mellen. We're going to my house and we're going to have champagne, OK?

Last question, even though I hate to end this because you are just delicious, Arthur.

No champagne, really?

We will find you some champagne in this building.

That's why I came here. I thought it was champagne galore.

We'll get you champagne. If you could put three people, living or dead, in a photograph together, who would they be?

My children, because there's three of them. Maybe we'll add Grethe to it.

That was a beautiful wrap-up: Arthur, his family, his work. Thank you, Arthur, this has been wonderful.

Thank you. Now do the lights come up?

SINCE FASHION ICONS

Arthur has gone on to publish two more books: *I Love…* , an homage to the beauty and the power of the supermodels who helped make his career, and *Ballet*, an ode to his first love. In 2020, Arthur met his long-awaited grandson when daughter Sophie and her husband, Eric Von Stroh, welcomed their second child, Artie. During the COVID-19 pandemic, Arthur and Sophie began hosting a digital series on Instagram called *Behind the Lens with Arthur Elgort*, in which they share the stories behind Arthur's most iconic photos. Sons Warren and Ansel continue their careers in film. Arthur and wife Grethe Barrett Holby split their time between New York's Upper West Side and Southampton. Follow Arthur on Instagram: @arthurelgort

BOB MACKIE

Sequins, sparkles, sheer, and sex are just a few of the words that describe the work of Bob Mackie. Diana Vreeland has said of Bob, "Mr. Mackie's superb clothes are not equaled in even French workrooms."

Long before we heard of, or followed, the Kardashians, Beyoncé, Lady Gaga, Nicki Minaj, Cardi B, Rhianna, or even J.Lo, who all think they were wearing the first nude sexy dresses with crystals strategically placed, the Sultan of Sequins, the Raja of Rhinestones, and the Guru of Glitter was dressing some real divas: Diana, Liza, Barbra, Dolly, Whitney, Tina, Elton, Michael, Madonna, Judy, Raquel, RuPaul, Mitzi, and Carol, for whom he designed over 17,000 costumes.

... and of course let's not forget Cher.

In the New York Times review of Broadway's The Cher Show, Jesse Green writes: "Designer Bob Mackie has kept on the right side of the line by making sure the level of craft supports the extravagance of the gesture."

While producer Jeffrey Seller said he's never been surrounded by so many sequins in his life: "It's a lot different from Rent."

Frank DeCaro said in the New York Times that "Cher and Bob Mackie have... over thousands of concerts, movies, television shows and award show appearances... forged as formidable a fashion partnership as Audrey Hepburn and Hubert de Givenchy, Liza and Halston, or Gaga and her butcher."

Did you know his very first job in Hollywood entailed sketching what became the most iconic dress ever? The "nude" beaded gown Marilyn Monroe wore to sing "Happy Birthday" to President John F. Kennedy.

Every star who walks the red carpet has been influenced by him whether they know it or not, and owe him a debt of gratitude.

But Cher says it best: "There is simply no one like Bob Mackie. I love him, always have, always will."

BOB MACKIE: You sure there's not a lot of drag queens out there?

FERN MALLIS: I hope so.

I hope so, too.

This is your life, Bob Mackie.

Oh, dear.

We start at the beginning. You were born Robert Gordon Mackie on March 24, 1939. That's two days before my birthday. Not 1939. That makes you how old?

That makes me seventy-nine. Almost eighty.

You were born in Monterey Park, California. You're an Aries. Obviously, my favorite sign.

Do you believe in or follow astrology?

Not really. But I read it every day, just in case.

Some of the Aries positive characteristics are: adventurous, courageous, versatile, lively, positive, passionate, enterprising, spontaneous, daring, incisive, fearless, natural born leaders, loyal, life of the party, inspirational, generous, amazing self-confidence, positive energy, and creativity. I added a lot of them.

OK, and some of the negatives.

Oh, what? Negatives?

Unfortunately, we've got a few: arrogant, stubborn, impulsive, confrontational, tendency to leave projects midway, opinionated, rebellious, competitive, impatient, short-tempered. Do you agree or disagree?

No, I don't agree with any of those. But I don't usually leave a project midway. That's something I just don't believe in. I guess that's because I worked so many times in television, movies, and stuff. You just don't walk out in the middle, you finish it. Or you don't work again.

…and last on the horoscope, we're in good company. Aretha Franklin, Reese Witherspoon, Rosie O'Donnell, Alec Baldwin, Robert Downey Jr., Steven Tyler, Mariah Carey, Lady Gaga, Celine Dion, Pharrell, Kourtney Kardashian, and of course, Diana Ross.

You know, a lot of those people are a pain in the ass.

Some of those negatives really worked for them.

Well, they do.

Tell us about your parents. Charles Robert Mackie and Mildred Agnes Smith. What did your dad do?

Well, my dad, he got in trouble a lot. I didn't know him till after the war. He was in the Canadian army and he thought he was quite hot with his kilt and his little beret. When he came back to America and he wasn't nearly as popular…

He was one of the 48th Highlanders. He felt like he was a big hero. And then he worked for the Bank of America. He didn't like me very much, because he just didn't get me at all. So it's kind of tricky…

Mom was a homemaker of some fragile health, but loved movies?

Yeah, she was fragile. My mother was a flapper in the '20s. When she was about eighteen, she had to get out of that small town. She got herself married and pregnant right away, moved to LA and had my half-sister, then divorced her husband. She was not a happy woman most of the time because it didn't work out like it did in the movies.

She always went to the movies, and when she would talk to you, it would sound like dialogue from a movie.

Did she keep any of her flapper dresses?

No, no, no, they were old. We didn't want anything old.

Don't you wish at a certain point you had those?

As she got a little older, she didn't want to be flamboyant or anything impressive. If I'd give

From left to right: Bob Mackie and sister Patricia Mackie; Bob with his son Robin and mother Mildred in Laguna Beach.

her something, sometimes she'd say, "Do people wear this?" I'd say, "Well, some people do." And one time, just to annoy the hell out of her, I was doing an African collection here in New York. I had all these African things. One sweater had a big Nubian princess on one arm, and her whole headdress went down the sleeve. I knew my mother wasn't going to like that. But I just gave it to her to see and she said, "I don't think I can wear this." She just didn't get it at all.

You were just testing her?

Yeah, well, I was, but it made me laugh.

Between the ages of six and fourteen, is it true that you lived with your British grand-mother? Who believed children should be seen and not heard?

Well, yeah, and stay indoors so she knew where I was. There were no kids in the neighbor-hood, so I stayed indoors and drew pictures all day.

Well, she was an important influence on your life like many of the designers I've talked to here; Grandma was the most important person in their lives.

She was the stability that I needed. When I was living with my mother and my half-sister, who was a teenager at the time, I was wandering around the streets and going into con-struction sites and playing around, you know, about to get in trouble or hurt or whatever. I was wandering.

Then she got a little sick, so my grandmother said, "Bring him over here, I'll take care of him." And I never left after that.

I'd see my mother once in a while on a weekend, a couple times a month. My mother was like my favorite aunt who would take me to the movies and buy me clothes and things and she could still have her dates during the week and not worry about babysitters. I was so unhappy as a child when I was living there because I had no structure. My grandmother and I had lots of structure.

You went to Rosemead High School. Were you good in any subject?

Almost nothing except decorating the classroom.

Bob Mackie as a student at Rosemead High School.

That's important.

It was right after the war, the big war, and there were no teachers in California. There were thousands of kids moving into California, and a lot of GIs: ex-soldiers and sailors. What do they call those people that just got out of the army? Veterans, yeah.

Anyways, the teachers were lousy. They were just out of school, and they were frustrated, and they had so many kids in a class. So I never learned to read.

I didn't read until the third grade. All of a sudden a teacher from Boston had come to California, and she realized half of her class couldn't read. She said, well, I'll come an hour early every day if I can get the kids to come in. That was the third grade, and we did pretty well. She said, "I think I need to move to the fourth grade next year." She had the same kids again, and by the time we finished the fourth grade, we were all able to read.

You describe growing up in Southern California in the 1950s where cinema was an escape. Tell us about seeing _An American in Paris_?

Well, let me start a little earlier, because when I was little, I had my favorite movie stars. For some reason, they were all Technicolor ones. The black-and-white movies didn't interest me when I was five, six, seven. But I loved movies.

Later, I started getting kind of fussy about what I watched. I did go to see _An American in Paris_ with Gene Kelly. I thought, oh, this is nice musical and I'm watching it, watching it... at the very end of the movie, there's a twenty-minute dream ballet.

I sat there and I watched it. And I went, whoa, I could do that. I want to do that. And I said, well, who does that? And I never thought about there being a costume designer in the movie. All of a sudden, I think, well, somebody has to do that. That was too beautiful for words.

When I see it today, I can't flip the channel if it's on television. I just sit there and watch it again and again. It's just one of those things. When I see it today, it is truly beautiful. Irene Sharaff became my favorite costume designer. She did _The King and I_ and some fabulous-looking films.

I always thought, well, one day, I'm going to do something like that.

Did you ever tell her?

I did. I got to know her later on. In fact, she had clothes made in my own workroom and I was so proud.

That's a nice whole circle.

Well, she was quite the number, that one. She'd sit in this little tight black dress, and a great big hat, and just smoke and watch them make the clothes.

It's a nice description. I read that when you were younger, you built mini movie sets, with stars and people in costume on the top of your dresser.

I did my own little shows in my bedroom. I'd have put on those little 45 records, I'd hold a flashlight, pull down the shades and that was my own little theater. I'd hear the music playing. I just started doing more and more and more until I got to high school, and then I sort of lost interest because we were doing real plays and real costumes.

When were you the Easter Bunny at Bullock's?

Bullock's was a department store in Los Angeles, and they were looking for somebody to be the Easter Bunny, and so it got to be me. Then I was the back-to-school clown and…

So you grew up in costumes…

I thought, well, I can do that, and I was good with the kids. I was only, I think, seventeen or eighteen. Then they said, "Well, do you think you could do Santa Claus?"

I said, "I don't think so," because I looked like a skinny fourteen-year-old at that point. But the kids liked me. They liked my costumes. They were smelly, rented costumes. But I'd always fix them up, and add more things to them.

Costumes were always a part of your life—without you realizing it.

Well, it wasn't so much costumes. I just love the whole idea and what it did and how it lifted the entertainment in movies. And then I started seeing a few stage shows, and I thought no, this is it.

For a while I thought I could be in plays and sing and dance, and then I realized I couldn't sing or dance. I thought, well, maybe I'd better design some costumes? It's never changed since then.

Then you went to the Pasadena City College, followed by the Chouinard Art Institute, which is now the California Institute of the Arts.

I went to the City College because with some of my arithmetic classes, I couldn't go to college because they weren't high enough, if you know what I mean… you know, the grades.

We know what that means.

But then I got a scholarship to the art school and they had a costume design department, and that was great.

But then you didn't graduate, but you got married in 1960.

I did. You know, you do things that you shouldn't be doing, but I did it.

That was Lulu Porter?

Yeah, that's her name. That's her stage name. She was an entertainer, you know.

She was a singer, actress, and later, you divorced her in 1963? Did you stay in touch with her?

Oh, I'm in touch with her all the time. She's my best friend.

Together you did have a son. A son named Robin who became a makeup artist, and unfortunately died in 1994, at thirty-three years old, from an AIDS-related illness.

He had a lot of drug problems and he was over them. It was hard. It was really hard.

… And then I learned that you found out years and years later that you have a granddaughter and two great-granddaughters.

I do. That is just the most amazing thing to go through your life and be, you know, I don't know, I mean how, what year did I find that out?

I don't have that.

I was already middle-aged and I find this out. I thought, oh dear, I'm going to have somebody that says they're related to [me] and they're not really. Lulu said, "Oh, God, I hope they're not living in their car," because you just don't know what's going to come out of the woodwork.

Bob Mackie with son Robin Mackie.

Then I saw pictures. The granddaughter, who's in her thirties now, looked just like my son. Then I saw the little girls, and they looked like they were related to me.

I said, "Well, this must be true." I went to visit, and it was wonderful. They're beautiful children, and they're all smart.

..and they're all girls so that's a nice legacy...

Well, two little girls, six and ten right now. I have a granddaughter and two great-granddaughters.

Are you saving a lot of clothes for them?

No, but when they visit, they like to play with the jewelry and whatever is around the office.

I think you need to save a big trunk for these kids.

You think so?

Are you kidding? [APPLAUSE]

I don't think they can wear any of Cher's old stuff.

Oh, they'll figure it out. If there's Mackie blood in them they'll figure it out.

So then it was time to get a job and you looked toward Hollywood for that work. Your first job was at Paramount Studios. Is that right?

Well, actually the first job I got was to go work for Jean-Louis on the Marilyn Monroe film.

Something's Got to Give.

Something's Got to Give, the one that was never finished. But while they were waiting to get it started, Marilyn was having some whatever done, and it didn't start on time. So Edith Head had seen my work and she called me [APPLAUSE].

And yeah, she'd like that. I was working over at Paramount, and I said, "Oh, I think this is good." I don't have any responsibility except doing sketches. I could watch them make mistakes, and see what works and what doesn't work. It was like college, really.

Early on, sketching was a very important part of your life.

Well, I was doing a lot of fashion illustration to make money when I was in art school. The drawing was an easy part for me. It still is kind of easy for me.

Tell us about how you met Ray Aghayan.

He was working at NBC. I'd met him at a guild meeting.

Then he was hired to do *The Judy Garland Show*. We'd had a couple of dinners, and he said, "Would you be my assistant on *The Judy Garland Show*?" I said, "Yeah, I'd love to do that," and so that worked out.

But he wasn't supposed to design for Judy at all. She had just done a film with Edith. She had asked Edith to do it, and of course, she never said no to anybody. But Edith didn't really want to do any television.

That was beneath her?

Well, kind of. I mean, in those days movie people were like, "Television [GROAN]," you know. It was all changing at that point, anyway—all the studios were changing. They were closing down their costume departments and their workrooms.

This page, clockwise from top: Bob Mackie and Edith Head; Bob and his partner Ray Aghayan in the 1970s; Bob adjusting Mitzi Gaynor's costume on the set of *Mitzi Zings into Spring* in 1977. Page 356: Bob's sketch for Carol Burnett's costume for the "Went with the Wind" sketch, 1976.

Anyway, she decided that Judy would have a plain black dress, and sometimes she'd wear a full skirt, and sometimes she'd wear a little wrap skirt over it. Edith said, "Well, next week, we'll put something else over the black dress." All of a sudden, the producer went, "I don't think this is going to work."

That week on the show, Mickey Rooney was on and they had this number where he was singing to all these beautiful, tall, gorgeous girls. We dressed the shit out of them. When Judy saw them, she went, "Oh, why can't I have some of that?"

From then on, Ray did the costumes for the show and Judy, and it was great for me because Judy was a big handful to deal with. I got all the guest stars and the chorus clothes and everything, I was in hog heaven.

Tell us a Judy story.

We all know the bad ones. The thing about her that I loved is if you went to her house, and I did often, on Sunday nights when the show was on, *The Ed Sullivan Show* would come on first. She'd sit there and she'd say terrible things about the other singers.

Then her show would come on, and she'd sit there, you know, like that [FLUTTERING HIS HANDS]. She'd laugh at her jokes. She was just fabulous. I always remember that I thought, "Well, she really liked her work."

Whenever there were really good singers or performers, she was fabulous. When there were ones that were "iffy," she might not come out of her trailer for an hour or two to do the show.

It's nice that she rose to the occasion when the talent was good…

Well, I know, but it's not good for the show.

When we had a show with Ethel Merman, Barbra Streisand, and Judy, all singing, "There's No Business Like Show Business," I just stood there like, "Oh, my God, I'll never forget this." There was the future, and there was history, and there was Judy. You didn't know what was going to happen. It was amazing.

Then President Kennedy was killed and Judy was a good friend. I was at her house one time when she called him up and sang "Happy Birthday" to him—it was one of those Sunday nights. It was just a wild kind of time. It was shortly after that that he was killed. That was kind of wild and she was very emotional.

Then around that time, Ray became your partner in life?

I finally found somebody that I could go out to dinner with and sit across the table. We would talk and talk, and drink and drink, and have the best time. You didn't even have to do anything special except eat good food and drink. I realized that I wasn't such a good drinker at that point. I'm down to one martini a night now. But it was interesting.

You're a cheap date.

Well, I was a cheap date, but I was a good date.

You were a good partnership.

We were a good partnership because we opened a workroom. We did shows together. We did movies together, and we did things separately. It was all very good. We kept a lot of people

Carol Burnett as
"Starlett"

working for many, many years.

In 1966, tell us how you met Mitzi Gaynor, who was putting together a Las Vegas review at the Riviera.

Well, Mitzi Gaynor, who had been this musical comedy movie star, had her own nightclub act. It was the 1960s and fashion was changing. She was the epitome of the 1950s girl, with a little waist and a big bouffant skirt and everything, which we never really gave up. But all of a sudden, they put her in little miniskirts and her legs were beautiful. Her hairdo changed. She did a nightclub act in Las Vegas.

The choreographer from that show was going to do *The Carol Burnett Show* the next year, 1967. Carol was pregnant at the time. They said, "Come up to Vegas and see the show." Carol and her husband went up to see the show and the next week, I got a call asking, "Would you be interested in doing *The Carol Burnett Show* next year?"

I was thrilled. I was thrilled to have a big show like that with a lady star. To have a show that had so much comedy.

Oh, my God. That is still the funniest show.

… And I love doing comedy. If you can dress somebody, and they walk out and the audience goes crazy before they even open their mouth—or if it's so beautiful, that they just swoon before they even open their mouth to sing, that's my idea of a good job.

Absolutely. Carol said that when you came to her door, she thought you looked like you were twelve years old and had the most beautiful baby face.

She was right.

… And that you designed clothes that could be both elegant and comedic. And helped develop those characters on the show with her because of the clothes?

We had the most wonderful musicians and singers. We had a huge band nobody had. We had the best singers in the business, like Ella Fitzgerald. Then we did all the comedy. To me, it was like being able to do the perfect show every week, and I love doing that.

When they do reruns and specials with her, every skit that they play, you crack up laughing.

Well, they don't play the bad ones. We had some fabulous ones.

Tell us about the *Gone with the Wind* dress. How did that come to be?

Well, that's a tricky one because it's a takeoff. We did a lot of takeoffs on famous films, which is my favorite thing to do. But that one was more famous than anything; everybody had seen it. The minute she took down the curtains, everyone said, "She's going to make a dress out of the curtains." I went, "Well, that's not funny."

We all saw Vivien Leigh do that, and it was funny in that movie when she came out in this perfectly gorgeous dress, made out of these old dusty drapes. I said, "Well, what am I going to do?" I just I didn't know.

We used to fit Carol on a Tuesday, and I had finally come up with the idea of putting the rod in, and letting her put it on, and be so proud of herself. She came in and I showed it to her

This page, from left to right: Bob Mackie and Cher preparing for her Las Vegas show in 2018; Cher on her *Love Hurts* tour in 1992. Opposite: Bob's sketches for *The Cher Show*, 2018.

and she got hysterical. Then Carol said, "I don't want Harvey to see this. He'll crack up if he sees this early."

Then with the audience, they recorded it, and it's one of the loudest, longest laughs in the history of television. It still is, it's amazing!

We just had the fiftieth anniversary last year. The dress was on a mannequin on the staircase. All these famous movie stars were going up and having their picture taken with the curtain rod dress. It was the strangest feeling to see it. It was like the donkey at the state fair, because everybody wanted a picture of themselves with it.

Now it's in the Smithsonian Institution.

Which is great. Tell us about 1967, when Cher was on the show?

She was on in the first year. On a new show like that, they thought, "Well, Carol will bring in the older folks, but we'd better do some young acts that will bring in a younger audience." That never really works in television, even though it's a rule.

Anyway, Sonny Bono and Cher came on the show, and they did their little song. They were in the finale. I thought, "What am I going to dress this hulking girl in?" I mean, she was a goth girl, but she wasn't really then, because nobody knew what goth was. She just looked like a new age cavewoman.

When they came on, they cleaned their whole act up and they were really crisp. Cher was adorable, with her little Audrey Hepburn body and her hair in two pigtails. I went, "Wow, I like her. She's got a good figure," not thinking that we're going to show it all in the next fifty years… but I really liked her.

At the end of the day, one of Carol's gowns had a little beading that was coming loose. I was fixing it in the hallway, which is a job I usually don't do myself. But there I am, fixing it, and Cher said, "Oh, I'd love to have a beaded gown one day."

One day.

… And I said, "Well, you could." Cher said, "Well, we're kind of low on the money now."

They had a huge hit as the duo Sonny and Cher, and then it just dropped right out. They went

Bob Mackie

to Vegas and they started working, and before you know it, they were a weekly television show, and a huge hit.

Did you dress Sonny at all?

I did in the early days. But then when her [solo] show came on, I couldn't possibly do that whole show, and Sonny's, and *The Carol Burnett Show;* which was the next studio over at CBS. I was busy in those days.

I'll say. Much has been written about Cher's 1986 Oscar outfit. She was presenting an award to Don Ameche, who said he's never been photographed so much in his career as when she presented the award to him, wearing that outfit.

I said to her, "You can't, you can't wear an outfit like this. It's great. It's fun. It's not fashion, but it's fun. It's kind of like, you know, drawing attention away from the man that's going to get this award."

She said, "Oh, he won't care. He'll be fine."

… And I went, "Yeah, all right." What do you do? She's the boss. She's ordering the dress.

It was after Cher didn't get nominated for a part. She really wanted to make a statement.

Yes, she didn't get nominated for *Mask*, and she was quite upset about it because she did a good job, but nobody listened. Nobody went to see that in Hollywood. But the people that vote in Hollywood weren't interested in a biker movie about this woman who has a deformed child. She didn't get nominated. She didn't understand that.

She said, "Well, what should I wear?" I think she'd already been on Broadway. She was in very small parts in movies and stuff. She said, "Well, let's do something kind of Indian, like we used to do in the old days on television."

… and I went, "OK. Would you want a headdress?"

"Oh, yeah, I want a headdress, a big headdress."

… and I went, "Really? OK."

Before you know it, it's a mohawk kind of thing made out of feathers … it was just the craziest outfit. She looked amazing in it, though. That's the thing: the girl can wear anything.

You know, she's never intimidated by anything that I ever put on her. She's never like, "Oh, I don't think I can really wear this."

She was game for whatever…

… For whatever. She never poses, like a poser. She's poses as if she's in her T-shirt and jeans, standing there, and that's what makes it work for her.

She's not showing off. She just is a show-off. She can't help herself.

How many of you have seen the Cher play? [APPLAUSE]

It's definitely theater that you have to see. Telling that story, and his costumes in it, it really is such a fun night at the theater. It is really, really worth it. I mean, if you don't get the Tony, there's something wrong on Broadway.

You know what, I've done a lot of jobs in my life, and you just don't do a show or a project to win an award. The awards aren't important. It's better that you do a good job.

... And that you did. Then tell us about when you opened a New York fashion business.

In the early 1980s, I guess. That's when she [Cher] was doing movies, in the 1980s, and someone said, "Do you want to come to New York and make some clothes for ladies?"

I had never done that. I had done a lot of TV and movies and stuff. I thought "Oh, OK, I'll try that." I didn't know how hard *that* would be. That was really hard. I'm not really a fashion designer. I'm a costume designer in my heart.

You do that so brilliantly. The fashion industry wasn't very kind to you?

They had lots of names for me, like "Barnum Bob." They always made fun of me. They didn't get it. If I was doing a fashion show, it wasn't like I was asking for singing and dancing, but at least I could have a theme and something that'll make you smile. But a lot of fashion people don't really understand.

I remember one of your shows, it must have been during New York Fashion Week in the Bryant Park tents. There were lots of incredible dresses and costumes. They were like Alice in Wonderland pieces. I remember distinctly that for almost the entire show, the audience was standing on their feet. And I'd never seen that. It was definitely memorable.

I don't remember what show that was, but I'm glad they were standing. I always had a theme. One time I did a whole collection based on Broadway. It could have been that one. That was in the tents.

I did American women icons. I had Mary Martin and Billie Holiday. It was fun, but I thought, "I need to do a show where people really clap and enjoy the singing and dancing."

Do you feel that you get respect now and admiration from the industry?

Well, I don't know about the fashion industry one way or another. I mean, I had a good time doing fashion. It was fun.

I had to do those horrible trunk shows all over the country. You go down to Texas, and I'm out in the middle of some ranch, and there's this really expensive store. When models came in, one is on her plane coming in, and the other one's coming down the street on her horse. I thought, oh dear.

The rich Texas farm girls were the models in the show. I'm going, "What are we going to do now?" All their husbands would stand by the door watching all the models get dressed. It was the worst experience in my life.

OK, we'll move on from that experience. Then you went back to work at one point with Bette Midler on the TV movie *Gypsy*. Was Bette fun to work with?

I did. I think we did fashion shows in New York for almost ten years, or a little less. Things just slowed down, and I thought, I've got to get out of this. It was a bad year for me. The business was closing. My son was sick. I wasn't doing any theatrical stuff to speak of.

I went back, and God bless Bette. She asked if I would do the television version of *Gypsy* and it kind of got me through a really hard time in my life.

I loved it. I mean, it's one of my favorite shows ever. I thought she was fabulous. We had Christine Ebersole, who was amazing, and all these great people in that show with her.

Then tell us about being hired to design costumes for Diana Ross and the Supremes and the Temptations for a TV special.

Well, that was early, it was 1968. She had another designer that was doing the specials. We say "she" because it was always Diana Ross and the Supremes. She was the star, and we knew that she was going to break away any minute. Then she had the Temptations with her and they did a whole salute to Broadway, and it was fantastic.

All of a sudden, Diana was out on her own doing her own act and trying to do movies and everything. We also did *Lady Sings the Blues* with her.

... And you were Oscar nominated for that. Diana was a good Motown legend for you to work with.

She was *the* Motown legend. Just ask her [LAUGHTER].

All right. Tell us about working with Elton John.

I love Elton John. I'm not sure Elton John ever knew what he was looking at when he looked at the sketches, but he'd go, "Oh, that looks like fun," and "Let me have one of those."

When I first went to see him I asked, "What kind of things do you want me to do for you?" He said, "Well, things like you do for Cher."

... and I went, "OK."

He was trimmer in those days and younger. I did jumpsuits with holes and mirrors and big fur coats that went across the stage. He had Mr. World, who was practically naked, holding him up [on his shoulders] in his cape as he went across the stage. I mean, it was like Liberace on acid. It was just crazy.

I mean that's a lot of fun, if you don't take it too seriously.

... And why a duck?

Well, he just likes costumes. He had a Minnie Mouse outfit one time, and he had Donald Duck. Then he had to do a big concert at Dodger Stadium, and I said, "Well, why don't we do a sequined Dodger uniform?" Everybody liked that idea and it got press everywhere. It was really fun.

Silly question, but did you have fun appearing as yourself on *The Love Boat*?

Yes. It took a week to do. But it was kind of an interesting thing because I wasn't really in fashion. I was doing a lingerie line in LA just as a side bar and doing my other work. I was doing a movie called *Pennies from Heaven* with Bernadette [Peters] and Steve Martin. It was a 1930s-style movie that had fantasy, Busby Berkeley numbers, and then realistic poor people, all in Chicago. I love doing that.

Right in the middle of that, they said, "Would you come over and be on *The Love Boat*?" At that point in time, I'd become kind of infamous, everybody knew who Bob Mackie was. They were giving me awards for being the "Best Designer in America," and what was I doing? Drag queen clothes for Cher? It just didn't make any sense. But it was fun, and I was on there. There was Bill Blass, and Geoffrey Beene, and Halston with all his girls.

It was a fashion boat.

It was a fashion boat day, and it was really fun to do. It's on all the time. Somebody always says, "I just saw you on *The Love Boat*. You look good." Did I still look good?

You still do. In 1999, FIT mounted a Bob Mackie retrospective. How did that come to be?

They called me and asked me if I would do it, and I said, "Yes, I'll do that." I had the best curator there, Dorothy Twining, who is the tea heiress. Anyway, she was fabulous and it was really a good exhibit. We had 250 mannequins.

It's almost time for another one, right? [APPLAUSE]

Well, I've got a few things in the back room.

Do you still go to malls to people-watch?

No, but I go to the airport all the time and that's horrifying enough.

Are you surprised about how drag queens and transgender people have become so mainstream?

No, it was bound to happen. It just needed to happen sooner. It's still not fair the way people treat people. But, thank God. When RuPaul becomes a big, moving, important person in the country, I'm thinking to myself, "OK, why not? Why not?"

Have you been on her show?

A couple times. I've done so much stuff for Ru. She had a Vegas act. When I asked her, "What do you want me to do," she said, "Well, I want a strip outfit with a big wings like Tina Turner, and then I want to kind of look like Barbie here, a black Barbie."

I said, "I think I could do that," because I have all these Barbie dolls that I did forever.

We've been trying to get Ru here at the 92nd Street Y.

You should. She would be fabulous. She's funny and she's smart. She's smart as can be. She knows how to do it. She is probably the best drag queen ever because she comes out looking gorgeous, and you know, she's eight feet tall.

I mean, when I stood next to her, and had a picture taken, I looked at it later, and I said, "How did Mickey Rooney get into that photograph?"

She actually asked me to do some stuff recently, and I turned her down because… it's not easy. Drag queens aren't easy.

In case you thought they were.

I do go up to Provincetown in the summertime to see my friend Marilyn Maye sing. She always plays about a week there. One time I went up there, there were like five different Cher drag queens working at different places on Commerce Street. Before I knew it, they were following me down the street. It was just too weird for words.

You more recently did work for Pink?

I did some work for Pink, yes. She's an amazing performer. You get her all dressed up, and she has to go up in her trapeze, and they spin her around, and they dunk her in the water. I don't know if that's show business, or if it's just her.

But it's amazing. She's very good. How many years have you been on QVC?

It's going to be twenty-seven years in May. When I first started, I was doing scarves, and they called it "wearable art." You could hang it in your living room. But I was only on like every two months, selling a few scarves and some earrings, or something. I would forget that I was even doing it. Now I'm doing it quite a bit more.

Do you enjoy talking directly to the customers?

I don't mind. It used to make me really nervous. But now I figure, you know, whatever. We don't have a script, so you just talk.

What are some of the strangest calls you've gotten?

Well, really early on, there was one, and I could hear the ice jingling in the glass. This lady, I don't know where she was, I guess she was in the South somewhere…

Page 363: Bob Mackie on the set of the *The Cher Show Special* with Bette Midler, Elton John, Cher, and Flip Wilson in 1975. Opposite: The FIT Museum's *Unmistakably Mackie* exhibition in 1999. This page, from left to right: Bob's Le Papillon Barbie; Bob and Diana Ross at the 2001 CFDA Awards.

It was cocktail hour.

… And she said, "Bob Mackie, you could put your slippers under my bed anytime."

Well, every model on the stage was bent over, laughing. It was good. It was a good time.

What other collections and licensees do you still do today?

I've had a lot of different ones over the years. I had rugs, and lamps, and furniture and all kinds of stuff like that.

I had a fragrance that was hot for a while, and then Elizabeth Arden bought it. I hear that it's still for sale in certain places. But I don't know, I don't see it. I don't have to do PR for it or anything. Thank God.

What do you think your greatest skill is? How do you build the dress?

Well, if you're building a dress for somebody, you'd better see them, you'd better take a good look at them. If they're a performer, you'd better know what they're known for. You'd better understand what they do.

I think a lot of costume designers just kind of want to make a fabulous outfit, and they don't worry about what the poor woman's going to do in it. It's very important that they can do what they need to do.

You see some people walking down the red carpet and they can't walk.

That's when someone gives you a sample to wear made for a six-foot-tall girl, and you're five four. The train is all over the floor and you're picking it up and stepping on it.

Let's talk about *The Cher Show*. Did you think it was a good idea to do a play about her life?

Well, I thought it was a good idea. I thought it was going to be a little different; it turned out to be a rather entertaining show, and people are having a really good time seeing it.

Our core audience are people that were probably young teenagers and young adults when the *Sonny & Cher* show was on. They know all the words. They sing in unison. They get up and dance. They put on their glitteriest outfit they can wear, and come to see the show, and really have a good time.

The show is pure entertainment. It is a jukebox musical. But she's a more interesting subject than a lot of people who have jukebox musicals.

Were you involved from the very beginning?

Not the very beginning. No, they had somebody else that they were looking at. They didn't even think I was alive.

You are very much alive.

Well, I wasn't making a big fuss out in California. I was just doing my work, and you know, feeding the cat.

Well, we're glad that they found you. Are the costumes made in New York?

All of them were made in New York. All the hand beading, luckily for me, was done in Los Angeles by the woman that works for me on a regular basis, and works for Cher. She had made some of the really early dresses herself when she was a young girl in the beading shop.

All the embroideries were done out there, and it was fabulous. I mean, you send her sketches for a full beaded dress with a cape and I think two or three days later, it would come back in the mail and it'd be perfect.

We had the real dresses. The iconic ones: from the Academy Awards, the ones that everybody has seen pictures of in those magazines year, after year, after year. We had the real ones so she could just look at them. I had the pattern. I had beading patterns. I do all my own beading patterns, which everyone thinks is crazy, but then I get what I want.

Absolutely. That's the only way to get what you want. Did Cher have to sign off on all of these pieces?

No. I avoided her like crazy, and somehow she didn't have time to come look. Then I was supposed to show her in California and she said, "No, I'm too tired." I said, "God, I don't have to go to Malibu, thank God."

She never saw any of it until she saw it when the show started. Some of them she's like, "I never really wore that." I said, "This is a musical, darling."

Those of you who have seen the show, she comes out in those wings in the beginning, and she said, "I never wore wings." I said, "But if I had drawn a picture and shown them to you like that, you would have, probably."

Clearly, she seems very happy with the show.

I think so. She had her moments when she was less than happy. But when the show opened, and she came onstage and she sang with Stephanie J. Block, the two of them together sounded like twins. I mean, it was the scariest thing. I'm standing there onstage, because they brought all the designers, the set designers, the lighting designers, everybody onstage on the opening night. There we are the next day on the news, grinning like idiots, behind her. I had the best time.

Did you have anything to say about the guy who they hired to play "Bob Mackie"?

I'd heard who was originally playing me and I knew what he looked like. When it was just a workshop, I got on the elevator to go up to the rehearsal hall. He got on, and I don't think he knew it was me.

I said, "Hi, I'm Bob Mackie. I hear you're playing me."

He said, yeah, and I said, "Please don't play me like an officious old queen."

His voice got really high, and it was funny. Then when I saw the run-through, they wouldn't even show me the number the first day I was there. He was playing it like, you know, he's flying off the ceiling. He was just, you know, lovely and gorgeous and fabulous. If you ever see a costume designer in an old musical or movie, and we've seen them all, they're just screaming pansy fairies. I love a good pansy fairy, they're usually funny and I enjoy that. But that isn't really my image. At least I'm working on not making it that. And besides that, he weighed about a hundred pounds more than me.

But I didn't say anything. I didn't say anything to the director. I didn't say anything to anybody. I just kept my mouth shut. Cher came to see one of the rehearsals, to see if she would pass

Previous spread: Bob Mackie and the cast of *The Carol Burnett Show* for the "Cinderella Gets it On!" sketch in 1975, guest-starring the Pointer Sisters. This page, clockwise from top: Bob and Carol fooling around during a photo shoot; Bob and Carol embracing in 1974; Bob and his many Emmy Awards.

on it. Cher said, "Well, if he'd been like that, I never would have kept him around."

He found a nice job playing Daddy Warbucks somewhere, and they got Michael Berresse, and I adore him. He sings, he dances, he's nice and trim, and he wears a blond wig with a big pompadour, which, you know, my hair would never do that. But it's fun. And he's a little grand. But it's Broadway, and he's playing one of those costume designers, so they have to do a little extra.

Well, the very fact that the first guy didn't even recognize you should have been enough for him to not play you.

I don't think he realized. You know, those elevators are full of dancers and singers and people doing auditions and he just didn't realize who I was, and I knew exactly who he was.

I like him, he's really fabulous. He's in a show right now and it's a hit. He's doing fine. I'm not worried about it.

Are there any costume designers working today that you admire?

Oh, yes, yes. I pay a lot of attention to costume designers. I don't get to see all the shows because I'm not always here. The worst part was being here all year last year, and I saw one show the entire year, because we were so exhausted by the end of the day.

What fashion designers do you think are doing great stuff?

I don't pay a lot of attention to fashion because I'm not doing it. When all of a sudden you're in the fashion business, you're watching what everybody's doing, and you don't want to do that, and you don't want to do any of it.

Then you have all your salespeople say, "Well, we need something for the ladies to wear to the cocktail parties, and we need something to wear to the Alzheimer's Ball, and the Kidney Ball..." All these women, all the gowns that they have in storage, they all had disease names on them.

The disease designs, I love it. I think there's a business there. Is there anybody that you really wanted to dress and never did?

I never thought about it very much. I was just sort of thrilled if somebody would come and ask me. I never minded when Totie Fields, some of you probably don't know who that is, she was a little round girl who was a stand-up comic, a real Jewish comic, and she was really tough. She had the best rings ever. She had the best jewelry, and she said, "Would you do things for me?"

Anybody you want to dress.

I will dress anybody. I don't care what shape they are. I hate dressing performers that aren't good. You want to be part of the whole thing and part of that team that makes that happen. That's when you're doing a show, all the people that work on the show, you want everybody to be fabulous. Sometimes they're not.

I'm afraid to ask you who's not fabulous.

I'm not giving any names. This is in the past. I love our cast on The Cher Show. They're just so talented and they're so beautiful. I mean, I've never seen a bunch of more beautiful men and women. It's a good thing that it's not a burlesque cast, or they'd just be playing with themselves. If you do a show like *The Cher Show*, where the leading ladies are half naked quite often, you can't dress the chorus like they are the preacher's children. You just can't, you have to make sure the pants are cut low and the boys are showing their muscles… you know, what's wrong with that?

Nothing. What would you advise a young fashion student who wants to be a designer or go into costume design?

Go work for somebody that you really like what they do, and watch them. Watch what they do, and what they don't do. Watch them make mistakes. Everybody still makes mistakes. It doesn't matter how long you're in the business. You do it, and you go, "I shouldn't have done that." But you do it, you fix it.

But you learn, you learn from them. Anybody that's just starting off, fresh off the block, and you haven't done anything, chances are you're going to screw up.

True. What would you like your legacy to be?

Oh, I don't know. Legacy is this—I mean, are you trying to tell me something here?

No. No.

You know, I am going to be eighty already.

Eighty is the new sixty.

Oh, it is. Can it be the new thirty-five?

That's pushing it.

This whole thing, all of a sudden, this year, I realized, "Shit. I'm going to be eighty." I was always the youngest one. If I wasn't, I looked like the youngest one.

You still look like the youngest one.

No, but I really looked young in those days. I mean, when I was brought in to meet Dinah Shore, remember her?

I had done some wide-leg pants for her back in 1960-something. She said, "Well, I can't wear these." About three years later, she was coming to me to have them made in all the colors. Then she had a talk show. But for years and years, she had a wonderful variety show on Sunday night. She got to be a good friend and a good client.

But it's hard when you're starting out and they don't trust you, because you look too young or whatever.

In the 1960s, all of a sudden, in Hollywood, no designer was worth anything unless they were kids. It was the youth quake that happened. The Beatles came and everybody had to have the right haircut and the right outfit, and I had some really good outfits. It was just crazy. I mean, all of a sudden, I was getting jobs that these people that were really wonderful designers in Hollywood weren't getting because I looked younger than I actually was.

It was an advantage.

It really was for a minute. But you know, if you get those jobs and you don't deliver, there were a few of those, too. Those kids never worked again.

But I was lucky I'd already, you know, been working for several years.

Audience questions, let's end with a couple of those. What do you attribute your success to? Short answer.

Just being part of the team. Working for the show, and to help the show, whatever it may be. To make your work, really work. And sometimes you have to fight to get it to work because unless they see it in the flesh, they don't understand. You can do a sketch, and think, "I don't know." There were sketches on *The Carol Burnett Show* that were about to be cut and I would say, "Please don't cut that. When they get in costumes, you're going to be so happy." Now they're on all these retrospectives and everything. You don't always make funny clothes. Sometimes you make people look normal, so the funny things that happen to them are funny. But you have to read the script and figure those things out.

How is your Broadway experience different from TV and film?

Well, TV was fabulous in the old days. I mean, you did a huge show every single week. You get your script on Friday at the end of the taping, and the next Friday you're standing there with a whole new show and a lot of costumes. I mean, we had incredible budgets for the time.

Bob Mackie and Bernadette Peters showing off his 2019 CFDA Geoffrey Beene Lifetime Achievement Award.

Carol, the other night, said we could never have those shows again because they would just cost too much. I'm glad I was there.

This is basically a compliment, not a question, but we'll read it because it's very nice: "I had the pleasure of wearing one of your costumes in *Pennies from Heaven*. You were the kindest, most thoughtful person in the industry I've ever worked with. Thank you, Robin Paulson."

Oh, that's good. You know, a lot of people treat extras and chorus people really badly. Like, "Oh, they don't matter. Don't worry about them. They're just a dancer."

They're a dancer, they're the most beautiful people on the stage. They're doing the best work. I have dancer friends that are as old as I am. That's a long time.

Well, even the people serving the food. I mean, everybody matters when you're doing the work. You have to be nice to everybody.

Absolutely. But it's like, "I'm only good to the stars." That's bullshit.

Let's end on this question, because this has been remarkable. This has been an amazing, wonderful night. What is the Bob Mackie definition of fabulous?

A lot of smiles and a lot of applause. We're all whores. We all like applause. Whatever I do, if it's well received, I'm happy.

Did I talk too much?

SINCE FASHION ICONS

In 2019, Bob received the CFDA's Geoffrey Beene Lifetime Achievement Award and won a Tony Award for Best Costume Design of a Musical for *The Cher Show*. In 2020, Bob designed an exclusive collection for *Wheel of Fortune*, kicked off by a week of his most iconic dresses worn by cohost Vanna White. In 2021, Bob published *The Art of Bob Mackie*, which includes hundreds of photos and dozens of previously unpublished sketches of his work. He continues to run his successful QVC fashion line. Bob lives in Palm Springs, California. Follow Bob on Instagram: @bobmackie

BETHANN HARDISON

I think I've known Bethann Hardison longer than any of the Fashion Icons I've interviewed so far on this stage, and she is the only one who has been a guest at my home in Southampton.

I've admired, respected, and feared Bethann since the early 1970s, when I first met her. Bethann is the sage, the conscience, and the principal of our industry; and like the principal in school, you listen up, pay attention, and do whatever she tells you to do. "Purpose" and "responsibility" are her important words and actions.

She is a very strategic Instagrammer. She doesn't post or boast about herself, but will surface when there is a cause that matters. Bethann says, "I think anyone who has a real point of view, you can't shut them up. You can't shut Kanye up, though you may want to." She is outraged at designers and businesses that ignore the diverse consumer, a population that spends $20 billion on fashion and cosmetics annually.

For her decades in the industry, Bethann has been honored with the CFDA's Founders Award, and most recently, the Harlem Fashion Row's Iconic Trailblazer Award.

But Bethann is so much more than a pioneer, a trailblazer, an award winner, an industry cheerleader, and a whistle-blower. She's funny and charming. She's passionate and committed to her many causes and her many friends, and I'm very happy to be among them. Let's welcome my dear friend Bethann Hardison.

BETHANN HARDISON: Oh, wow. Thank you very much.

FERN MALLIS: In eight years, this may be the second time somebody got a standing ovation coming out.

Are you already starting to cry?

Yes. You are making me teary-eyed. That says a lot. It is well deserved.

Thank you so much. That says a lot, too.

There is a lot of love here.

Yes, and a lot of respect. God bless you.

We start at the very beginning, the very beginning. You were born on September 30. But we do not know what year?

That's a fact.

Why won't you reveal your age?

It's a combination of things. I think one thing is because it is in my DNA. My father never told his age. My mother never told her age. I think that's my excuse.

But my real reason in my own mind: it always delights me when people want to know what a person's age is. There are many people who don't mind saying how old they are. I like to go without anyone ever knowing. Then when it's all over, you can say, "She was that old?" Right?

That's what they said about me when I revealed my age on the stage. You're the only one in eight years whose age has not been outed on this stage.

Oh, well done, Bethann. Well done.

In respect to her, I actually do know it, but I will not reveal it. You'll have to kill me to find out.

Exactly right.

You're a Libra. Do you believe in astrology?

Yes, I was raised by my father, who believed in the solar sciences.

Some of the positive characteristics of Libras are: tactful, charming, diplomatic, balanced, eloquent, affectionate, peaceful, idealistic, clever, intelligent, and spontaneous. Do you agree?

Yes. They all sound positive. They don't say anything negative.

Detached, controlling, condescending, self-indulgent, manipulative…

Wait, wait, wait, what? I don't like that one, take that one out.

I'm crossing that out. Lazy?

I love that word. I love that. I am. I love saying, "I'm lazy." No one believes me, no one agrees. But I feel so lazy.

So lazy is a good one for you then?

Yes, very good.

Some of the famous Libras are Bruno Mars, Simon Cowell, Gwen Stefani, Snoop Dogg, Kim Kardashian, Cardi B, and Will Smith.

No Vladimir Putin?

No, I didn't have Putin. Do you really want to be associated with Putin? [LAUGHTER] You were born in Brooklyn. Where in Brooklyn?

Bedford-Stuyvesant.

You have said, "You've got to leave Brooklyn to be proud of where you come from."

Absolutely true. I think truly, you have to leave Brooklyn. Many of us have. I meet people around the world or in business, and we all are so proud to say that we came from Brooklyn.

I'm from Brooklyn, too. It wasn't so cool and clever when I was growing up there. Now, it's the hottest place on the planet.

No, that's bullshit. It was always cool. Maybe not in your neighborhood. You were in the wrong neighborhood. It was always cool.

I was in Mill Basin. I watched Jimmy Kimmel and found out that he actually grew up in Mill Basin, and went to the same grammar school I did, many years later.

Yeah, he is a Brooklyn boy.

Tell us about your parents. I have here that your father was a practicing Muslim and a supervisor in the local housing authority?

Wow, I don't know how you find this stuff. How scary. I'm scared when you go down these roads. Yes, this is true. Albany Projects.

Tell us what he was like?

He was an extraordinary man, I mean, in so many ways. It's wonderful when you can really—not because they're gone—admire your parents from the time you got to know them. I admired my father greatly. He was just mad cool because he was an important adviser to many people at that time.

When Elijah Muhammad wanted to come from Chicago, he called my father. All of the jazz musicians, a lot of people were coming up and embracing Islam at that time. My father was someone who was a mentor. Malcolm X was someone that looked to my father as a mentor. But for me, growing up with him, he just kept me so wise. He made me read many things. He let me have choices. He made me read the Torah, the Koran, the Book of Hadith. But he also allowed me to have a choice of reading, so I chose Greek mythology. My father also made me aware of the world. He had me send telegrams to world power leaders. He was just so smart about so many things. He was very cool. I went to live with him when I was twelve.

There are a lot of things about me that are very funny. I was in a gang from the age of nine. Were you in the gang, too? [TO THE AUDIENCE]

I was in a gang when I lived with my mother. When you leave the neighborhood, I was at the chapter in Bedford-Stuyvesant, and then I had to go to Crown Heights, where my father lived, you had to join that chapter. I told my father about it. He was so mellow about it. He was so cool. He said, "Really? What do you all do?" I told him, "It's basic, and it's nothing terrible."

He just was so easy. He was so smart about what to take on. He picked his battles. But he really was someone who educated me. He took me from my mother when I was twelve. He knew his responsibility was for me, because by thirteen there are a certain amount of things you had to know. That's when I became Muslim. But the fact of it is, I'm ever so grateful to him. I disappointed him greatly when I was a young girl, too. But in the same sense, I came back.

Was there anything you learned from being in that gang?

Oh, yes. I took on the war counselor role. A war counselor is the one who can go to the other gang and really define what you're going to do, and what's going to happen. If anything happens, you "take the bullet," but there's no bullets back then. We had zip guns. The most violent thing that would ever happen is a stabbing. But more often than anything, if you went to the wrong neighborhood, you got beaten up. Like if your mother doesn't know, and says that you're going to visit your aunt, she lives in the wrong neighborhood. But not to the girls. The girls of the gangs were always easy-breezy.

It was a good experience for what you started to do later in life because you had to deal with a lot of professional gangs.

Yeah, I think so.

Did you have any siblings?

No. I have someone you'll always hear me refer to as my sister, but she was my foster sister that came along in the later part of my life.

Tell me about your mother. What I read somewhere is that she loved dancing and dressing up, and that she was a domestic?

Yes, she was a domestic worker, as was my grandmother. I lived with both of them. I was a latchkey kid; they both worked. At the age of seven, I had to take care of myself.

My mother and my father were jitterbug partners; that's how they first met, dancing. My mother was a good-time girl. My father was the intellect. My mother was someone who thought that being intelligent was too much work. She was not concerned about reading and all that stuff. But she was a very wonderful woman.

They divorced?

Yes. It was so funny. Sophie, my mother, I don't know what she could have done, but he got an annulment and then the judge gave me to him. I still don't know what she ever did. But the good news is he let me stay with her, because my grandmother came to take care of me. He didn't want to take me away from my grandmother.

Your grandmother helped raise you. You know, most of the Fashion Icons I've interviewed, their grandmother was the most important influence in their life.

Yes, same thing with me, with Willi Smith, and Stephen Burrows. Our grandmothers—that's one of the things that connected the three of us. I knew both their grandmothers. Grandmothers are everything.

You are one now?

I'm a grandmother. I'm gangster with my granddaughter [Sophia Hardison].

What school did you go to in Brooklyn?

PS 44, Junior High School, and then I got into the School for the Performing Arts. But then this man came to my school at junior high school and talked about a school that was being redeveloped. I didn't know at the time what this whole thing was, but I got fascinated by the aesthetic of the school.

So I chose not to go to Performing Arts, which you have to really prepare for and get selected for, and go to this new school in Flatbush. I learned many years later, many years later, that we were being bused. That was the beginning of busing.

You went to Wingate High School. Were you a good student?

I was a very good student in elementary school, as well as junior high school. Wingate changed my life. I mean, I changed Wingate and Wingate changed me. I got selected to do so many things.

I wind up being the first Black cheerleader. I wind up being selected to do SING! [the annual student-run performing arts competition across New York high schools] SING! was something that every high school participated in. I was the one who was in charge of that. For two years. Each time I was in charge of it, we won. I learned to play chess when I was in high school. I loved my high school. It was a great experience for me.

Then you decided to go to NYU, to the art school?

No, it was my uncle. He was a well-known art director out of J. Walter Thompson. He just

Clockwise from top: Bethann Hardison and Stephen Burrows at the premiere of *Tommy* in 1975; Bethann models with Karen Bjornson, Pat Cleveland, and Iman for Stephen Burrows in 1977; Stephen and Willi Smith in 1975.

kept telling me that I had the ability because everybody in my family was an artist. But I just had no ability to draw or paint anything. He believed in me, so he had me go to NYU, and I failed. They just gave me Fs because they liked me.

They gave you Fs because they liked you?

I mean, they gave me Ds because they liked me. They wanted to fail me, but they just liked me. I was so bad. I didn't know how to draw. I didn't know anything. Then he made me go to, what's on 57th Street? The Art Students League.

I had to draw nude people. It was a mess. No bueno.

Then you went to FIT?

Then I went to FIT, for merchandising. I just went for two years.

Did you enjoy that?

You know, you think you know what you're supposed to be doing. It's so funny about life. I didn't get the opportunity to go to college like I was supposed to. All those things you think you're supposed to do. I was just trying to find a road to be able to go down so that I could become something. You think that's what's going to do it. You go to school, you go on with that thing, you take it to a corporation, and you become something. It's not true, not in every case.

Your life took a turn around that age because you had sex for the first time, and what happened?

Oh, I got pregnant. I don't know how you know these things… Memories.

That's the trade-off for not talking about your age.

Yes. I'll give you that. Yes, I did. That was a pretty awful situation. That's when my father really was devastated because everybody was so shocked: my mother and my grandma. Because I was someone that you didn't think this would happen to.

I always loved boys. I always had a boyfriend since the time I was seven years old. You all are slow if you didn't have a boyfriend. I mean, you've got to be kidding. Well, that's

This page: Bethann Hardison and son Kadeem celebrating the 100th episode of his series *A Different World* in 1991. Pages 387–389: Bethann's modelling test shots taken by her friend Bruce Weber in Central Park in 1969.

Puerto Ricans and Blacks; we have boyfriends at eight, nine, ten, eleven. You know, it's easy-breezy.

We don't have sex. I didn't, because I wasn't interested in that. Even with the gang, all the tough guys in the gang always protected me. They would tell the guys, "Don't you ever touch her." I never had interest in that, ever. I was always attracted to a boy or I always had a boyfriend, but never went any further because I had plans.

And then, you know, it was one of those times when he said, "Come on." He keeps talking to you and keeps talking to you. The next thing you know you're laying down. The next thing you know, it's not a nice experience. All that you ever heard somebody say is how wonderful it is. It was the worst thing that you ever felt. I don't know if anybody remembers their first time, but believe me, it was no picnic.

Then, to become pregnant, who lets that happen to them?! Thank God, my mother and grandmother were so cool. They were so supportive. God bless them. But my father, you know, what father would be happy, right?

But you dealt with it. You have a son now, Kadeem Hardison, who's about fifty-three years old?

Did he tell you that?

There's no candles on the birthday cakes in your family. He was looked after by your mom and your grandmother.

Up until he was nine.

He became a very successful actor on the sitcom *A Different World*. He played Dwayne Wayne. Has he continued to act?

He's still an actor, yes. I have to give a shout-out to the Akils [Salim and Mara Block] when they created *Love Is ___*. Kadeem had a great part in that. *Love Is ___* was on OWN. It was unfortunate that it had to be taken off the air recently due to the #metoo situation. But Kadeem was in that, and I liked it. Then he just recently was in *Black Monday*, which is on Showtime. He just got hired to do a new Lee Daniels show that's going to pilot. Lee is a stroke of gold. It's going to be on Amazon.

Are you still his manager?

I was. I just sort of played it, just to keep my hands on it at the very end. Just a little bit. He always had an agent out in LA, so it didn't really require too much.

He has a daughter, Sophia. Do you know how old she is?

I don't try to think about it too much, but she's twenty-two. I don't have any problem with that.

They live in LA. Do you see them often?

I try to see them at least once a year.

Let's talk about your early work. You did a lot of different things at the beginning. I read you worked for a telephone company and a prison.

How do you find out this stuff? Wow, I never even checked myself out. Everything you just said was true. My first job I think was AT&T as a long-distance telephone operator. I always wanted to work in law enforcement. I had this fascination, but don't ask me why I wanted to work in a prison. I was the youngest officer ever to be appointed in the state prison of New York in Bedford Hills.

What did you do?

I was a corrections officer at a state prison. I took the test at nineteen, I was appointed at twenty, and I went in at twenty-one. But instead of the women's prison, I was in the reformatory, which was for people who were really my age. Which was scary. They are scary. I had to act tough. I mean, all the gang stuff. My ability to act was really on because they challenged you, but I won. I came through. Also, I had a lieutenant who saved me and got me out of there for a little while.

All of that experience still helped you later on. I mean, if you can deal with prisoners, you could deal with the fashion industry.

Yes, it seems to be so.

Then you were at a company that made hand-painted buttons for design houses. You were quoted as saying, "That first day, I wore a white straw hat, an off-white suit, and slingback shoes. The owner was worried I'd get covered in paint, so he decided I should be the one to take the buttons to the designers."

Oh, that was my first job in the Garment District. That was at Cabot Button Company. That was great. I looked at the *New York Times*; you looked at it to get a job. You go and you dress up. That's what you're taught to do; you're taught to dress up. I didn't know what it was—a button factory? He just kept saying, "You have to tone it down. I'd love to hire you." I said, "I can tone it down."

I toned it down. I came in the next day and he said, "No, I mean, really tone it down." Because no matter how I toned it down for him, it wasn't enough. He said, "Well, let me just send her out."

That was great, because I would go to all the designers on Seventh Avenue. I would go and show them the swatches, let them check it all out. Because back then, coat and suit companies were really big. Custom buttons and stuff like that was a big thing for Cabot.

Then you were discovered on the street by one of the first and most talented African American designers, Willi Smith?

I was discovered by Willi Smith. I was on Broadway between 39th Street and 40th Street. He always saw me down on Seventh Avenue because we were juniors. I worked for a juniors dress house. He also had just started working at a company called Digits.

What did he say to you?

He didn't know who I was. He thought I was a designer. He kept watching me. He thought I had a lot of style. We had buying offices back then those days. The kids, they would come out and go to different design houses. He saw this girl he knew that came to his office. He asked, "Do you know this girl?" He described me. She said, "Oh, I think I know who that is." He said, "Could you get her to call me?"

She came to me and she said, "Willi Smith is looking for you."

I said, "Who's Willi Smith?" and then she told me. So I contacted him. He asked me to have a meeting with him and a friend of his, down at 1407 Club, remember that? That's how we met. I met him and he told me that he really thought I was great, and asked who did I design for? I said, "Oh, no, I'm not a designer. I'm a showroom girl." At that time, I was in sales with Ruth Manchester.

Now that he knew that I wasn't a designer, he said, "Well, I would love if you could just maybe consider being a model for me."

I said, "Model? Wow. How would that work? I don't know how that would work. I have a job." He said, "No, no, no, just sometimes. I get calls and I need somebody." He was looking for something like a muse.

I told my office, who was always so supportive of me. They were like, "That's wonderful!" Those are my Jewish mothers, sisters Sylvia and Ruth Manchester. Bernie Ozer was the one who really put me on the map. You all know Bernie?

I remember Bernie.

Yes. God bless you. He was very special for me. The first time I ever did a fashion show was with Bernie. He used to put on the shows for his junior buyers.

Bernie, for those of you who don't know, worked in one of the big buying offices. Those offices were the ones who really told the stores what to buy. They were the eyes and ears of the entire market. They saw and sourced everything, domestically, internationally. They were the bible, not the fashion editors, and Bernie was a big man. Bernie was the oracle.

He would go over to Europe. He had this flair. He had an incredible style.

Because he loved the theater so much, whenever he did a fashion show for his buyers, he put together a show. I was taking my junior dresses from Ruth Manchester over to them. I had been a well-known child tap dancer back in my day, when I was nine to twelve years old. My hoofer was Duke Baldwin; he taught me to tap.

I went up to him, and I just couldn't resist. I leaned in his ear and said, "If you really want to have a great show, you'll have me in it."

He asked, "Where are you from?" I said, "Ruth Manchester."

He said, "OK, get those dresses over there," and he didn't say anything else to me. By the time I got back to my office, oh, Sylvia was so excited. "Oh, my God, Bernie wants to put you on the show!" And that was the beginning.

Did you tap in the show?

No, I didn't tap. But, you know, I found out that I was theatrical. I didn't walk like the other girls. I performed a bit.

The first show you did was a Bernie Ozer production?

It was Bernie Ozer. Then he started using me all the time. He was so impressed with me. The crowd would just clap and clap. He said, "Where did you come from, with all that?"

I told him, "I used to be a tap dancer."

It was very easy for me because when you tap, you had to "wow" the crowd. Duke Baldwin used to have these big shows he put on at night. My mother would have to wake me up. I found two girls to tap with me that were my age, too. They would take us out at night. We couldn't get paid, so they would throw us money. We had to collect the money up off the floor. It would be ten, eleven, twelve o'clock at night, and then the next day, I had to go to school. He was mad cool.

After modeling in Bernie shows, you then start to work for Willi?

Yes, I worked with him as a muse. Then eventually I didn't work for Ruth and Sylvia anymore. Willi had me be his assistant.

How would you describe what Willi's contribution was to fashion?

I want to tell you that Alexandra Cunningham is here. She's a curator and she's going to put together a Willi Smith exhibit, which is major because that's not easy to do. It's going to be at the Cooper Hewitt Museum. That's not easy because with people like that, you don't always have a lot of the things you can find. I have to gather the clothes, like what I did for Stephen Burrows.

That was a huge thing because Stephen didn't have a lot of his things, either. A lot of his stuff got burned in a fire, even the dress I wore at Versailles! You had to do a lot of work to try and find the garments. His show was at the Museum of the City of New York. We pulled that off.

Fantastic, but tell people what Willi was about.

When people talk about streetwear, which is really a tricky word right now, because if you're old, you basically resent hearing these words drop so easily. If anyone truly created streetwear, it was Willi Smith. We called it streetwear because whenever you were out on the street, you always saw people in WilliWear. It became streetwear. Everybody had Willi Smith.

Willi was a basic sportswear designer, but his shapes were great. He was so special. He was that kind of charming guy that all the editors loved. He was wise enough to send you flowers. He was such a well-raised Black kid.

He had the taste, the style. He was very good friends with many people in the art world. His taste for art was very good. I was telling a story about how Willi always wanted me to introduce him to Jean-Michel Basquiat, and I did. Jean-Michel was very happy with that, because he needed someone to buy some art. Willi bought, like, six paintings and stuff like that from him. It was really kind of a good situation.

He has a great, fabulous sister, Toukie Smith. She was also a muse to him.

Yes. She became that.

That was an interesting time. Was it from there that you started doing runway shows for Anne Klein, Oscar de la Renta, Calvin Klein, and Perry Ellis?

Yes, at some point I became a model. I tried it because I was encouraged by Willi. Willi really thought I should take it on, that I had the goods. He introduced me to Bruce Weber. Bruce Weber had just begun to take up the camera. Every Saturday, we go out and he'd

photograph me. His pictures were the best of me, really, truly. Everybody else afterward, I was, like, "Oh, my God, I can't."

I'm not a print model. Runway was my thing, you know?

That was where your personality came out.

Personality and all that. I know you want me to tell that story about Jean-Michel Basquiat, no? I took Willi down to Jean-Michel's studio, which was still on Great Jones Street at that time. I was watching what he was showing, and Willi was just buying this and selecting that. There is one black and white that I loved, and I kept thinking to myself, "Oh, my God, I wish I could get that." But of course, I'm not able to buy anything like that.

Afterward I thought, well, maybe they'll give me one, just because I'm doing such a big deal for Jean-Michel and he was just so happy. Jean-Michel called me up. He said, "I got something for you," and I was so excited. I was like, "Oh, he's going to give that to me."

He comes by the house, and he brings me a bag of marijuana, about this big [HAND MOTIONING A LARGE BOX]. I looked at it and I go, "Jean-Michel, Jesus Christ, it will take me a lifetime to smoke this." And he said, "So we're good then, huh?"

And it took me a lifetime.

Did he at least draw on the bag or something? Back to those modeling days. I remember I met you back when you were modeling for people like Clovis Ruffin. That's when all the girls would just dance down the runway. It was a party.

I became a fit model for Clovis as well. I was a fit model for Willi, at different times.

In that time frame, we could do anything we wanted. The designers hoped that you would come prepared to bring them inspiration. But that's what they anticipated. You know, there was a freedom at the time for modeling. You could do whatever your personality was, and the audience expected it.

One of the greatest times I ever had… Jeffrey Banks, who worked with Calvin then, will remember it. Talk about bringing it. Calvin, being the great marketer he was, he took the show out of the showrooms. Calvin found a loft and had them build a runway there. That was the first time a designer ever did that, and his music was always banging. Always banging.

I never got the great clothes because I was so skinny, and not curvy, and not that girl. I was always a sportswear girl and they put the worst clothes on me because, "Oh, Bethann, you could sell this." That's what they tell you when they're putting clothes on you and you're hating everything. "But you can sell it. You can sell it."

It was lower Broadway because that's where all the lofts were. Calvin sent me out, and that song came on, and it was my moment. I had to go out and it was just me. It was just a plaid cowboy shirt. That song was so good. From the moment I hit that stage, I danced that whole runway. The audience went wild.

When I came back, Calvin said, "What were you doing out there?" But the shirts sold like you couldn't believe. I always remember Jeffrey saying that, because he was working for him as an assistant designer, "You can't believe how that shirt took off." I had a good time.

So they were right putting that stuff on you?

Yes, a lot of times. They were always right about it. But it just was so sad, you know? You look at Pat Cleveland, and she had the cute dress, and everybody else had all the great things, and I had these same corny clothes.

How did you connect with Stephen Burrows?

That was Willi Smith, again. His O boutique was right across the street from Max's Kansas City, on Park Avenue South. Those kids were extraordinary. They were a little tribe. You didn't see anything like that. I only wish something like that could happen again. Stephen Burrows and these guys and girls, they just all were together all the time.

Willi used to tell me about Stephen, and I sort of knew of him. I'd see the O boutique. But when he finally got to Henri Bendel— it was the first show he had at Bendel's—Willi called up Bobby Breslau and told him, "You've got to see Bethann. She's so great." But Stephen never really liked me. He didn't like me as one of his girls.

When he left Bendel's, and Ben Shaw invested in Stephen and brought him to 550 Seventh Avenue, Roz Rubenstein, who was Stephen's right hand at the time, asked me to come in as their showroom girl. That was the beginning of my relationship working with Stephen, because of Roz. Roz was a great teacher. She used to work for Bendel's, too.

That's how I began to work with Stephen.

What wound up happening is slowly everything started to change. Roz left. I slowly went into the design area and started to actually work with him more as heading the design studio, overseeing it, and becoming his right hand.

I mean, Stephen is an extraordinary talent. Why do you think he didn't have the staying power?

Stephen is not a businessman. A lot of designers are. They are much more business savvy than you think. I could name the ones that we still know are around. It takes something; you can't just be the person who understands design. It helps to have some sort of passion, of ego. If you do not have some passion, of ego, oftentimes things fade. I think he went back and forth to Bendel's. It's about finding that right person that can connect the dots for you.

If you've got the goods, you've got the goods. Even after all of this, when we didn't see him in the industry for ten years, Bendel's brought him back. He lasted there for two or three years. Then he went off and did his own company again, when a friend named John Robert Miller went in to help him. Then John passed away. It's always a journey; you have journeys.

It's not easy to be a designer. I was just being interviewed for the BBC on Radio Four, speaking about the state of fashion and the designer of color, the Black designer: where is he? That always pisses me off. Because it's not an easy thing to be a designer, period. But it is not easier for someone of color to be that, either. That's one of the reasons why I want to help designers.

But there was a moment back then with Stephen, Willi, and Scott Barry, Jon Haggins… There was a big community of Black designers and Black models.

There was a huge number of designers that were of color and that were Black. That was at the time when it was a much easier game. It was a much easier game.

OK. Let's go to 1973 and the Battle of Versailles. You were one in the group of incredible Black models who were brought over.

There were white models, too. I'd just like to say that.

But the Black models were the ones who captured everybody's imagination. It was something revolutionary.

When I interviewed Bill Cunningham at the 92nd Street Y, the last question of our interview was, "What was your favorite fashion show?" He went on for quite a while about the Battle of Versailles, and specifically singling you out for when you walked across that stage with this reed through your hair. He said, "She had such a fierce look and she just owned that stage. The audience was riveted. They didn't know what to do." You were such a power in that show. It was a marvelous moment, how he talked about you. It was really beautiful.

I remember talking about it, too, as Bill cried that time. I remember talking to the BBC, and I started to talk about that moment, and I'm actually there again. It really was quite unique.

The different thing with me is even when I was a model, I always had a full-time job. With the other girls, they were just models, which is a wonderful thing; that's their career at that moment. I had a full-time job, and then I modeled. With Stephen, I was his assistant, I ran his design studio, and I fit the clothes.

I could always go out and model with other designers. He was fine with it. Ben and Guido, the owners of the company, were fine with it because I always delivered. But this time, I almost didn't make Versailles because each girl had to have three designers who selected them. I only had two so far. One was Anne Klein because she needed me to help her. She was doing an African collection. She all of a sudden needed Black girls, which she never used before. I had to come over to her and explain things to her, so I definitely had her. I had Stephen.

But up until like ten days before, I didn't have the third designer. Halston told Stephen, "Tell Bethann not to worry." Stephen said, "I have to have Bethann there because you know she is not just a model, but because she does other things." I worked for him. Halston said, "I'll take her if nobody else takes her," but I wasn't a Halston girl. Then Oscar stepped up, and that was the greatest thing.

So, going there, I'm working. The other girls have a different life. They're freer. It was terrible. The atmosphere, it wasn't as comfortable for us as we would have liked. The hall was very cold. It was not an easy thing.

At the same time, I had to pay a lot of attention to Stephen and the details of what we had to do as a team. The designers were all fighting, and poor Anne, she was miserable.

There were a lot of battles about who went first and who went next.

Yes, exactly. It was a wonderful experience in many ways, even with all the little nuances of

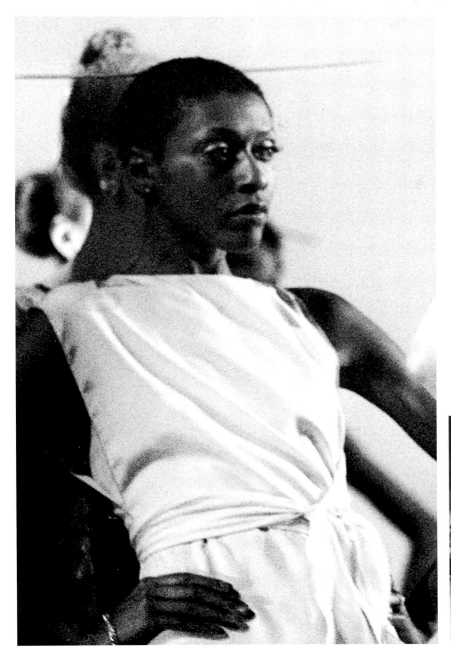

Pages 392–393: Models (Bethann Hardison wearing a blue beret) lifting Stephen Burrows in the air for a spread in *Vogue*, 1977. This page, clockwise from top: Bethann wearing Stephen Burrows at the Battle at Versailles in 1973; Another view of Bethann at Versailles; The American models at the Battle of Versailles flanking Josephine Baker.

Iman, Bethann Hardison, and June Ambrose at the Kenzo x H&M launch in 2018.

how and what didn't happen. Anne being sad because she was the only woman. She probably knew then that she had cancer. I learned about it when she got back. I had to really stay close to her and help her.

Every time we did rehearsals, I would just pace it. Halston was always saying, "Come on, Bethann, we need you now! Come on now! You know what to do."

I'd go, "Yeah, yeah, I got it," because I'm just pacing it. I can't really give it to you like I'm going to give it. The other girls, they're just doing their thing. I'm an actor. I'm a performer.

I get the dress on, and the dress was very special to Stephen because he was always designing in knits, and this was a woven piece. It was a canary yellow, silk dress, and he built it in a way that it was like a couture dress. I knew the significance of this.

In all the rehearsals, I had Halston in my ears saying, "Now come on, Bethann." Well, I knew when I hit that stage, I was going to bring it. That was that moment, and I really brought it. I defied everybody in that entire audience. I defied that entire room. I really wanted them to know that we're here to take this because we have been put down so much. They were saying, "The American designers are nothing. Who are they to come over to Paris?" All the people who were supporting us and who were going to come with us for months before, they started fading—all the editors. The only ones who were excited to go were Bill Cunningham and Marylou Luther.

Marylou's the best. She's always here at Fashion Icons.

She was gung-ho to go. But otherwise, everybody was so nervous for us. They were not there to support us. We looked like we're going into a dungeon. That was our beginning.

I stayed, instead of moving like I was going to move. I stayed there for so long. The longer I stayed there, the more they screamed. When I turned and looked at them, I gave them that look, like, "Don't you even try it." We knew we had them. Yes, that was the moment.

And that standing ovation would make it all worthwhile?

They threw their programs in the air! They started storming backstage! I didn't know what was happening. It was like a graduation.

That was the moment. Shortly after that, this model that Peter Beard discovered in Somalia came to Stephen's showroom?

That's right.

Shall I read what Iman said about that experience with you, when I interviewed her for Fashion Icons?

You can.

Iman said that she came into Stephen Burrows's showroom and she was very nervous about being there. She was trembling a little bit. She couldn't tie her shoes. She said, "Bethann got down on her knees to help me put the shoes on. The whole room erupted, telling her, 'Don't do that; now she will think she is a princess, and we all will have to go down on our knees.'"

It was not the whole room, it was only two girls. It was my fitting girls, just to be clear.

You put the heels on Iman, and you looked up at Iman, and you said, "You speak English and you understand everything they're saying, right?" Iman said to you, in English, "Yes." When I interviewed Iman here, and you were here that night, she said that people didn't think she spoke English at all.

Well, she just let them believe it, yes.

You helping her in that moment was a big deal for Iman.

She considered that a moment, yes. As life went on, she always regarded me in that moment as her Statue of Liberty.

She said you were the first face to welcome her in the country.

She always said that, yes.

When Iman married David Bowie, you were her maid of honor. What was that like?

I was blown away that she had asked me to do that. I couldn't believe it. I thought to myself, "You're kidding." She said, "Who else would I have asked? Who else would I want?" I was so stunned by it all, you know. It was wonderful.

We went to Florence. Joe, David's son, was the best man and it was just the four of us. It was a small gathering of people that came, some notables, of course. I was always David's favorite in so many ways, too. It was a wonderful thing to be part of.

In 1984, you formed Bethann Management. Your focus then was diversifying the fashion industry. You worked with a lot of models: Roshumba Williams, Veronica Webb, and Tyson Beckford.

Well, let's start and get real-real. Bonnie Berman. That's the real deal. She and Talisa Soto were the two who wanted me to be on my own. Little seventeen-year-old Talisa, and Bonnie who was just out of Princeton University. They just wanted me to be on my own. Ariane Koizumi wanted me to be on my own. It was five girls, including Mariama, Angela Alvarado.

And Gina Figueroa. And then, God bless, Nick Kamen, who basically gave me the opportunity to represent these kids. I found my little office on North Moore Street.

Bonnie found the money. Everybody that was going to come with me, I told them I couldn't afford to do the voucher system that all the model agencies had, where you were paid every two weeks. Bonnie and all the models said they'll take the risk with me. That had never been done before. We were a tiny, smaller agency.

I pioneered a lot of things. I pioneered moving to North Moore Street, rats and all. Someone determined like Bonnie found the money. David Irving's family gave me the money and believed in me. I'm very proud of this.

How many years did you have the agency?

The corporation is there, but I sat at the agency for thirteen years.

Tyson was a big breakthrough client for you.

He was a breakthrough for Ralph Lauren. I just want to keep it 100.

I was in an emotional moment right then thinking about Bonnie, the girls, and my initial team. You know, that was big for these kids to do that. They had to walk in and say, "I'm leaving." Tahnee Welch, she was the first. Tahnee Welch is Raquel Welch's daughter. She was my first. Veronica learned about me from Matt Robinson. I think she was at NYU or something like that. He said, "You need to go to see Bethann Hardison. She's at an agency called Click." She went to Click and found out I had left. She said, "What are you doing here?" That's the story I heard, anyway.

She's here tonight and she could verify that. Your relationship with Naomi Campbell… she apparently got you out of your hammock in Mexico at a certain point when you were there and said, "We need you back"?

When Naomi came calling me, it was because the models of color had disappeared off the runway. That was in 1997. The Black Girls Coalition was created in 1988.

Why do you think they disappeared?

The industry had changed. Casting directors came into play. Big stylists and things like that changed our industry. The design companies no longer were on their own to decide who the models were. Also scouting was big in Eastern Europe. The Eastern European girl was really the flavor at the time. They had the silhouette of what we sketched as models: they're narrow-hipped, very long, and hardworking. It was just a change of time.

There was no guard. If you have no moral compass of somebody saying something, then it just changed.

Where was Regis Pagniez from *Elle* at that time?

Oh, Regis! Oh, my God, thank you for bringing him up. Regis Pagniez: his coming to set up American *Elle* was our savior. He just liked beautiful women, and he loved beautiful women of any color. When he came along, he started putting girls of color in American *Elle*—on the pages, on the cover, and that ignited the competition because that magazine took off so fast and was doing so well.

Bethann Hardison with granddaughter Sophia Hardison and Tyson Beckford at the premiere of *About Face: Supermodels Then and Now*, a documentary by Timothy Greenfield-Sanders, in 2012.

That pushed Condé Nast and Hearst to have to move their asses. Then *Vogue* and other Condé Nast magazines had to catch up with what he was doing. That helped to bring those girls out. That's what made me start the Black Girls Coalition. Seeing these girls come about.

What do you think now about the groundswell of Black designers in the forefront? I'm thinking of Kerby Jean-Raymond at Pyer Moss, Telfar Clemens, Virgil Abloh, LaQuan Smith, Romeo Hunte, Heron Preston, Tracy Reese. Ozwald Boateng is having a show in New York in two weeks. What's your take on diversity in the industry now, from the designers' point of view?

From the designers' point of view, I think there are probably many more people whose names we don't even know yet. The important thing is for their companies to become strong. That's my objective right now, to help designers have a good business.

When people say, "Where are they?" I don't know if they think we're supposed to be in a clubhouse, where there is a whole bunch of them. It just pisses me off. It really gets me a little annoyed. The fact of it is that there are designers out there. It's not an easy business. That's what Ralph Lauren said at the CFDA. It's one of the hardest businesses. He has been in it for fifty years, and he didn't act like it was easy.

There's a lot of good energy and good talent out there.

I think that we can't be judged by the fact that someone who is very successful, and gets the chance to represent a luxury brand, gets compared to the guy who is just trying to make sure he doesn't go out the back door of his business. I think that's the most important thing.

Now you are a consultant to the CFDA to cultivate the next generation of Black designers.

No, you know, I don't like that. You see where I'm going, right? I just like designers, and if you look at them, they're Black. I mean, because "Black designer" sounds like a cult or a rash.

If we know of some young, up-and-coming talented designers that need guidance can we send them your way to get some advice?

As long as they have a business and they are not "wannabes." I'm not interested in "wannabes." I'm interested in people who have a business.

Fashion is reflective of so many things in society. You're also consulting now for Gucci about their diversity initiatives, and they've taken a very strong stand with removing controversial products from the market. Was that racist, the products that they were putting out there?

Definitely not. It's not racist. Many people saw it as something that looked like blackface.

I want to be real-real with you. I would have never necessarily flagged the Gucci sweater as racist, I didn't see it that way. Rihanna wore it two months before. I have girlfriends and they're begging for that sweater. I didn't see it the way somebody else saw it. I didn't see it that way but that doesn't matter. It's how someone else feels.

If someone sees something and feels something, that's fair, but that wasn't the intent. The person making it was not saying, "I'm going to go out there and make some racist things for people." Nobody's doing that. No design company or firm is trying to do that. But sometimes they will make something, and with society now so sensitive…

… With social media that reacts in a nanosecond.

… If you present something, somebody may not have thought about it that way. The same thing happened with Burberry and Riccardo Tisci and the rope necklace. It was a rope necklace. But for many people, it was indicative of suicide or lynching. It all depends on how you look at it.

I didn't see it that way. I have many friends who didn't see it that way. I said to the company, you didn't do anything wrong, but what you did offended some people. That's the most important thing to understand.

How do you advise these companies? Should they apologize and remove the product at great cost? Or should they explain that there was no malicious intent?

Everybody immediately tells you that that's not what the intent was. First it was Prada, then it was Gucci, then it was Burberry, and these things happen. It's not the intent of the design firm. It's just unfortunate. I'm an old-school Gucci fan. I'm not about hip-hop and any of that. I knew Aldo Gucci. I knew the brothers.

Do you remember when the store was on Fifth Avenue and they closed at lunchtime for an hour, like in Milan?

That's right. It was so different. Oh, God, Fern. God bless age.

We have some questions from our audience.

Oh, I love this.

Somebody here says they met you several weeks ago in Marrakech at the Sufian Concept Shop. What attracted you to Morocco, and Marrakech in particular?

Oh, wow. What attracts me to Morocco? That's because of my dad, too. I mean, many years ago when I was young and lived with my father, I used to have a fascination with Morocco. A lot of wise men, religious men, used to come into town to see my dad from Yemen to Saudi Arabia, Egypt, Pakistan, Karachi.

My father said to me, "What is this fascination with Morocco? I don't know anyone from Morocco." I would go, "I don't know."

I think there was a movie called *Joanna* that I loved back in the day, and I always wanted to know it. Someone I knew had just built a *riad* in Marrakech. He always promised he was going to take me when it was finished, and he did. I was working for Dolce & Gabbana in

Opposite: Bethann Hardison at the CFDA and Google's Black Fashion Founders Summit in 2018. This page, from left to right: Bethann and Fern Mallis at the 1994 Ralph Lauren fashion show; Bethann and Edward Enninful at the RL50 fashion show in 2018.

Clockwise from top: Bethann Hardison receiving CFDA's 2014 Founder's Award, presented by Iman and Naomi Campbell; Bethann holding her award; Then-CFDA president Diane Von Furstenberg and Michael Kors congratulating Bethann.

2010. That was the beginning.

Will you buy a place there?

No, never. I'll never buy another place, ever. But I've been very lucky because my friend there, he just built me a little something there.

That's a nice friend to have.

You have a documentary called *Invisible Beauty* that's been in development a long time.

Oh, my God. The bane of my existence is my documentary. I think it's a dance.

It will happen.

Inshallah.

A potential book? An autobiography?

Inshallah. I hope so, in both cases. I owe it to the community, right? I know that. I'm doing my best figuring it out. I said something the other day: "I want to be a fly on my wall," and someone said, "You should make that a book title."

Sometimes things that happened to me, I am just so taken aback. That's why it's important that you never know how old I am, because there's a story to be told.

Is there something still that you haven't tackled that you want to do?

There's nothing I've ever wanted to do, never. There's nothing I've ever wanted to do. The only thing I ever said I want to do is lay in the hammock. But I never have any ambitions and things like that. It's always been what lands at my feet.

That's the lazy part.

That's the lazy part, exactly.

What would you like your legacy to be?

Oh, wow. I always used to say as long as it doesn't say, "There lies Bethann, who had a model agency." As long as they don't say that, I don't care what else happens.

This page: Bethann Hardison in Gucci arriving at the 2019 Met Gala; Bethann at the Metropolitan Museum of Art's tribute to the models of The Battle of Versailles in 2011. Next spread: Bethann and Pat Cleveland in 2015.

Not a chance. That's not going to be it. Who would be your dream lunch date?

My dream lunch date? Vladimir Putin. I know, but I'm fascinated. I know. I know. I could say Cardi B, but everybody would say that, so Putin.

At what point did you realize you were contributing to a movement?

Oh, that's a good one. I never thought I was contributing to a movement because I always sort of thought that when things are happening, we are the movement. I think we're creating a revolution. I'm the person who pokes the bear. I'm the one who starts it. I never think I'm contributing to it, because I *am* it.

It's a scary thing sometimes, to take things on. I always joke that I called Fidel Castro. And I would say, "I spoke to Fidel this morning," because that was my way of trying to understand how to step into being this person that was a revolutionary. What that meant was that you were going to take the hit.

That's the reason why I don't have any problems stepping into the "mental danger zone" when I work with these companies, or when I help to educate white people, or when I want to go and fight for something that I think is so important to our society. I think it's so important to do that.

I noticed in myself that I'm that person who feels very comfortable doing it. I don't know how, or why. I'm always glad that I have the young people behind me who are my backup band. I'm the front of the band, and I take the hit of course if something goes wrong because I'm the one who did write those letters.

I'm still learning who I am.

… And that keeps you young, at whatever age you are.

Yes.

Do we dare end on this question? How will we move forward post-Trump? I hope there is a post-Trump. How will we overcome this racial divide?

Yes, that's a hard one. I think that every one of us is so responsible for how we think and what we do. It's really tough right now because we were always told to suppress, or when someone is not nice to stay mellow. Then you have someone that comes along that allows people to think that it's OK to be a certain way. It's going to be really tough. I really don't know.

All I do is shake my head. I'm sure you all do every day.

Every hour.

Yes, I do, too. I just shake my head. You know, I have a home in Mexico in the mountains. Everybody was moving to this town because of President George W. Bush. They couldn't stand it. I couldn't imagine leaving my country because of its politics. I couldn't imagine leaving my country because I really am an American.

I don't know what to do. I really feel my hands are tied. I stay in my neighborhood.

I think one of the things we can do is keep raising our children. If you are young parents, please be strict with your children. The most important thing in the world is to give them a great deal of boundaries. I think it starts with the kids, in the homes. I know everyone's so busy, and so distracted, and we just want to stay in our lane. That's the best thing I can do: stay in my lane.

… And your lane has been a very powerful, impactful, and important lane. On that note, thank you.

SINCE FASHION ICONS

In 2020, Bethann launched the CFDA's Designer Hub, a mentorship program for young designers of color, enlisting industry veterans Patrick Robinson and Tracy Reese to serve as its advisers. Also in 2020, Bethann made her acting debut on the CW's series *Black Lightning*. Bethann, Iman, and Naomi Campbell continue to work together to advocate for a more diverse and inclusive fashion industry. Bethann is working on her autobiography and a documentary about her life, both tentatively titled *Invisible Beauty*. Bethann lives in the Gramercy Park neighborhood of Manhattan. Follow Bethann on Instagram: @bethannhardison

ZANDRA RHODES

I am so thrilled to be here with Dame Zandra Rhodes. She has been a true inspiration to me and a designer I have admired forever. On my very first trip to London I shopped at Biba, Mary Quant, Foale & Tuffin, and Ossie Clark. I can kill myself for giving them all away, not that any of it would fit me now.

But I didn't buy a Zandra Rhodes dress. I actually kept dreaming that I would be married in one of her floaty white-on-white chiffon dresses with the little pearls dangling from the borders. Well, there hasn't been a wedding yet. But now, several decades later, even better, we've become friends. Zandra and I bonded on the inaugural Fashion Week crossing of the extraordinary Queen Mary.

As Suzy Menkes says in the foreword in 50 Fabulous Years in Fashion*: "With shocking pink hair and dresses decorated punk-style, with safety pins—Zandra Rhodes burst into a fashion era that was named for a new energy: 'Swinging London.'" ... And yes, this was before Vivienne Westwood and Versace's safety pins.*

When Pierpaolo Piccioli of Maison Valentino chose her to create the textile designs for his Spring/Summer 2017 collection, she reinterpreted Hieronymus Bosch's painting The Garden of Earthly Delights. *Of this collaboration, Piccioli said: "I still remember the emotion of seeing Zandra's first sketches. I could not have asked for a more vibrant and unconventional vision. I was astonished by her talent for combining pictorial and pop symbols such as flames, hearts, lipsticks, and thunderbolts, in shades of red and pink. Meeting Zandra, to me, meant facing the beauty of revolutionary artists. She is incredibly strong and kind at the same time, and she is a good friend, and I love her."*

... And I couldn't say it any better myself. Let's give a colorful welcome to Dame Zandra Rhodes.

ZANDRA RHODES: Well, what can I say? Lovely to be here. Thank you.

FERN MALLIS: You've been all over the world in the last few weeks: London, India, California...

... Shanghai, and then I landed here.

I think you haven't had a lot of sleep yet, either, so I'm going to keep kicking you to keep you awake tonight. I really am thrilled that we're finally here. Congratulations on your beautiful and informative book. Does fifty years feel like it went by in a flash?

It definitely went by in a flash. It goes by and you suddenly realize it's gone, and it's passing by quicker and quicker.

That seems to be the case. But now we're going to go back and start even before your fifty years in fashion. You were born on September 19, 1940. The math's easy, how old does that make you now?

From left to right: Zandra Rhodes's mother, Beatrice Rhodes; Zandra, Beatrice, and Beverley Rhodes on the steps of the Sacre Coeur, in Paris.

Seventy-nine [APPLAUSE].

We do know that seventy is the new fifty. Eighty is the new sixty. We heard the other night that ninety is the new eighty-five. How old do you feel?

I sort of just keep going. As long as I don't look in the mirror, I don't feel any different.

Yeah, mirrors are a problem. You were born during World War II.

Yes, there were bombs going overhead in Chatham. The bombs would go across and then when they stopped buzzing, that's when you knew that the bomb would come down.

I read that you said, "I can remember being held up to the sky to see the doodlebugs, and drawing chalk butterflies in an air raid shelter."

That's about all I can remember. My mother drove an ambulance during the war and I was brought up by my grandmother, who had a news agent shop. My mother would be driving the ambulance, so she'd be working. My father was in Egypt at the time, I think.

You're a Virgo. I'm going to read you some positive Virgo traits. Tell me if you agree with them: intelligent, analytic, honest, reliable, artistic, hardworking, faithful, patient, and modest.

I always think of it as boring and hardworking.

Boring? "Boring" is not a word I would ever use with you. Not even close. Negative traits: critical, judgmental, old-school, fussy, slow, stubborn, uptight, and picky.

Oh, I think they're pretty true, yes.

You're the first person that's agreed about all the negative traits. Some of the famous Virgos: Cameron Diaz, Beyoncé, Michael Jackson, Pink, Sophia Loren, Amy Winehouse, Mother Teresa, Hugh Grant, and Freddie Mercury, whom you've dressed. OK, so as you said, you were born in Chatham, Kent, right? Where exactly is that in England?

If you were to go by the train from London to Dover, it's about halfway. In those days, in the time of Turner and even before, it's a branch of the River Thames. It was considered a naval town, but for small ships in those days.

How long did it take you to get to London?

It was an hour by train. It's probably now about twenty-five minutes.

Your mom's name is Beatrice?

That's right.

I couldn't find your father's name anywhere.

My father was Albert James.

Your mother apparently walked down the hill to the hospital to have you in the middle of an air raid?

That's my understanding. I mean, the air raids were going on, yes.

OK, and as you said, your mother was an ambulance driver, but she was also a fitter at the House of Worth?

She drove an ambulance during the war, yes. Before she got married, she was a fitter at the House of Worth in Paris. Later on she taught in the local art college that I went to. She was always draping on the stand at home and everything like that.

She was teaching there when you went there?

She was teaching, but I pretended she wasn't my mother. I didn't want people to think I got special treatment. I didn't particularly want to go into making clothes. I first thought I'd be an illustrator, and there was a fantastic teacher then, Barbara Brown, that interested me in doing textiles.

But I read that when growing up, your father's mother, your grandmother, was a prostitute who was stabbed to death in the street, when he was a small boy? That has to have been somewhat dramatic.

My mother told me that. He never talked about anything like that, but my mother said that later on. She met him ballroom dancing. He was very handsome. He looked like Errol Flynn. She said, "Oh, you're that boy." He was only about four when this happened. It was a naval town and this was a big scandal in the town apparently.

Your mother was much more influential in your upbringing than your dad?

Oh, totally, my mother was the influence, yes.

... And grandmother?

She was just very hardworking and supportive.

Your siblings: you have a sister, Beverley? Is it just the two of you?

She's married to a doctor and they live in Amersham. She's got four children and seven grandchildren.

You're Auntie Mame?

I suppose I'm Auntie Mame. But I don't see them very often now. Years ago when I had to tidy up, I'd always say, "Could you bring the goblins so we could play games?" Then they would tidy up my shoes and my jewelry.

What was the dynamic like growing up at home when you were both kids? Is she younger?

She's three years younger than I am. I would say, in truth, if you asked me to describe myself

as such, I'd say I was just a boring hardworking Virgo. I liked school. I didn't need to go out to a lot of different things. I always did my homework. I would say boring things like, "Oh, I think I should do my work because I want to do it, and I like sitting in the front row." Totally boring.

You said you wanted to be an illustrator. I read you also wanted to be an archaeologist.

You've read a lot of notes. You remember more about me than I do. How? I mean, I did love to read books on archaeology and the Egyptians, and all those things, when I was at school.

Then it was Midway College of Art in Kent, that's where your mom taught. In 1961, that's when you went the Royal College of Art in London to specifically study textile and prints?

Yes, I got a scholarship from Midway College of Art to the Royal College, for textiles. Printed textiles.

That was the most acclaimed design school in London at the time?

Yes, [David] Hockney was there. Who else was there? Well, all sorts of different people.

Were you friends with David Hockney?

Yes, funny enough, I got to know him through my great friend Joan Quinn, who is here, when I was in LA. I didn't know him when I was at college because you worshipped him from afar.

But now you can worship him up close?

That's it, yes.

I also read this: is it true you had a boyfriend who you'd only go out with on Saturdays?

Well, that's right, because I was working the rest of the time.

Were you at that time dressing colorfully?

I like dressing up. When my mother was at the college we used to model in the college dress shows and I used to like wearing the clothes from the shows. You know, the pretty little embroidered things and bonnets. I'd put them on on a Sunday to go to see my grandmother, and I would have to run through the park because the children would throw stones at me because they'd say I look funny.

I know this probably happened a little bit later, but when did you start to dye your hair?

About 1970. After I'd left Royal College, Vidal Sassoon brought out those lovely green wigs. I thought the wigs pinched your head and I thought, you know, if sheep hair can be dyed, why can't we dye our hair? I went to Leonard Louis. At that time they would bleach my hair and we tried textile dye on it because I thought that would work. Well, it used to come out on the pillow. But it was green first of all, and then later purple, and then became pink. I used to stick feathers on the end of my hair with eyelash glue.

You did pink, and you did red, and you did blue, and orange, but then you settled on pink?

Pink is so easy to keep. I don't have much of a problem with it, except growing out of it.

Does your pink hair have a Pantone color?

Well, it's a mixture of Pinkissimo and Cerise. The dyes are now made in Belgium and they're pretty permanent. They're very good.

Have you let it grow out at all in your later life?

When I first came to live in California, I once thought I needed to be maybe a bit more conservative. I had my hair dyed brown and I went to a cocktail party and, you know how people say, "I'm Mary Jane." I'd go, "I'm Zandra Rhodes." They'd go, "I'm sorry. I'm sorry." They felt embarrassed when I said, "I'm Zandra Rhodes." They didn't realize it was me. I'd much rather keep my hair pink.

All right, good enough reason. Then you met Marylou Luther, I think in 1969, when she was the fashion editor of the _Los Angeles Times_. Was that when you met her?

Yes. I met Marylou, who I know is somewhere in this audience.

… And you told her, "I decided I must be an extension of my designs. I used myself as

Opposite: Zandra Rhodes with _Los Angeles Times_ fashion and beauty editor Marylou Luther in 1977. This page: Zandra working in her studio, 1985.

a canvas with no compromises, experimenting with my image using cosmetics and my hair to make an impact."

I think if you're a designer and you're creating a product. If I'm not wearing my stuff then what am I telling people to wear?

When you graduated, what was your first job?

My first job was teaching. I taught textile design at the Royal College. It was only a part-time job. I'd be teaching two days a week, and then I tried to sell my work to manufacturers. We would go up to Manchester to show the designs. They would go, "I wouldn't sell any of this." Then they would get some terrible texture and go, "a million yards of this." I discovered that I couldn't sell my textile designs. I realized that I'd have to print them myself and get other people interested in them. I took my designs to Foale & Tuffin, who were then the queens of Carnaby Street, and they commissioned me. I did work for them for three years.

Then you decided to open your own place?

While I was teaching, I met Sylvia Ayton, who had been at college with Sally and Marion, of Foale & Tuffin, and we decided we'd do a collection together using my prints on the garments, with her designs. Then I had ideas that I wanted to do things and she started to show me how. We met Vanessa Redgrave, who sponsored a shop, the Fulton Road Clothing Shop. Not sure on the name of this store, Fern. We stayed open one year. Sylvia got offered a job at Wallace Shops and I was without a job again. I thought, I can't face teaching anymore. I'm going to put my own collection together.

How did you do that? I love hearing how people start a collection and start a business.

I already had a studio that I shared with another designer, Alex MacIntyre. I had a place to work. I got sewing machines and things. People used to say, "Well, if you're a textile designer you can't be a fashion designer." I thought, well, when I was at Royal College, people who designed fashion didn't look that much more intelligent than I was. I think I'm going to have a go. I did a series of prints. I showed them to English *Vogue*. They photographed them on amazing Ukrainian American models. They said, "You've got to go to America. You've got to go to America. You'll make your fortune." I got myself a ticket to come to New York and a letter of introduction to Diana Vreeland.

Who gave you a letter of introduction?

That was from the head of English *Vogue*. Diana Vreeland then photographed my designs on Natalie Wood and also introduced me to Henri Bendel. That was 1969.

That's a nice way to start a business in America. Diana's blessing and Henri Bendel in its heyday.

That's it. I did a collection each season with them. I'd come over and bring the collection to show them. People at that time came to London as well. Then in 1975, I founded a shop on Bond Street. Then I started to do my huge spectacular shows.

But first, your success in America: it was at Bendel's and then you also sold to Sakowitz.

I went to Houston for Sakowitz, and then to… I'm trying to think, who was the next one? It

A brunette Zandra Rhodes in her Notting Hill Gate studio, 1969.

was Martha's. Martha's Palm Beach, where I went down and did a show with Bill Blass.

You also did Martha's in New York, where you did a show at the Pierre Hotel.

But that was a bit later. That particular show is in the Andy Warhol Museum and it's one of my favorites.

Because Andy photographed it. That was a surprise to you when you went to the museum.

He filmed the whole thing, yes. When I went to the Pittsburgh [Andy Warhol] Museum, when I was doing the *Pearl Fishers* opera in Pittsburgh, I went to the museum and there was my show playing in there, which is wonderful.

Wonderful surprise. The success in America really made a difference for your business, right?

That was really the key of my business. I gradually did tours for both Neiman Marcus and for Saks.

Then in the UK, Fortnum & Mason also created a little shop for you.

Fortnum & Mason had created their shop with me, Jean Muir, and Bill Gibb. That would be 1967 through 1969, and then I founded my shop.

In the 1970s you were part of the big wave of British designers that was really propelling London to the forefront of the fashion scene. Were you friends with lots of the other British designers?

Yes, I've been friends with them. Most of my close friends are really sculptors and artists more than anything else. Like Andrew Logan, whose jewelry I wear, and Duggie Fields, whose paintings I collect.

Clockwise from top: An invitation to celebrate Zandra Rhodes at Henri Bendel; Zandra's first appearance at Henri Bendel in the 1970s; Behind the scenes of a photo shoot of Zandra's 1984 collection Fables of the Sea. Page 420: Freddie Mercury wearing a Zandra Rhodes design.

When did you start dressing clients such as Princess Margaret, the Countess of Snowden, Blondie, Jacqueline Kennedy, and Freddie Mercury?

Let me see. Freddie Mercury, I got a phone call in my funny little Bayswater studio, which was sort of like in the back of Paddington, up a rickety staircase. Once, Baby Jane Holzer came around, and said, "Oh, these stairs are very dangerous." With Mike Nichols, that's right.

Baby Jane and Mike Nichols. That's a nice visit.

Anyway, so I have a phone call and it was Freddie asking if they could come around for me to do an outfit for them. Any of you that know me closely would know that I wouldn't have at all have known what they played. I had to ask the people in my workroom who said, "Oh, it's that pop song that's on at the moment." But they were still what I would call a small teenybopper group in 1975. I said, "Well, you'll have to come around the evening," because I didn't have changing rooms. I only had the girls, and the machines. They came around and I pulled out a wedding top. I said, "Now dance around and see how you feel in it." Then I made the outfit for him. They gave me tickets to go to one of their shows at Earls Court. I went with my great friend Duggie. We were at least ten years older than most of the audience. I never saw them again until I got called, because it was one of the photographs that everyone likes, and all his fans wanted me to sign them, when he died. I've never seen them play otherwise.

How did it feel when you were called when the movie *Bohemian Rhapsody* was being filmed?

I was very thrilled. I think the movie is lovely. I've only learned the songs recently.

Did they ask you to re-create that specific top?

I re-created that top and the top that Brian wears, which is again a sort of pleated top.

It's full circle?

Full circle.

You saw the movie?

I've seen the movie several times.

That's very special. Tell us about your Lovely Lilies collection. What were those dresses about?

That was a very exciting time, 1971. I was in Japan at the same time as Antonio Lopez, and he's got a drawing of me somewhere. Antonio and Karl Lagerfeld were there. I had my dresses and Issey Miyake wanted me to do a show. He organized that I do a show for Seibu. It was all very, very, very electric. Tina Chow was my model and I introduced her to Michael Chow at that time.

You introduced Tina to Michael?

Yes. That was 1971 in Tokyo.

I didn't find that in any of my notes. But I did read that Michael is the one who told you to make posters of your shows, and to number them.

Michael choreographed my first show in London, which was midnight at the Roundhouse. I

had a lot of the Warhol girls. I had Donna Jordan and Pat Cleveland very early on, which was fabulous. It happened to be just the most magical show. Oh, you asked me about the lilies. Sorry I'm jumping. When I was in Japan, it was at the time where you couldn't get around easily, so a wonderful flower arranger brought me all these wonderful lilies and I sat in my room drawing the lilies, and that's how Field of Lilies started. It started as a textile design and then it became the collection.

Was that the dress that Princess Anne wore for her engagement announcement?

The one that she wore was a sea shells net design.

In 1981 *Vogue* magazine asked you and several designers to create a gown for the future princess, Lady Diana. Describe that dress.

Well, my dress that I designed was all gold with wonderful swirls and a crinoline pannier. I think it was probably quite over the top. In my book there's a wonderful picture of Diana Ross in one of those.

It was much more suited for Diana Ross than Princess Di?

I mean, they didn't consider me for that wedding dress, even though they had used one of my dresses for Princess Anne's wedding. But it was one of my favorites, the Elizabethan collection, with all the swirls and the panniers. That was on show in the Metropolitan Museum's costume exhibition, *Camp: Notes on Fashion*.

And then Diana Ross was photographed by Richard Avedon in that?

In that one, yes.

Tell us about other work for the [British] royal family, because you've dressed a lot of people. Do you do fittings? Do they come to you?

I go to the palace. Princess Diana would come into my shop and pick out what she liked. I'd take the measurements. I would go to Kensington Palace to fit her for the dress.

Was that an out-of-body experience doing that for you there, or it's just, "Ah, the royal family"?

I mean, a lot of people say, "How did you get to know them?" If you're English you don't really get to know them. There is a sort of barrier there, do you know what I mean? You just sort of curtsy, and answer the questions, and slightly get to know them.

You also hung Christmas ornaments in Buckingham Palace with the Queen.

Well, I did the pink-haired fairy on the top of the Christmas tree one time when they asked personalities to do different things. I did the pink-haired fairy. With the Queen, well, and all the royal family because they all look at the Christmas tree before it gets given to charity and auctioned.

They probably have an archive of all these ornaments.

They might have. I'm sure they are given so many things they don't really remember.

Then tell us about your early collaborations. How you took your first trip to India in the 1980s with Rajeev Sethi?

In 1981, Rajeev came to London for this amazing, grand Indian lady, Mrs. Pupul Jayakar.

They were organizing the very first festival of India. He said that they had chosen me to go to India, to see the crafts and all the things, and to see what I would come up with.

Is it because of your pink hair, which is the navy blue of India?

Pink hair in India gets you anywhere. You can go in the middle of the country and little old ladies that wouldn't normally talk to you have to come up and touch the hair to find out if it's real. They might not now, but they did in those days. I found India a wonderful influence to go around and see all the arts and crafts.

India has been influential in your work.

Someone once said they thought that I was influenced by the Indians first coming over here and doing shows because I made lots and lots of friends in India. I was very influenced by both the makeup, those wonderful braids with color, the exotic blue makeup. I did two really influential Indian shows, with wonderful Indian music. Then I found that all my close Indian friends I'd made wouldn't wear anything I was making because they're always in saris. I thought, well, I'm a textile designer, why don't I design saris? I designed a sari show that I took to Bombay and Delhi in 1987.

Didn't the government ask you to come and work with the local artisans and craftsmen on this?

I worked with local craftsman and I had everything done there. When I showed them, I showed the saris with panniers underneath and wonderful feather headdresses. I did a little couley bodice. I gave shoulder pads to everything. I think a lot of the ladies in the audience were very shocked at that time. But it was a wonderful experience.

You know that India is one of my favorite places in the world. You also were a judge of the Miss India contest.

I was a judge of the Miss India contest to an audience of something like fifty million. I'd walk through the airport then and people would ask for an autograph.

Do you still go back to India frequently?

I've just done a program in India. I hope I'll be going back more. They've got a TV series in England that's followed on from the movie *The Best Exotic Marigold Hotel*, where they take eight ancient people of retirement age, and they ship them to India. You're over there for a month experiencing it. I was there with Britt Ekland, and the wonderful man with the golden voice who commentates on cricket [Henry Blofeld], and several different other people. But it hasn't come out yet in England.

It will be out in England and then we'll get to watch it on BBC America. You'll have to keep us posted about that. I definitely want to see that. Then in the mid-1990s, you met your future life partner, the Egyptian-born Salah Hassanein. He was the president of Warner Bros. How did you meet him?

I met him at a cocktail party in New York. But then he came to London and invited me to some lunch he was doing, when he was expanding the Warner Bros. cinemas. I don't like lunch because it cuts up the day. I said, "Well, I could meet you for a cocktail and you could

Clockwise from top: Diana, Princess of Wales on
a trip to Kyoto, Japan, in 1987; Anne, Princess
Royal, in a Zandra Rhodes design, announcing
her engagement to Captain Mark Philips in
1973; Zandra's sketch for Diana's Kyoto dress.

This page: Zandra Rhodes and her partner Salah M. Hassanein. Next spread: An exhibit of Zandra's iconic looks at The Fashion and Textile Museum in London.

tell me about your project." That was the beginning of something like a twenty-five-year-old relationship.

He just passed away this year at ninety-eight years old.

That's it, this June.

And you traveled the world together.

He built fifty multiplexes in Japan alone. He went to different places. If I was lucky enough to be doing a project somewhere, he might also be there.

He was doing multiplex theaters in Europe, Japan, and Australia for Warner Bros. So that was very advantageous for your work to dovetail on to. But he semiretired in 1993 and became president of a postproduction company. Then moved to Del Mar by the Sea in San Diego. You split your time between London and San Diego.

That's right. We had a home there. Luckily, he was a workaholic. He knew that he could continue to do his work from there. He knew that I wanted to continue my work and that I didn't want to not work.

Did San Diego embrace you?

They have been very, very nice to me. Yes, I like it there.

Do you still have the place in San Diego?

At the moment, I'm now finishing the house. We had a huge house on the beach. I'm now going to something smaller, and then working on what I'm going to do. While I was there, I had commissioned these amazing, big, Andrew Logan sculptures both of him [Hassanein] and me. I'm going to ship them back, so they go into the museum. I couldn't have found it if it wasn't for him.

Was there a time when you would have married Salah?

There was, and then it went past that. It's a thing in the past now.

You don't regret that or regret not having had children with him?

I don't regret that because I always think my work is my children. I don't think that makes any difference.

And they don't talk back to you.

The work doesn't talk back to you, but you have to continue to do it.

Living in San Diego opened up some other creative opportunities for you with the opera.

Yes. If I hadn't been in what I very rudely call the village of San Diego....

The village of San Diego?

You know, in London, I don't know the head of the opera. But I got to know the head of the opera [in San Diego] and he said to me, "Why haven't you ever designed an opera?" I said, "I met Zeffirelli once but he never phoned me back." He said, "Would you be interested?" I said, "yes." He asked me first to do costumes for the *Magic Flute* that now belongs to Seattle. Then he asked me to do *The Pearl Fishers* that's done twenty-eight tours around this country.

You did the costumes and everything?

Costumes and sets. Then I did *Aida* in Houston. In January, I've got the John Wayne Airport to display the costumes from *Aida* in one terminal and the costumes for *The Pearl Fishers* in another one.

How did they come to be displayed at the airport?

Well, through my great friend Joan Quinn down there. We got to know the man who ran the airport. What more do friends do for you? It ended up that he asked me if I'd then do an exhibition. The costumes are good because opera doesn't always get enough people seeing what goes on. We put my original drawings, the headdresses, and the costumes up for people to see when they've got nothing else to do but wait around in an airport.

Have you ever been asked by the Met or any of the New York companies to do anything?

No, unfortunately, but if anyone's here. . . [LAUGHTER]

That's why I'm putting it out there to our audience. Also, in ballet and dance, Sarah Jessica Parker has been chairing for many years the New York City Ballet benefits where they always have a designer doing the costumes.

If you're a designer, I think one is always interested in different projects that come along. You know, you never know where they lead and they can stretch you in a different way.

I think in opera, the thing that's wonderful is making a very large opera singer still look like a wonderful princess on a stage, with printed fabric. They had my *Aida* costumes in San Diego this last month and they look fabulous.

Were you an opera fan before you started designing for it?

No, I didn't know enough about it. I think you realize when you work on it, how wonderful opera is. It works on not just your visual senses, but your hearing senses, all of your senses.

Now you consider yourself an opera fan?

I consider myself an opera fan, yes.

Tell us how you came to buy a warehouse in London?

Around the mid-1990s, I was finding that no one was taking much notice of my work as a fashion designer. One minute you're in, one minute you're out. Or you float around, you know. My friend Andrew Logan said there's a warehouse. He knew I saved all my historical costumes, the ones I like best. And he said there's this empty building.

Where did you save them?

Oh, boxes and boxes. Just everywhere. Silver chests, I was being buried by them. I had some in a warehouse that even got flooded because the warehouse was closed one Christmas. …And anyway, he said, "Zandra, you've always wanted to do a museum. Why don't you look at this building?" I said, "I'm not a millionaire." But it was a very unfashionable part of London, rather like Alphabet City in New York. I found that I could sell my house in Notting Hill Gate and pay for that warehouse, which I then did. It was very unfashionable. I'd seen a building by Ricardo Legorreta and it's all lovely rainbow colors and gorgeous. Through Salah, I met some people who lived in one of his houses and they introduced me. They said, "He doesn't do secondhand buildings," because it was really a makeover. I was introduced to him and then I flew him over to London.

And he saw your pink hair and he must have been intrigued.

Maybe that. Well, I flew into London first class on my American Airlines mileage ticket. I got all the top architects of London together to say that this is an up-and-coming area, and he agreed to design it for me. Then they built the Shard, and that's history. It's now a very lovely crowded area. You know, we had a show there.

It's very brave of you to hire somebody like that. Did the neighborhood go crazy?

No, I think it's become a landmark. It was a very working-class area. It still has that aspect, but now they've got all the warehouses that have been converted. It's also become quite expensive, but very crowded, now.

That warehouse now has a museum.

It's a fashion and textile museum.

And you live there.

The way we made it, two-thirds of it is the museum. Down one side is my print room and my workrooms. Then we got another architect, whom Legorreta approved of, and we built ten apartments on the top and we presold eight. Selling the apartments paid for doing the building. The one at the front on the top is mine.

Tell us what your mission statement is for the museum, because originally I read it was just for English designers, but then that's changed.

I felt that with a lot of British designers, people didn't notice them enough. Like the wonderful jersey work by Jean Muir or Thea Porter, who was really one of the British designers who perfected the caftan. It's to highlight also textile design because I think people never realize that when you're looking at a garment, the invisible textile designers put a lot of work into that, too.

How often do you change the exhibitions there?

Well, at the moment, mine is on for four months: *Zandra Rhodes 50 Years of Fashion*. It can be for maybe two months, three months, depending on what we think is going to go well.

Princess Michael of Kent cut the ribbon at that exhibition or at the opening?

She cut the ribbon for the opening, and she also opened this exhibition, my *50 Years of Fashion*.

And you recently also mounted *The World of Anna Sui* there.

We did indeed, and it was her first exhibition, I believe, and definitely the first in Europe.

That led to the exhibition happening here in New York.

Oh, in that fabulous museum [Museum of Arts and Design]. Wonderful, yes.

Anna said you were her ultimate designer idol. She bought your clothes when they were at Henri Bendel's. The first fashion show she ever attended was one of yours with her pal Steven Meisel.

There's a marvelous picture of Anna and Steven in the book. It's worth buying the book to see that picture. "The Circling Square," it was a very imaginative show. I had Pat Cleveland, a lot of really amazing people in it. It was on the eve of Passover.

You didn't have any Jewish people there. Well, that's too bad. You have subsequently done some collaborations with Anna, and textiles for her.

I don't know if that one's in the book, but I have done a collaboration with Anna. Yes, rather like I did one with Valentino. It was a great honor.

It's a great honor. Describe to us what it's like to be appointed a Commander of the Order of the British Empire?

It makes you feel a lot older. I mean, you come into a wonderful group of people like Helen Mirren, Paul McCartney, or whatever. I mean it's really just an honor from the country, that your work is valued somehow, I think.

Absolutely. You were named Chancellor of the University for the Creative Arts.

Well, they just sacked me. You apparently only get it for eight years. What it is, I shook hands with something like five hundred people. I kept thinking, "Why have I got a pain here?" It was a repetitive strain injury. It was from shaking hands as they [the graduates] come across the stage. There were a lot of people in three or four days.

You've done quite a few books. How many books have you done before this?

I think this is my fourth or fifth. Yes, they were not my life history, you'll only learn about my work.

This one is the life story. How many sketchbooks do you have? Because you're sketching all the time.

I wish I sketched all the time, but probably I've got at least a couple of hundred. I use Japanese rice paper and I try to draw things when I go to places. It isn't always anything that you particularly think would go into a garment. It could be a cup of tea.

Well, the drawings you did on the *Queen Mary II* were quite beautiful.

Oh yes, when we came into the harbor at four in the morning. We went underneath the Verrazzano Bridge.

The sun coming over the bridge. The Statue of Liberty. You did beautiful sketches for me.

You remember it.

I'm happy to have it framed and hanging in my office. Did you ever do children's clothes?

No. Sometimes it's really whether or not someone comes to you and you feel that they could do the project in the right way, that you then say you'll do it, and that it will be remembered.

I mean, your look, color, and personality just would be so fabulous for children's clothes.

I always listen if people come up with projects.

Paula Friedman, did you hear us? Maybe that will come up in the future. Tell us about getting the call from Pierpaolo Piccioli at Valentino?

Well, it was his first collection when he was working on his own. It's a great honor. He came over with his team. I showed them all the different things that I've done. They had a pick of what they wanted. They asked me for one key collection, which was the Garden of Earthly Delights. He then then decided he wanted the Lipstick [collection] that hasn't been reborn since 1965, when I first did it. You know, he just brought them to life in his collection, which was great.

Did you get a dress from that collection?

Yes, I've got a dress from the collection, which I wear.

Is there another designer out there that you would love to do prints for?

It's just lovely when it occurs. You know, like when Anna Sui asked me to do something, you just think, "Would they do something lovely with it?" That influences whether you do it or not.

But you never look around the fashion press and go, "God, I would do some great prints for that person."

I don't have enough time [LAUGHTER].

We talked about Freddie Mercury and *Bohemian Rhapsody*.

You've done too much homework here, I can tell.

We're almost through here. Barbra Streisand?

Page 428: Performers wearing Zandra Rhodes designs in Seattle Opera's *The Magic Flute* in 2011. This page: Queen Elizabeth II and Zandra at a reception at Buckingham Palace in 2010.

That was lovely when I got a call from a friend of mine that knows her very well—she was going to sing in London. She hadn't sung in Hyde Park, I don't know if she'd done it before, but she hadn't been singing in the park for such a long while…

And she didn't ask Donna Karan to do the dress, she asked you.

I think she had one of Donna's already. I went up there and gave her sketches, and that was the pink one that you saw.

What was it like meeting her? Did you enjoy her?

I've met her before, but it was the fact that she needed to feel confident, and that she wanted something of mine for that concert. My friend said, "Look, you've already got black, you might as well have something that isn't black."

Now, the *50 Fabulous Years in Fashion* book. Was it hard to figure out what to include in there? Is everything that you want people to know about you and your life in there?

I don't know about me and my life. It's done in, like, ten-year sections. Decade by decade, and my assistant Dakota had to chase like mad to keep following through to get the photographers to let us have pictures and things like that. It's those follow-ups, that's a lot of work. Apart from being lucky enough to have people say they would do the essays, you've then got to find the different pictures that are associated with what we're writing about. I'd already had my work recorded for twenty years when I got a grant to do recordings of my work that people can get on the web.

Where on the web do we find that?

It has to do with University for the Creative Arts; that has got a lot of my work that they can refer to. But then the last twenty years hadn't been done. We had to find all the clothes in the chests and organize all of that.

There's a documentary being made about your life and your work?

There is a documentary, I don't know where it's got to, but it's coming along.

It's coming. I was interviewed by the director, so I know that it's happening. You don't know where that's going to wind up?

No, I don't know. I mean, there was another one. Someone, when I got them to record the work I was doing for the opera, and other things, went ahead and put a lot of stuff out but didn't ask us. Then it wasn't worked out properly. You never know what happens to these things.

So you're just going to wait and see?

I'm going to wait and see. I haven't got time to do anything but wait and see, because I'm so busy. I've got the exhibition that's coming out in the airport. I'm working on new collections. I've got the IKEA collection. I've just done a range of furniture with prints on it in China. I would like to be saying I'm taking it a bit easier, but it's not the case at the moment.

No, you're not going into your eighties relaxed.

Not yet.

But you also just did *Celebrity Master Chef* in England.

Page 432: Zandra Rhodes is made a Dame Commander of the British Empire by Anne, Princess Royal in 2015. This page: Zandra in her home and studio at The Fashion and Textile Museum in 2020.

I only got through six episodes.

Are you a good cook?

I consider myself a reasonable cook and several people in the audience have come to dinner with me. I like cooking. I thought I was better than the people that they kept in.

What were some of the bigger challenges that you had to cook on the show?

We had to feed, let me get the numbers right, I think we had to feed three hundred at London Zoo between four of us, in freezing cold winter. Of course, the worst thing was if you come from San Diego, which has got the world's most wonderful zoo, and you go around London Zoo, it's very difficult to look enthusiastic. But then we had to feed the staff.

What do you make for three hundred people at the zoo?

We were divided up. We had to do one meat course, one vegetarian course, and dessert. The girl I was with, we did some chicken with lentils. What else do we do? Mixed vegetables, and then I did baked apples. Now, one of my specialties is apple crumble. I could have done that standing on my head, but the guy who was interviewing me later said, "You got food blindness, didn't you, because you're looking at all this food." Do you know what I mean? You know you suddenly panic because they only give you ten minutes to make a decision on what you have to do. Then we worked in an Indian restaurant where I had to put skewers into one of those big, fat tandoori ovens. I had to grill my broccoli and I burned myself on that. Then I did poached salmon with mango salsa and quinoa with vegetables. I thought I did a really good job, and then when I watched the tape later, they said, "What do you do with this funny sauce, with this salmon?" I thought that I should have gone further.

Has the program aired yet in the UK?

The programs aired because they had a festival in London at Bermondsey and people kept saying, "How are you going there? Did you get through?" They rooted for my cooking. But

BILLY PORTER

Are you ready? Tonight's category is: Billy Porter realness.

I've been a fan of the movie Kinky Boots *for many years, and could not wait for the Broadway production. Luckily, I was there on opening night, and what a night it was! There wasn't a person in the theater who wouldn't agree that Billy Porter would be bringing home the Tony. I didn't realize at the time how influential that role would be in Billy's life and career. He carried the message of that play, and took the red of* Kinky Boots *to every red-carpet appearance since.*

I met Billy during New York Men's Fashion Week, when he was a CFDA ambassador. About his first fashion shows ever, Billy said, "It really is astonishing how much of an effect clothes have on your spirit."

Shortly after Fashion Week, he showed up for the Oscars in Christian Siriano's black tuxedo gown and the New York Times *said, "Billy Porter shut down the red carpet." Does anyone even remember what movies won that night?*

Billy got everyone to binge-watch a controversial series on FX: Pose. *His compelling and compassionate portrayal of Pray Tell led to his history-making Emmy for lead actor in a drama series. He was just nominated for a Golden Globe and a Critic's Choice Award. He'd better make room on his awards shelf.*

Then, at the Met Gala for Camp, Billy paid homage to their Egyptian Collection with a showstopping red-carpet entrance... and I said, "Get him to the 92nd Street Y stage!" Let's hear it for the one and only Billy Porter.

BILLY PORTER: Wow, that was amazing. Wow, that was like the best intro I've ever had.

FERN MALLIS: Well, that's a good start.

I like it when folks do their research. She has all the information.

I do my research. He's wearing Michael Kors tonight from the Studio 54 collection.

Because I get to go sing with Idina Menzel after this, so I have to look cute and festive.

Do you mean you didn't dress that way for us?

I'm dressed this way for both.

Billy, let's talk about all that good stuff. Let's start at the beginning. You were born on September 21, 1969. How old are you?

Fifty. I turned fifty the day before the Emmys.

Was that a big birthday party?

It was a big birthday party.

That makes you a Virgo.

Virgo on the cusp of Libra.

Some of the positive Virgo traits are: intelligence, analytic, honest, reliable, perfectionist.

Billy Porter and Michael Kors at the launch of Michael's Studio 54 collection in 2019. Billy wore the collection to "Fashion Icons."

Do you agree?

Yes.

The negative ones: critical, judgmental, old-school, slow, fussy.

I'm old-school. I'm not judgmental. I'm not fussy. But that's the Libra side that creeps in.

Do you know who some of your other famous Virgos are? Beyoncé, Michael Jackson, Pink, Sophia Loren, Amy Winehouse, Mother Teresa, Hugh Grant, and Freddie Mercury.

Well, that works! That's a good list to be a part of.

Tell us about your parents. Your dad, what was his name? What did he do?

I am named after my father, William Ellis Porter I. He was a security guard. I wasn't very close to him. I didn't really have a relationship with him. My relationships were with my mother, my grandmother, and my great-aunt.

Your mother is Cloerinda Jean Johnson Porter Ford. That's a lot of names.

That's a lot of names. She's got her maiden name. She had her first married name, and then her second married name.

Your mom was physically disabled since birth? But you called her handi-capable.

That's my sister. My sister came up with handi-capable. She's very, you know, of the moment.

That is a good thing.

It's great. Listen, teach me. I'm a vessel. My mother lives at the Actors Fund nursing home in Englewood, New Jersey. She is close to my sister and me. Closer now than she was. We get to see her a lot and hang out with her.

She gets to enjoy your success?

She gets to enjoy my success. Not the way that I would like her to. It's very difficult for me because she doesn't have any mobility. She needs somebody to take care of her all day, every day. While she's living to see this moment, it breaks my heart that she can't come and, like, be here. That's not something that she can do anymore, really. That's heartbreaking. But she is alive, and we get to go see her. I took her the Emmy the last time. She said, "Bring

442

that Emmy over here."

Now you're going to have a couple of other awards to take her.

Yes.

When your mother remarried I understand that was a very challenging time in your life. You were sexually molested by your stepdad.

It's something that I write about a lot. I was sexually abused by my stepfather from the time I was seven to the time I was twelve. Once again, it was really, really difficult. I do not, however, know that I would be the person that I am had that not happened.

It was in some ways the best thing that ever happened to me. I grew up in a very religious environment. While I do believe there's a higher power, while I do believe in God, while I do believe in all of those things, religion is man-made. Spirituality is divine. I was forced to understand that difference very early.

Because when that stuff happened to me, I looked around the landscape, and there wasn't one of those religious people, not anybody, who was present to help me. To help me. I had to save myself. Because of that trauma, I was able to see clearly, you all don't have nothing for me and I've got to save myself. No adult around me has the tools to do what needs to be done, so I'm going to do it myself.

If that trauma hadn't happened, I wouldn't have been able to see that. A lot of that for me, in that space, was extracting myself from religion. Extracting myself from the church. Not spirituality, but from the church. I had to leave.

Did your mother know this was going on?

She didn't until I told her. I told her around the time I was sixteen years old. You know, from the time of twelve to sixteen, I didn't really realize what had happened. I went into that place that everybody talks about, where it's like you don't even know what happened. Then it all came flooding back to me when I was sixteen.

But when you were eleven, you did a sermon at the church?

Yes. Well, we are very much products of our environment, right? Where I grew up in Pittsburgh, in the church, there's a language. Everybody has their little bubble, right? The church was our bubble. Nobody explored outside of that.

When they looked at me, they felt something special there. I know the only thing they know is "preacher man." The only thing they know in their bubble is that, "Oh, he's special, he's going to be a preacher." That's all they know. They don't understand that there are different ways of having a ministry that's not necessarily from a pulpit.

Do you feel like you're preaching now in your career?

I do, this is a ministry. What I do is a ministry. I know. I don't call it preaching, but I do call it a ministry. I know, it ruffles a lot of church people's feathers. I don't care.

We can all pray at the Ministry of Billy Porter?

If you want to [LAUGHTER].

You went to Reizenstein Middle School, then Taylor Allderdice High School, and then

Pittsburgh Creative and Performing Arts School.

… And Carnegie Mellon, all in Pittsburgh.

How were you treated in middle school and high school?

You know, it's interesting, because there was bullying early. Like, extreme bullying. Then I got to Reizenstein and there was an afterschool program called Reizenstein Musical Theater, I didn't know what theater was. I went to this thing and I also simultaneously got hooked up with All City Junior Choir. There were teachers whom I caught, the people in my life who were like angels, just plopped all over. They literally lifted me and pushed me in the right direction. When I sang, the bullying stopped. I just sang all day, every day. As high and as loud as I could for as long as I could. My voice was my weapon.

… And what a weapon it is.

But prior to that, before sixth grade, I didn't know if I was going to make it. After that it was cool. Because I was an artist, so it didn't matter.

You told your mom three times that you were gay?

This woman did a lot of research. How do you know that? Lord have mercy, yes.

You know, living in that religious environment, also this was the 1980s, there wasn't a whole lot of language about that in the world. People weren't really talking about it like that. My mom was a little church girl. She didn't really understand what it was. All she knew was that it was a sin. She didn't want her son to be sinful. So, yes, you know, denial, denial.

But then when she believed it, it was 1985, in the height of the AIDS crisis.

No, that was when I first started telling her. Part of that time, it was like gay and AIDS, and nothing in between. But it was more like in my mid-twenties and in my early thirties, where it was like, "Boo, it ain't going to change. We should really have this conversation for real. It's not another passing fad."

Let's go back to the Pentecostal Church. You describe it as theater and a fashion show every Sunday.

I think, you know, the Black church is high theater and a fashion show every week. Your runway is the aisle that you walk down to get to your seat. Where you sit in the sanctuary is how good you felt that day. If you were in the front, you felt good. You sashay down that center runway, "Praise the Lord, praise the Lord." That hat was on. That suit was fierce. That pump was strapped in. Yes, please. They are the best and the worst. You know what I mean? It gets a little catty in the church, too. People will talk about what you're wearing, honey. "Did you see sister So-and-so? Sister So-and-so and brother So-and-so."

That was an early fashion education for you?

It was an early fashion education. We would put on our own fashion shows. The church would have a fashion show fundraising, "blah, blah, blah, blah, blah." It was fabulous. It was so much fun, but everything was a tableau. Tthe thing [MOTIONING A DOOR] would open and everybody would be, like [POSING LIKE A TABLEAU], you know.

It was good training for *Pose*?

Clockwise from top: Billy Porter at age ten with sister Mary Martha Ford-Dieng. Billy, husband Adam Porter-Smith, Mary Martha, and mother Cloerinda Jean Johnson Porter Ford; Billy at age three, surrounded by clothing; Billy, Cloerinda, and Aunt Dot in Pittsburgh.

Clockwise from top: Billy Porter performing at Pittsburgh's Creative and Performing Arts School; Billy singing with Carnegie Mellon University classmates Kena Tangi-Dorsey and Vanita Harbour; Billy performing with the Kennywood amusement park cast of *FLASH*.

Yes! There was a moderator, too [IN A CHURCH PREACHER ACCENT]. "The model is wearing a cream, bone, brown, beige, off-white, powder blue pants suit from Sears and Roebuck. $13.99, praise the Lord." You know, it was like that.

[TO THE AUDIENCE] You laugh too much! We need time! Tell us about the aha! moment you had watching the Tonys on TV in 1981 when *Dreamgirls* won?

Well, I didn't know anything about the theater, right? I had done my first musical—it was *Babes in Arms*. I played one of the leads. I was singing Rodgers and Hammerstein music the original way. I came from the church. I didn't make the correlation that a) singing was something that you could make a living doing, and b) that this thing that I had just done was something that people did for a living. Like, I didn't know.

I just happened to be washing dishes in the kitchen and the Tony Awards came on. There were all these Black people who were so gorgeous, because it was the fight scene. They were already the Dreams. They were in the wigs, and the jewels, and the sequins, and the gowns. Then Jennifer Holliday sang "And I Am Telling You, I'm Not Going" and I was like, "Well, wait. If can do that, that's my ministry."

I didn't even really realize what it was because even for us at that time they were on television. It was the Tony Awards, but they were on television. In my little brain, they were on television. Black people were beautiful on television, I hadn't seen anything like that before. You didn't see a lot of glamorous Black beauty in 1981 on TV.

Why did you pick Carnegie Mellon?

It was picked for me. Once again, the angels in my life. I had these wonderful teachers like Lenora Nemetz. I don't know if any of you know who she is? She's a big Broadway woman. She was from Pittsburgh and she had understudied Chita Rivera and Gwen Verdon in the original *Chicago*. She was my mentor and she was back in Pittsburgh teaching. Peggy Hughes-Ruslander was my acting teacher, and they caught wind that I was making decisions. I was making decisions to move to New York after graduation.

I wasn't going to college. I was just going to do it, and I got dragged by my ear. They were like, "You're going to Carnegie Mellon."

"I'm, like, where? That thing down the street?" Once again, we talk about access. We talk about opportunity. I lived in Pittsburgh my whole life. I had no idea that Carnegie Mellon was one of the top drama schools in the country. I should have known that, and ultimately, I did.

You learned a lot there?

Yes. They said, "You can sing, you can dance, and when you open up your mouth, it's a disaster. You've got to learn how to talk." That's how I ended up at Carnegie Mellon.

I saw a great interview you did with one of the professors at Carnegie Mellon. It was terrific. You were so positive about what you learned there. You took a costume behavior and etiquette class that taught you how to work with all the stage garments like petticoats, bustles, trains, fans, and parasols. You didn't realize that would really come in handy?

I had no idea! It was a styles class that we had in drama school. The men learned how to use all of the accoutrements from the top hat, to the cane, to the waistcoats, to the tails, to how to stand. The women had to learn all of the different ways to work a garment, and I paid attention because I was more interested in the girls than I was in the boys, because the boys are boring. You know the boys are boring. I paid attention to the girls.

From university, you went right to Broadway in the original cast of _Miss Saigon_ in 1991. That went on to win three Tonys and was one of the longest-running plays on Broadway. How did you get in that?

I went to the audition. Everybody asks that question. It's, like, "I went to the audition, and I got the gig." Really, that's what everybody does.

You've got to show up.

You've got to show up and go to the audition. You know.

What was it like being in that?

There's only one first. At that point, Cameron Mackintosh, the producer, was the biggest name in the business. It was the biggest, grandest thing I had ever been a part of. It was just lovely. I wish I was more present for it. In retrospect, looking back, I really could have been more present for it, but I was just trying to be a star child. I was in the chorus. It's like, "You ain't going to have me here long in the back underneath these coolie hats in the dark. That's only going to happen for so long, kids."

Then you became a teen angel in _Grease_?

Well, I did _Five Guys Named Moe_ first. _Five Guys Named Moe_ was my second Broadway show. I covered three of the leads. Then I did the revival of _Grease_.

I have a whole bunch of things that you did after that. If we go into each one we will never get you to Carnegie Hall. _The Merchant of Venice_, _Songs for a New World_, _Smokey Joe's Café_, _Miss Saigon_ again, _Jesus Christ Superstar_, and in 2001, _Dreamgirls_.

That must have been iinteresting to you… getting into _Dreamgirls_ after that epiphany?

Well, I had already done it several times, but that was the twenty-fifth anniversary concert recording.

Then: _Topdog_/_Underdog_, _Little Shop of Horrors_, _Musical Feast_, _Ghetto Superstar_, which you wrote? Tell us a bit about that?

Well, there was no work. When I decided that I wanted to go down the road less traveled, which was: I don't want to be this clown. I'm going to stop doing that and do the work. That dried up.

I had a number of years when I wasn't working, where the door was closed, and the phone was not ringing. I went to graduate school in UCLA's screenwriting program. I was in LA for like two years and nine months. I just wrote a one-person act. I did a residency under George Wolfe at the Public Theater. He decided to put it up and do it for me. That was 2005.

During that time, is that when you were singing at the Duplex and the Don't Tell Mama piano bars?

I was singing at the Duplex and Don't Tell Mama from the time I got to town. That started in

Sardi's managing partner Max Kilmavicius presenting Billy Porter with his portrait in 2013.

the 1980s. You know, I'm the one who was like, I'll go do my Broadway show and then I'll sit in this piano bar and scream all night till four in the morning. It was a great training ground, though.

Then how did you get to work on the soundtrack for *The First Wives Club*?

I had a record deal at the time at A&M Records. I was doing an R&B album. This song just came to me and I recorded it. Bette Midler heard it at a party and said, "That would be great for this movie I'm doing," and it ended up in *The First Wives Club*.

You said that the music industry broke your heart. That it was very homophobic.

The music industry was the first place where my voice didn't save me. It was the first time that when I opened up my mouth to sing, nobody cared. All they were concerned about was who I was fucking. All they were concerned about was, "What will people think if they figure out he's… " It was really, really debilitating. I didn't really know it until I was out of it.

Well, if you really look back at the music industry, there weren't a lot of people who were out.

Still not a lot there. It's better. It's hard. That was a hard time.

When 9/11 happened here in New York, I read that you were traumatized. You said you lost your voice and that God took your voice. You would learn that you were more than your voice.

Yes, I kept saying, "I'm more than my voice, I'm more than my voice, I want people to experience me as more than my voice." Then I would just keep making the same choices. Because if I wasn't singing, I wasn't making any money.

9/11 happened and I lost my voice to acid reflux disease. It became erratic. I had cords of steel, and then all of a sudden, I couldn't even make a sound. But it pushed me once again. It pushed me into a deeper understanding of myself, in a deeper place.

When was it that you first saw *Angels in America*, and you saw what your future could be?

It was 1994. I was doing *Grease* around the corner. I heard about this play called *Angels in*

Billy Porter, Robin Weigert, and Christian Borle in Tony Kusher's 2010 revival of *Angels in America*.

America, and I took myself to it on my day off. It really did change my life forever. It was like I saw myself for the first time in the character of Belize.

It's like, "Oh, he's a human being. He's three-dimensional. He has a job. He's a nurse, and as quiet as it's kept, he's the emotional compass of the whole piece." I was like, that's me. That's me. I had never seen it before. To have that circle back in 2010 and be a part of the…

You were manifesting?

Well, I guess, yes. I was a part of the 2010 revival, the twentieth anniversary production.

What was it like working with Tony Kushner?

It was everything that I ever dreamed of. To be in the room with somebody who has that much to say. I really feel like he's one of the greatest artists of our time. You know, to be in the room and be able to absorb from those kinds of people.

What was the ghetto smack?

The ghetto smack? [MAKES A SNAPPING NOISE WITH HIS MOUTH] People tell me, "I'm too much, I'm too much, I'm too much." I'm playing Belize, I don't know if you know the play, but in "Millennium Approaches" [Part One of *Angels in America*], there's a scene with Louis that's like thirty minutes long when they're sitting at a diner. Louis is talking and Belize lets him have it at one point, after he talks for literally twenty minutes. Then Belize finally cuts him off and lets him have it for real.

At one point, in that moment, I'm talking, I'm talking, I'm talking, and I went [MAKES A GHETTO SMACK NOISE]. I was like, "this is pushing it." I did it in rehearsal, and I said, "This is pushing it. This is one of those times when they're going to tell me I'm too much."

But nobody said anything. Then one day I forgot to do it in previews. I forgot to do it, and Tony Kushner ran over me and he said, "Where's the smack? Where's the ghetto smack? Don't take that out! Don't take that out!"

While you were in *Angels*, you learned about the Broadway production of *Kinky Boots* happening, and you manifested the part of Lola and a Tony Award.

Yes. Thank you. I had seen the movie. I remember seeing the movie, and once again, feeling like I don't fit in anywhere, feeling like there are no parts for me. Then it was, like, that was a part! I was like, I could do that. I can really do that. When I heard about the musical, I was like, all right, that's mine, that's going to be mine.

You knew Jerry Mitchell [the director and choreographer of *Kinky Boots*]?

I knew Jerry Mitchell. I called him on the phone, and I was like, "Bitch, why are you having readings of this thing without me?" Because there were readings going on. Other people were being called, because I hadn't been in the business for a decade, because I had extracted myself, trying to change the narrative around me. But when you do that, in this business, I don't know about the rest of the world, but when you do that in the business, and then you don't talk about it, people start making shit up about you.

You're hard to work with. Then I was having my voice issues. "Oh, he lost his voice. He can't do it no more." You know, like that kind of shit. I was not the first on the list. I had to literally pick up the phone to the director and be like, "Hello! You're not even going to let me have an audition? Please just bring me in and let me audition. I'm the one for this."

You were not a "shoe-in," no pun intended?

No, I was not a shoo-in. They try to act like it was always me but it wasn't. You know, people get selective amnesia. They made me jump through hoops of fire to get that part. Just so you all know. No shade, we all should do that. That's how you get it, right? I don't have any problem going to the audition.

How much fun did you have doing that part?

It was the time of my life. It changed everything. It was like the dream, it was the original dream coming true.

How many of you saw *Kinky Boots*? [APPLAUSE] You won the Drama Desk, the Tony, and a Grammy? Not bad, right?

Not bad at all.

At that point, did you feel like, "OK, my career is now on track and it's where I can do anything I want?"

No, because unfortunately, the kind of shine you get from Broadway is not consistent across the board. It doesn't always register beyond that sort of twelve-block radius. It doesn't always register in a sort of broader, mainstream way. I won a Tony Award for playing a drag queen, and that's how I was treated. It's all good once again. But the phone wasn't ringing. I wasn't getting a whole lot of extra stuff.

You know what I mean? It wasn't springboarding me like I saw it do for other people. It doesn't do it for everybody. I'm not a single case. That's what Broadway is. But once again, I did that shit for three years. I had the time of my life. The time of my life. It was like wherever I am is where I'm supposed to be. I'm not going to worry about that. I'm here. Let me just be here.

Clockwise from top: Billy Porter in *Kinky Boots* at the Al Hirschfeld Theatre in 2017; Billy accepting the Tony for Best Performance by an Actor in a Leading Role in a Musical in 2013; Cyndi Lauper and Billy pose backstage with their Tony Awards in 2013.

PARIS
L'ORÉAL
VANITY FAIR
VANITY FAIR
L'ORÉAL
PARIS
VANITY FAIR
L'ORÉAL
PARIS
VANITY FAIR
L'ORÉAL
PARIS
VANITY FAIR
L'ORÉAL
PARIS

Then you married Adam Smith. You guys met eight years earlier. Dated, split up, got together again in 2015.

All the information, she has all the information. Yes, we met in 2009. We dated for a year. We broke up for five. We got back together five years ago.

You proposed in London. on the forty-second floor?

On the forty-second floor. City Social is the name of the restaurant.

Cartier ring and all.

Cartier ring and all. I asked my friends. I was like, "This should be a thing, right?" I'm not, like, a romantic person like that. I didn't have a lot of romance in my life. I asked my friends, "This has to be a thing, right?"

Then comes 2018 and *Pose*. You originally were not there for the role of Pray Tell?

For those of you who haven't seen it, Charlene Woodard plays Damon's dance teacher. That was the role that they had originally called me in for.

Now here's what I say did change with *Kinky Boots*. I had a Tony, I had a Grammy, I was also forty-five years old, and people would listen to me now, which hadn't happened before. That is how it changed, because I could go into that audition, prepare it, slay it, and then say to the casting director, "I think this is the wrong part for me."

That's what a Tony Award lets you do. That's how it changed. Alexa Fogel was open to hearing me. I said, "I lived it. I've been here. It would be a waste of everybody's time if you're doing it about the ballroom culture and you have me over here as a dance teacher, not even in that world. I think that's a waste of time for everybody."

Ryan Murphy agreed?

Ryan Murphy agreed, and he called me back and essentially said, "If you can be an announcer,

an impersonation of the ballroom people, then I'll just create something for you."

How important was the movie *Paris Is Burning* to you for this role?

Well, that was, once again, visibility and representation. You know that was one of the only things that we as Black queer people had, period, to look at forever. That was the thing.

I said, "Can I do an impersonation?" First of all, the whole world is doing an impersonation of these people. Let's be clear about that. Some people don't even know, because it's so removed from where it started. That's what I love about *Pose*. It's reclaiming our time.

Madonna did not create vogue. I love Madonna. She's a wonderful ally, I love her, I love her. This is no shade, but the world thought she created vogue. She did not. She appropriated it. Listen, all good, you know. I love *Pose* because you get to see what the source of all this stuff is in our culture.

I was involved in the initial Love Ball that Susanne Bartsch did in 1989. You were a great MC for the recent revival of that as well. That was an extraordinary time.

Thank you.

Let's talk fashion. You obviously loved fashion from way back when. When you were asked to host the red carpet for the Oscars in February, did you go to Christian Siriano? Did your stylist Sam Ratelle do that? How did that happen?

I went to Christian. You know, it came out of the blue. I had no intention of being at the Oscars. They said, "Would you come and host it?" I'm like, "OK." It was during New York Fashion Week and I was like, "What am I going to wear? What am I going to wear?"

We went to a Christian Siriano fashion show like a half hour after I got the call. I remembered why I loved him. He's always been the designer that understands that everybody wears clothes. Everybody on the planet wears clothes, whether you're a size zero or a size four hundred. Everybody has to put clothes on.

It's in his DNA to design for everybody. We had already been coming up against the wall with a lot of designers because I wanted to do this gender-bendy, fluid thing. We just got flat-out "no's" from a lot of people. "We don't think he should be wearing that." That sort of silencing thing that happens. I'm older now so I knew what it looked like when it was coming. I'm going to do it anyway. I said, "Well, I need to wear a ball gown and this is the only person who will do it."

I said he's the only person who will look me in the face and say "yes."

He said "yes."

He said "yes," and he did it in a week. He did it in nine days.

It's incredible. We had Christian here for Fashion Icons.

It was my idea. The top and the bottom because I didn't know what the shot was going to be, but I thought if it's shot from here first and it looks like a traditional tux, and then you pull out, and it's just a ball gown bottom, the world will change.

It sure did. You told me one night about how heavy that dress was. It was huge.

It was heavy. But my styles class in college… you pick that shit up, you pick it up, it's heavy. You know, it's not delicate, it's heavy. Treat it like it's a heavy garment [WALKS ACROSS THE STAGE SHOWING THE AUDIENCE HOW TO CARRY A HEAVY DRESS].

I wore some Rick Owens boots underneath it.

You said they were the most comfortable ones you've ever worn?

Well, yes.

I mean, you really need kinky boots.

I do need kinky boots. Since *Kinky Boots*, I've always had an obsession with heels. My mother and her handicap could never wear heels. I always say I'm wearing heels in proxy for my mama.

Opposite: Billy Porter as Pray Tell in Ryan Murphy's *Pose* in 2018. This page: Billy winning the Emmy for Outstanding Lead Actor in a Drama Series for *Pose* in 2019.

Above and right: Billy Porter hosting the CFDA and Susanne Bartsch's Love Ball III in 2019, a fundraiser for the fight against HIV-AIDS. Page 461: Billy arrives at the 2019 Oscars in a Christian Siriano-designed tuxedo gown.

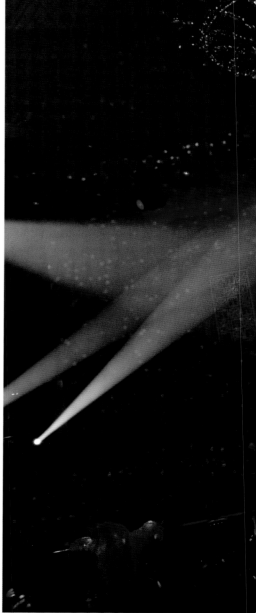

Kinky Boots sort of gave me a reason, I guess, that was acceptable. But I haven't been able to get out of them since I left that show. Give me some pumps, honey!

Where is that dress now?

The dress is in a museum in Boston at the moment.

You're keeping all these dresses in an archive?

I don't have space right now. Maybe someday.

I think you need to rent a warehouse somewhere and start keeping the "Billy Porter Archives."

Soon. Let's not get ahead of ourselves. But it's going to Kensington Palace in like a year.

You've said your life is described as "B.O." and "A.O."

Yes, "Before Oscar" and "After Oscar."

Now, we're "A. O." Let's go to the Met Gala. The exhibit is named *Camp*. Now, how many people did you have to get that approved by, to get that entrance to happen at the Met Gala?

I didn't have to do anything.

Well, somebody did.

My stylist did it and I let him do his job. He did all of it. It was his idea to have… [MAKES A LIFTING MOTION]

He arranged that with the Met, and with the PR people, and everybody to have that moment? That's a very big deal.

A big deal. Ms. Anna Wintour said, "Yes!" My stylist Sam had the idea and I was like, "Child, please. That ain't going to happen."

… And two weeks later, he was like, "Girl, you're getting carried in by six shirtless men, darling."

That effort was done by The Blonds.

Yes, we worked with The Blonds.

You did a terrific stint in The Blonds' fashion show on the *Moulin Rouge* set in the Al Hirschfeld Theater. You were wonderful.

Thank you. That was fun. You know, their clothes make me feel like a rock star. I'm about to come back and do that shit, too. Grandpa is coming back to the music industry. Y'all get ready!

OK. Then your big Tony dress was called the "uterus dress," bringing attention to women's reproductive rights. It was made from curtain fabric from *Kinky Boots*?

Yes. There's this company called Scenery Bags. They take curtains from all of the Broadway shows when they close and they turn them into different kinds of bags and stuff. Once again, it was my stylist's idea to have the *Kinky Boots* curtain made into a dress. That's one of the places that you can sort of do that, at the Tonys, and so I'm glad that we were able to do that, and I'm glad we were able to pay homage, too.

Now you seem to be wearing a lot of Thom Browne?

In the last couple of months, I have been wearing a lot of Thom Browne. It's good to travel

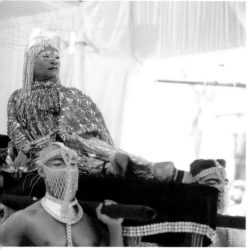

This page: Billy Porter makes a grand entrance at the 2019 Met Gala in a Sun God ensemble designed by The Blonds. Next spread: Billy wearing a tuxedo made of the curtains from his run in *Kinky Boots* to the 2019 Tony Awards. Page 466: Billy revealing his HIV-positive status on the cover of the *Hollywood Reporter* in 2021.

AFTERWORD

Our evenings with Fern Mallis and her—Fashion Icons—are always brilliant. The doyenne of fashion very quickly established the 92nd Street Y as an indispensable hub in the world of fashion—a place for you to come and to connect with and learn from the great icons in the business. Fern knows all the players: the designers from the big fashion houses, the couturiers from the most exclusive ateliers, the stylists, the editors, the photographers, the models, the men and women whose contributions to the art, to the craft, and to the business of fashion are legendary.

Her greatest skill is coaxing the most intimate stories, personal reflections, and profound insights from her interview subjects. She makes all of us, her entire audience, feel as though we are on the inside of the fashion scene in New York—the biggest fashion city in the world. The 92nd Street Y is all about building community. Thanks to Fern and "Fashion Icons," the 92nd Street Y has become a community for fashion enthusiasts, and I've been lucky to have a backstage pass since day one. I recall Donna Karan doing yoga in the green room. Tom Ford was all-around charming. Valentino and Oscar de la Renta were simply legends. Iris Apfel regaled us with her fabulous stories of New York in years past. And the great and unassuming Bill Cunningham was one of my favorites. You'll have to check out both volumes of *Fashion Icons* to enjoy all of these spectacular conversations.

What I've learned from "Fashion Icons" so far:
- Fashion Icons take their business seriously. You have to love it and be passionate to be successful
- Fashion Icons know how to celebrate and to have fun
- Fashion Icons have unique personalities, which come to life through their brands

You can be sure that the audience cheers at the introduction and gives a standing ovation at the finale. Though these conversations frequently ran over time, the audience never left until the final curtain call. At the receptions afterward, guests clamor to take a photo and ask one last follow-up question about the personal stories they just heard for the first time from the stage.

When it was time to reopen our doors post-pandemic, Fern was one of our first calls. We can't wait for more memorable evenings with Fern and her iconic friends. Aren't we all ready to add a little more glamour and fashion back into our lives?

—Susan Engel, Director and Executive Producer of 92nd Street Y Talks

APPRECIATION

Nordstrom has long been a champion of designers and their craft. From celebrating Missoni's twenty-fifth anniversary at Nordstrom with an in-store retrospective and hosting the first US runway show for Burberry Prorsum to celebrating Christian Louboutin's museum exhibition at the Palais de la Porte Dorée in Paris, Nordstrom has always been part of the designer conversation.

Over the years, Nordstrom has curated inspirational designer offerings. Iconic staples, seasonal trends, and the latest must-haves from both heritage and new brands alike are presented to both new and existing customers through the unique perspective of our team of fashion experts.

In the same way Nordstrom is synonymous with fashion, Fern Mallis is synonymous with Fashion Week—and not just in New York, but around the globe. A respected innovator, Fern has been an integral part of many of the key moments that have defined the way the industry sees fashion. She has spearheaded some of fashion's biggest events and is a long-standing champion of the Nordstrom brand.

From her "Fashion Icons with Fern Mallis" series at the 92nd Street Y, where time and time again, her unique storytelling approach and designer anecdotes leave you wanting more, to her first book, she's a valued voice in our community and a true friend of Nordstrom.

We're excited to be a part of the second volume of *Fashion Icons: Fashion Lives with Fern Mallis*, and we're excited to celebrate Fern once again.

Love,
Nordstrom

FASHION ICONS
WITH FERN MALLIS 92|Y

Follow Fern Mallis on Instagram to Learn More

FERN MALLIS - March 26, 2018

VALENTINO GARAVANI - November 18, 2014

LEONARD LAUDER - February 24, 2015

TIM GUNN - March 31, 2015

VICTORIA BECKHAM - June 4, 2015

STAN HERMAN - November 17, 2015

ANGELA MISSONI AND ROSITA MISSONI - April 21, 2016

IRIS APFEL - May 2, 2018

CHRISTIAN SIRIANO - June 12, 2018

ARTHUR ELGORT - October 9, 2018

BOB MACKIE - January 29, 2019

BETHANN HARDISON - April 25, 2019

ZANDRA RHODES - November 11, 2019

BILLY PORTER - December 11, 2019

ACKNOWLEGMENTS

There would be no "Fashion Icons" series, or books, without the brilliant photographer and filmmaker Timothy Greenfield-Sanders, who introduced me to Betsy Berg, who in turn introduced me to Susan Engel at the 92nd Street Y... where this all began in 2011.

Ashley Graham, I love you for writing the beautiful foreword to this book. I have been your biggest fan since you arrived on the scene. Your beauty, your candor, and your confidence in your body is an inspiration to me and millions of others. I always love greeting you at fashion events and hugging you backstage.

To the stellar team at Rizzoli: Charles Miers, publisher, I am so thankful for your unwavering support of this series. Of *Fashion Icons Book 1*, you said, "It's really original and intelligent. Charming and astute. Historic and stylish. Rewarding visually, but demands to be read. It feels effortless to browse, though I know nothing could be further from the truth." That comment means the world to me. Associate publisher Anthony Petrillose, you went to bat for us and ensured we met every deadline to get this book out on time. Working with you is a joy. Gisela Aguilar, editor, you were available 24-7 to help us navigate the trials and tribulations of writing a book. Copy editor and researcher Victoria Brown, you deserve a job in the CIA for your investigative skills. Who's ready to start working on *Fashion Icons Book 3* (and even *Book 4*)?

The entire team at the 92nd Street Y, led by the fearless and enthusiastic Susan Engel. David Schwartz-Leeper, Alyse Myers, Kevin Green and his security staff, Walt Taylor, Sean Fogarty, Catherine Pollock, Paolo Mastrangelo, Andrew Krucoff, Casey Jordan, Celeste Lannen, and especially Kent Davidson and Carrie Oman, who helped make this COVID-era project a possibility. You are my Upper East Side family.

Gigi Ganatra Duff, I will never forget your instantaneously positive response when I told you about *Fashion Icons Book 2*. This herculean effort would not have been possible without Nordstrom's support. Your entire team has been a dream to work with: Jin Churchill, Michael King, Rachel Friedman, Sam Lobban, Olivia Kim, Paige Boggs, Toni Forslund, Rosa Barney, and Charlotte Toates.

I've had several terrific assistants over the years (although not as many as Murphy Brown). They have helped me with every aspect of "Fashion Icons"—securing the talent, researching biographies, writing questions, organizing guest lists, helping the audience to their seats, and even getting me to the 92nd Street Y stage on time! I could not have done this without them. I'm especially grateful to Elliot Carlyle, Chloe Burney, Steven Almeas, and Tyler Pauly. Thank you, Michael Weston, for corralling the guests at each talk.

Sam Shahid, a dear friend and brilliant art director, you are the only person I wanted to design this book series. So much of the success behind the *Fashion Icons* books is because of how you visually bring each story to life. I can't wait to continue my journey with you. This could not have been possible without the Shahid/Kraus & Company team, especially Matt Kraus and John MacConnell. John, you blew me away with your commitment to quality and your creativity.

Ruben Baghdasaryan, you added a brand-new dimension to this project with the gorgeous portraits you painted of each Fashion Icon. You made each painting come to life. Thank you for sharing your amazing talent.

... And while we are on the topic of visuals, a big thank-you to the photographers who have been beyond generous and supportive of "Fashion Icons": The Billy Farrell Agency and their army of photographers and support team (Billy Farrell,

David X Prutting, Neil Rasmus, Joe Schildhorn, Connor Norton); Patrick McMullan and his team (Anita Antonini, Sharon Shalinski), who seem to be at every major event in my life; the team at Little Bear Inc. (Bruce Weber, Nan Bush, Nathaniel Kilcer); Bill Cunningham, I miss you always; Bill Clegg and Lindsey Sandberg at the Clegg Agency; and two of my oldest friends, Arthur Elgort and his right-hand woman Marianne Houtenbos. Joyce Culver and the Michael Priest Studios (Michael Priest, Maricela Magana), thank you for being the archivist for every "Fashion Icons" interview and reception. The Griffin Editions team (Charles Griffin, Junko Sakuno) for making sure every photo in this book is museum quality. Josh King, thank you for making all the Fashion Icons look their very best.

To the many agencies and archives, your researchers left no stone unturned to provide us with a collection of rare and never before seen images: Ivan Shaw, Cole Hill, Natalie Marcum at Condé Nast; Mary Ellen Jensen at Alamy; Michelle Press at Getty Images; Jina Park and Debbie Paitchel at Penske Media Corporation; Laurie Feigenbaum, Cary Georges, Nicole Burrell, Megan Victoria, Samuel Maude, and Nina Garcia at Hearst; Prosper Assouline and Andrea Ramirez at Assouline; Joyce F. Brown, Philips McCarty, Valerie Steele, and Faith Cooper at FIT; Jennifer Brown, Julie Zeftel, and Diana Reeve at the Metropolitan Museum of Art; Matthew Lufts at Associated Press; Sally Braid at Happy Socks; Matilda Beach at EMI; Holden Johnson, Anthony Baah, and Daniela Goes-Udoff at Shutterstock Editorial.

Jackie Adams, Patrick Anderson, Joan Agajanian, Christopher Bierlein, Mary Martha Ford, Tierney Gearon, Bruno Karlson, Kate Kuhner, John Kurdewan, Stephen Leek, Robert Bonanno, Russell Morrison, and Matthias Olson for offering up their personal photo archives to bring these Fashion Icons stories to life.

Richard Dickson, Shelby Powell, Daria Ruiz, Ernesto Bustinza, Bill Greening, and Kaitlin at Mattel, for understanding the important role Barbie plays in all things fashion.

The phenomenal PR teams who are crucial for making each "Fashion Icon" evening happen. We couldn't have done it without you—neither the interviews at the 92nd Street Y nor this book. Your assistance and support make it all happen and I am most appreciative: Giancarlo Giammetti, Carlos Souza, KCD's Rachna Shah, Nathan Kovach, Sofia Corti Maderna, Kelly Robinson, Caroline Adams, Lauren Ashdown, Rhiannon Wastell, Jacqueline Martinez, Alexandra Traber, Kegan Webb, Maddalena Aspes, Maddalena Giani, Elizabeth Covintree, Jocelyn Warman, Emily Gelber, Mallory Brown, Catherine Lewis, Joe McFate, Melanie Hanson, Lindsey Feinstein, Megan Herd, Mallory Cutler, Viveca Ortiz-Torres, Kelsey McWilliams Versha Sharma, Darnell Storm, Jason Lee, Chantal Artur, Chrissy Maron, and Ken Sunshine.

Estée Lauder's Bari Seiden, Alexandra Trower, and Jane Hertzmark Hudis, who moved heaven and earth to get Mr. Lauder onstage and in this book. It was worth the wait.

Luisella Meloni, you are truly a "jack of all trades."

WWD's Ed Nardoza, James Fallon, and Rosemary Feitelberg, who always report on each "Fashion Icons" interview.

To all the sponsors who made our receptions truly VIP events: Nicole Miller Wines, Susan-Anne Cosgrove at Legende by Domaines Barons de Rothschild (Lafite) and Taub Family Selections, Dom Perignon, and Lisa Carley. Steve Abrams, you are a very dear friend for always generously providing Magnolia Bakery's mini cupcakes and banana puddings.

Attorneys Douglas Hand and Rachael Skigen, for always giving our releases, contracts, and trademarks a legal look over. I am a lucky woman to have such esteemed attorneys on my side.

Jonathan Gray, Bruce Meyerson, BJ Perlmutt, Aleksa Kurbalija, and Lisa Immordino Vreeland, for guiding me through defining the next great chapter of "Fashion Icons."

PC Chandra, there is no way that this book would be in anyone's hands without you. You are my special Fashion Icon—for negotiating releases and licensing agreements, for communicating with every designer and their PR teams, and communicating with Rizzoli, with the art director, with the copy editor, with the 92nd Street Y team, and with everyone else who has been involved in this process, all the while smiling and laughing and keeping me focused and on track. "Fashion Icons" now has a digital presence thanks to you. You've touched every single aspect of this book with your humor, brilliance, and organizational skills. You have branded my "Fashion Icons" series in a way I couldn't have ever imagined. Thank you for "having my back," your belief in me, your love, and your friendship.

With everything I do, my family is in my heart and on my mind. I love them madly and I'm so proud of each and every one of them. While they weren't able to attend the talks in person, I know they were there in spirit. My sister, Stephanie Mallis, an architect and artist in Rockport, Massachusetts, who watches every "Fashion Icons" via livestream. My niece Brooke Lampley is beyond busy being chairman and world-wide head of sales for global fine arts at Sotheby's, along with her husband Chris Papagiannis and her extremely cute sons, Theo and Milo. My niece Victoria Lampley Berens, who is building a new jewelry advisory business in California and West Palm Beach, her husband Michael and their two angelic children, Rex and Lila. My niece Alexandra Metcalf,

a brilliant artist in Brooklyn. And of course, their mother, my late sister Joanne. You are always with me and give me love and strength. I miss you so.

My loyal "friends of Fern" who came to almost every interview, cheering me on: Scott Bromley, Tony Impavido, Jeffrey Banks, Stan Herman, Ivan Bart, Grant Greenberg, Brett Beldock, Mickey Ateyeh, Cindy Lewis, Steve Gold, Ron Roberts, Lisa Silhanek, Dan Scheffey, Mae Mougin, Lucy Suarez, Judy Agisim, Gary Van Dis, Charlotte Neuville, Ellen Zornberg, Ginger Puglia, Robert Verdi, McKenzie Liautaud, Ty Yorio, Marylou Luther, Nicole Fischelis, Freddie Leiba, Brandon Sun, Maury Hopson, Julie Britt, Lee Mindel, Hedi Kim, Paula Friedman, Christina Neault, Margaret Brathwaite, and Emma Snowden-Jones. Knowing that they were in the audience during so many of these interviews means more to me than they will ever know. To the best next-door neighbor possible, Josh Bell, for constantly bringing me my lattes and treats while in the office working on this. Michael Flaherty for sending me gorgeous flowers every week during COVID to keep me happy.

Bevy Smith, my love, who happily accepted the challenge to interview me.

The journalists, bloggers, and social media fans who tweeted, posted, Facebooked, and Instagrammed these interviews. Your energy and love for this series keeps me going back to the stage!

… And finally to the Fashion Icons who shared their stories with me and the rest of the world: thank you to Valentino Garavani, Leonard Lauder, Tim Gunn, Stan Herman, Victoria Beckham, Angela Missoni, Rosita Missoni, Arthur Elgort, Christian Siriano, Bethann Hardison, Bob Mackie, Iris Apfel, Zandra Rhodes, and Billy Porter. Without you, I would not have had so much fun at the 92nd Street Y, and this book would not have been possible. I love you all and will be eternally grateful.